SECOND EDITION

INTRODUCTION TO
80x86
Assembly Language
and Computer Architecture

RICHARD C. DETMER

Middle Tennessee State University

JONES AND BARTLETT PUBLISHERS

Sudbury, Massachusetts

BOSTON   TORONTO   LONDON   SINGAPORE

World Headquarters

Jones and Bartlett Publishers
40 Tall Pine Drive
Sudbury, MA 01776
978-443-5000
info@jbpub.com
www.jbpub.com

Jones and Bartlett Publishers
Canada
6339 Ormindale Way
Mississauga, Ontario L5V 1J2
Canada

Jones and Bartlett Publishers
International
Barb House, Barb Mews
London W6 7PA
United Kingdom

Jones and Bartlett's books and products are available through most bookstores and online booksellers. To contact Jones and Bartlett Publishers directly, call 800-832-0034, fax 978-443-8000, or visit our website www.jbpub.com.

Substantial discounts on bulk quantities of Jones and Bartlett's publications are available to corporations, professional associations, and other qualified organizations. For details and specific discount information, contact the special sales department at Jones and Bartlett via the above contact information or send an email to specialsales@jbpub.com.

Production Credits
Acquisitions Editor: Timothy Anderson
Editorial Assistant: Melissa Potter
Production Director: Amy Rose
Associate Production Editor: Melissa Elmore
Senior Marketing Manager: Andrea DeFronzo
V.P., Manufacturing and Inventory Control: Therese Connell
Composition: Northeast Compositors, Inc.
Cover and Title Page Design: Scott Moden
Cover and Title Page Images: © Xelena/Dreamstime.com; © Szefei/Dreamstime.com
Printing and Binding: Malloy, Inc.
Cover Printing: Malloy, Inc.

Library of Congress Cataloging-in-Publication Data
Detmer, Richard C.
   Introduction to 80x86 assembly language and computer architecture / Richard Detmer. — 2nd ed.
      p. cm.
   Includes index.
   ISBN-13: 978-0-7637-7223-9 (hbk.)
   ISBN-10: 0-7637-7223-2 (hbk.)
   1. Computer architecture. 2. Assembler language (Computer program language) I. Title.
   QA76.9.A73D48 2009
   004.2'2—dc22
                              2008038794

6048
Printed in the United States of America
13 12 11 10 09   10 9 8 7 6 5 4 3 2 1

For my mother, Emma Langenhop Detmer Baldwin Toombs, and my uncle, Carl E. Langenhop, both of whom encouraged me to become a scholar.

CONTENTS

PREFACE

The first edition of *Introduction to 80x86 Assembly Language and Computer Architecture* emphasized computer architecture over assembly language. In the years since it was published, assembly language use has declined but the need for a computer scientist to understand how the computer works "on the inside" has not. This second edition emphasizes basic 80x86 architecture even more than the first. I remain convinced that learning a real instruction set and writing assembly language programs for a real computer are excellent ways to become acquainted with the basics of computer architecture.

New to the Second Edition

There are several major changes in this edition. For many people the most significant will be the use of the Microsoft® Visual Studio® environment instead of stand-alone software. Visual Studio is widely used in academic and professional settings, and provides a robust environment for editing, assembling, debugging, and executing programs. The Microsoft® Academic Alliance (http://msdn.microsoft.com/en-us/academic/default.aspx) makes Visual Studio and other development software available to academic institutions at very low cost. All programs presented in this book have been tested using Visual Studio® 2008, Professional Edition.

The 80x86 microprocessor family has expanded considerably in the past few years. This book continues to emphasize basic architecture; that is, features that are found on most CPUs, not just the 80x86 line. Since 64-bit processors now commonly power new PCs, this book includes 64-bit architecture—although at the time of its writing 64-bit operating systems are not widely used. Much of the time 64-bit instructions are just "more of the same," but there are a few major differences. This book's topics are arranged so that 64-bit operations can be covered or omitted at the instructor's discretion. It is impossible in a textbook to provide full coverage of all 80x86 instructions.

Intel® provides comprehensive documentation on their website (http://www.intel.com/products/processor/manuals/).

This edition has decreased emphasis on input/output, with corresponding increased emphasis on using the debugger to see what is going on inside the computer. Macros for I/O, macros for converting from an ASCII string to a 2's complement integer, and macros for converting from a 2's complement integer to an ASCII string are included. The macros for I/O now use dialog boxes and message boxes instead of console I/O. Additionally, all program examples in this text are provided for students on the book's website at http://www.jbpub.com/catalog/9780763772239/.

Chapter 6, "Procedures," has been changed to focus on the *cdecl* protocol. Using a standard protocol makes it possible to cover calling assembly language procedures from a high-level language or an HLL procedure from assembly language. The very different 64-bit procedure protocol is also covered.

Chapter 9, "Floating Point Operations," has major updates. Since all current 80x86 CPUs have floating point units, it no longer discusses how to code floating point operations using processors without an FPU. It covers some SSE instructions because these are normally used instead of the FPU for FP operations in 64-bit mode. It omits in-line assembly but includes calling assembly language procedures with floating point parameters from a high-level language.

The chapter on binary coded decimal (BCD) has been omitted from this edition, although BCD representations are still covered lightly in Chapter 1, "Representing Data in a Computer." Chapter 8, "String Operations," has been retained because these instructions provide a striking example of the complex instruction set nature of the 80x86.

The first edition listed the number of clock cycles required for each instruction on different 80x86 CPUs. With current pipelined CPUs this information is almost irrelevant, and thus has been omitted. The previous chapter-ending "something extra" sections have been eliminated, but much of their content has been incorporated in appropriate places within the chapters.

Instructor and Student Resources

I always remind my students that they don't receive answers to exercises on an exam or in real life and need to develop confidence in their own answers. However, at the request of a few instructors and many students, I have included answers to selected exercises in Appendix C. These exercises are marked with an asterisk (*) within the chapters.

Answers to all exercises are available to registered instructors at http://www .jbpub.com/catalog/9780763772239/. PowerPoint lecture slides, code from the text, and sample Visual Studio projects are also available at this site.

Acknowledgments

Thank you to the reviewers, Cynthia Fry, Baylor University; Bruce Johnston, University of Wisconsin–Stout; and Evan Noynaert, Missouri Western State University, for their valuable feedback. Thanks also to those who reviewed the manuscript of the first edition.

I would like to thank the many students who have taken my 80x86 assembly language classes over the last 20+ years. They have always made teaching worthwhile.

CHAPTER 1

Representing Data in a Computer

When you program in a high-level language (like Java or C++) you use variables of different types (such as integer, float, or character). Once you have declared variables, you do not have to worry about how the data are represented in the computer. When you deal with a computer at the machine level, however, you must be more concerned with how data are stored. Often you have the job of converting data from one representation to another. This chapter covers some common ways that data are represented in a microcomputer. Chapter 2 gives an overview of microcomputer hardware and software. Chapter 3 illustrates how to write an assembly language program that directly controls execution of the computer's native instructions.

1.1 Binary and Hexadecimal Numbers

A computer uses **bits** (binary digits, each an electronic state representing zero or one) to denote values. We represent such **binary** numbers using the digits 0 and 1 and a base 2 place-value system. This binary number system is like the decimal system except that the positions (right to left) are 1's, 2's, 4's, 8's, 16's (and higher powers of 2) instead of 1's, 10's, 100's, 1000's, 10000's (powers of 10). For example, the binary number 1101 can be interpreted as the decimal number 13.

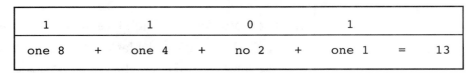

1		1		0		1		
one 8	+	one 4	+	no 2	+	one 1	=	13

Binary numbers are so long that they are awkward to read and write. For instance, it takes the 8 bits 11111010 to represent the decimal number 250, or the 15 bits 111010100110000 to represent the decimal number 30000. The **hexadecimal** (base 16) number system represents numbers using about one fourth as many digits as the binary system. Conversions between hexadecimal and binary are so easy that **hex** can be thought of as shorthand for binary. The hexadecimal system requires 16 digits. The digits 0, 1, 2, 3, 4, 5, 6, 7, 8, and 9 are used just as in the decimal system; A, B, C, D, E, and F are used for the decimal numbers 10, 11, 12, 13, 14, and 15, respectively. Either uppercase or lowercase letters can be used for the new digits.

The positions in hexadecimal numbers correspond to powers of 16. From right to left, they are 1's, 16's, 256's, and so on. The value of the hex number 9D7A is 40314 in decimal, since

$$
\begin{array}{rcrrl}
9 & \times & 4096 & 36864 & [\ 4096 = 16^3\ ] \\
+\ 13 & \times & 256 & 3328 & [\ D \text{ is } 13,\ 256 = 16^2\ ] \\
+\ 7 & \times & 16 & 112 & \\
+\ 10 & \times & 1 & 10 & [\ A \text{ is } 10\ ] \\
& & & = 40314 &
\end{array}
$$

Figure 1.1 shows small numbers expressed in decimal, hexadecimal, and binary systems. It is worthwhile to memorize this table or to be able to construct it very quickly.

You have now seen how to convert binary or hexadecimal numbers to decimal. How can you convert numbers from decimal to hex? From decimal to binary? From

Decimal	Hexadecimal	Binary
0	0	0
1	1	1
2	2	10
3	3	11
4	4	100
5	5	101
6	6	110
7	7	111
8	8	1000
9	9	1001
10	A	1010
11	B	1011
12	C	1100
13	D	1101
14	E	1110
15	F	1111

Figure 1.1 Decimal, hexadecimal, and binary numbers

binary to hex? From hex to binary? We show how to do these conversions manually, but often the easiest way is to use a calculator that allows numbers to be entered in decimal, hexadecimal, or binary. Conversion between bases is normally a matter of pressing a key or two. These calculators can do arithmetic directly in binary or hex as well as decimal, and often have a full range of other functions available. One warning: Many of these calculators use seven segment displays and display the lower case letter b so that it looks almost like the numeral 6. Other characters may also be difficult to read.

A calculator that does hex arithmetic is very useful. Some handheld calculators have this capability (typically ones that have keys labeled A through F). A calculator accessory is available in a Microsoft Windows operating system. If the Windows calculator looks like a four-function calculator when you start it, choose View/Scientific to reveal the hex mode, and select the Hex and Qword radio buttons. (The meaning of Qword will be explained later in this chapter.) Use the keyboard or click the display buttons to enter a hex number, and then click the Dec radio button to convert to decimal. Figure 1.2 illustrates this for the conversion of 9D7A to 40314 done by hand previously.

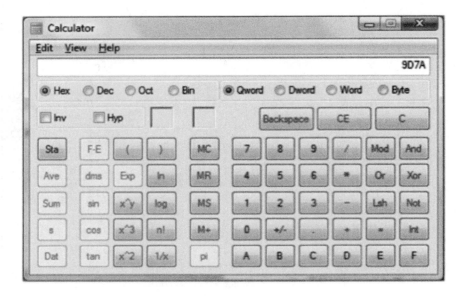

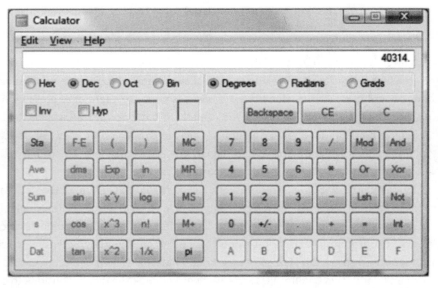

Figure 1.2 Base conversion with Windows calculator accessory

With the Windows calculator, the Bin radio button can be used to obtain a binary result. However, a calculator isn't needed to convert a hexadecimal number to its equivalent binary form. In fact, many binary numbers are too long to be displayed on a typical calculator. Instead, simply substitute 4 bits for each hex digit. The bits are those found in the third column of Figure 1.1. Pad with leading zeros, as needed. For example,

$$3B8E2_{16} = 11\ 1011\ 1000\ 1110\ 0010_2$$

The subscripts 16 and 2 are used to indicate the base of the system in which a number is written; they are usually omitted when there is little chance of confusion. The extra spaces in the binary number are just to make it more readable; vertical bars (|) work just as well as separators. Note that the rightmost hex digit 2 was converted to 0010, including leading zeros. It was not necessary to convert the leading 3 to 0011, although it would have been correct since leading zeros do not change the value of a number.

To convert binary numbers to hexadecimal format, reverse the previous steps: Break the binary number into groups of four bits, starting from the right, and substitute the corresponding hex digit for each group of 4 bits. For example,

$$1011011101001101111 = 101|1011|1010|0110|1111 = 5BA6F$$

You have seen how to convert a binary number to an equivalent decimal number. However, instead of converting a long binary number directly to decimal, it is faster to convert it to hex, and then convert the hex number to decimal. Again using the above 19-bit-long number,

$$1011011101001101111_2$$
$$= 101\ 1011\ 1010\ 0110\ 1111$$
$$= 5BA6F_{16}$$
$$= 5 \times 65536 + 11 \times 4096 + 10 \times 256 + 6 \times 16 + 15 \times 1$$
$$= 375407_{10}$$

Figure 1.3 shows an algorithm for converting a decimal number to its hex equivalent. It produces the hex digits of the answer right to left. The algorithm is expressed in pseudocode. It illustrates some of the pseudocode conventions that will be used for algorithms and program designs in this book: := for assignment; = for logical equality; repeat-until for a post-test loop; semicolons to terminate statements; indentation of loop bodies; and liberal use of words. This algorithm can be slightly modified to convert a number in any base system to its equivalent in any other base system. Just do the arithmetic in the original base system, repeatedly dividing by the new base.

```
repeat
     divide DecimalNumber by 16, getting Quotient and Remainder;
     Remainder (in hex) is the next digit (right to left);
     DecimalNumber := Quotient;
until DecimalNumber = 0;
```

Figure 1.3 Decimal-to-hex conversion algorithm

Example

As an example, the decimal-to-hex algorithm is traced for the decimal number 5876:

- Since a repeat-until loop is a post-test loop structure, the controlling condition is not checked until after the body has been executed the first time.
- Divide 16 into 5876 (*DecimalNumber*).

$$
\begin{array}{r}
367 \\
16\,\overline{)5876} \\
5872 \\
\hline
4
\end{array}
$$

   367 Quotient   the new value for DecimalNumber

     4 Remainder the rightmost digit of the answer

                       Result so far: 4

- 367 is not zero. Divide it by 16.

$$
\begin{array}{r}
22 \\
16\,\overline{)367} \\
352 \\
\hline
15
\end{array}
$$

   22 Quotient   the new value for DecimalNumber

   15 Remainder the second digit of the answer

                       Result so far: F4

- 22 is not zero. Divide it by 16.

$$
\begin{array}{r}
1 \\
16\,\overline{)22} \\
16 \\
\hline
6
\end{array}
$$

    1 Quotient   the new value for DecimalNumber

    6 Remainder the next digit of the answer

                       Result so far: 6F4

- 1 is not zero. Divide it by 16.

      0   Quotient   the new value for DecimalNumber
    16)1
      0
    ――
      1   Remainder   the next digit of the answer
                        Result so far: 16F4

- 0 is zero, so the until loop terminates. The answer is $16F4_{16}$

The **octal** (base 8) number system is used with some computer systems. Octal numbers are written using digits 0 through 7. Most calculators that do hex arithmetic also handle octal values. The Oct radio button on the Windows calculator is used to display results in octal. It is easy to convert a binary number to octal by writing the octal equivalent for each group of three bits, or to convert from octal to binary by replacing each octal digit by three bits. To convert from decimal to octal, one can use an algorithm that is the same as the decimal to hex scheme except that you divide by 8 instead of 16 at each step.

Exercises 1.1

Supply the missing two forms for each number.

	Binary	Hexadecimal	Decimal
1.	100	―――	―――
*2.	10101101	―――	―――
3.	1101110101	―――	―――
4.	11111011110	―――	―――
5.	10000000001	―――	―――
6.	―――	8EF	―――
7.	―――	10	―――
*8.	―――	A52E	―――
9.	―――	70C	―――
10.	―――	6BD3	―――
11.	―――	―――	100
12.	―――	―――	527
13.	―――	―――	4128
*14.	―――	―――	11947
15.	―――	―――	59020

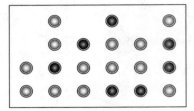

The author's office has a "binary clock," the display of which is an array of LEDs as shown above. The first two columns give the 10's and 1's digits of the hour, the next two columns give the minutes, and the last two give the seconds, each in binary where a lit LED means 1 and an unlit LED means 0. The illustration shows 02:49:16. Identify the time shown on each clock display.

16.

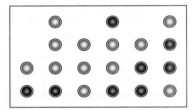

17.

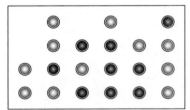

*18.

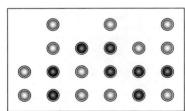

1.2 Character Codes

Letters, numerals, punctuation marks, and other characters are represented in a computer by assigning a numeric value to each character. Several schemes for assigning these numeric values have been used. The system commonly used with microcomputers is the American Standard Code for Information Interchange (abbreviated ASCII and pronounced ASK-ee).

The ASCII system uses 7 bits to represent characters, so that values from 000 0000 to 111 1111 are assigned to characters. This means that 128 different characters can be represented using ASCII codes. The ASCII codes are usually given as hex numbers from 00 to 7F or as decimal numbers from 0 to 127. There are several extended versions of ASCII. One common version assigns characters from 80 to FF; you may have seen some of their graphic representations if you tried to display a nontext file on your screen. The **Unicode** system uses 16 bits to represent a character, with 65,636 values making it possible to represent characters from most of the written languages in the world. ASCII characters are the first 128 Unicode characters, 0000 to 007F, each formed by simply appending nine leading 0 bits to the ASCII code.

Appendix A has a complete listing of ASCII codes. Using this table, you can check that the message

    Computers are fun.

can be coded in ASCII, using hex numbers, as

43	6F	6D	70	75	74	65	72	73	20	61	72	65	20	66	75	6E	2E
C	o	m	p	u	t	e	r	s		a	r	e		f	u	n	.

Note that a space, even though it is invisible, has a character code (hex 20).

Numbers can be represented using character codes. For example, the ASCII codes for the date October 21, 1976 are

4F	63	74	6F	62	65	72	20	32	31	2C	20	31	39	37	36
O	c	t	o	b	e	r		2	1	,		1	9	7	6

with the number 21 represented using ASCII codes 32 31, and the number 1976 represented using 31 39 37 36. This is very different from the binary representation in the last section, where $21_{10} = 10101_2$ and $1976_{10} = 11110111000_2$. Computers use both of these representations for numbers: ASCII for input and output, and binary for internal computations.

The ASCII code assignments may seem rather arbitrary, but there are certain patterns. The codes for uppercase letters are contiguous, as are the codes for lowercase letters. The codes for an uppercase letter and the corresponding lowercase letter differ by exactly 1 bit. Bit 5 is 0 for an uppercase letter and 1 for the corresponding lowercase letter, while other bits are the same. (Bits in most computer architectures are numbered right to left, starting with 0 for the rightmost bit.) For example,

- uppercase M codes as $4D_{16} = 1001101_2$
- lowercase m codes as $6D_{16} = 1101101_2$

The **printable characters** are grouped together from 20_{16} to $7E_{16}$. (A space is considered a printable character.) Numerals 0, 1, . . ., 9 have ASCII codes 30_{16}, 31_{16}, . . ., 39_{16}, respectively.

The characters from 00_{16} to $1F_{16}$, along with $7F_{16}$, are known as **control characters**. For example, the ESC key on an ASCII keyboard generates a hex 1B code. The abbreviation ESC stands for "extra services control" but most people say "escape." The ESC character is often sent in combination with other characters to a peripheral device like a printer to turn on a special feature. Since such character sequences are not standardized, they are not covered in this book.

Carriage return (CR) and line feed (LF) are two frequently used ASCII control characters. The $0D_{16}$ code for CR is generated by an ASCII keyboard when the Enter key is pressed. When CR is sent to an ASCII display it causes the cursor to move to the beginning of the current line, without going down to a new line. When CR is sent to an ASCII printer (at least one of older design), it causes the print head to move to the beginning of a line. The $0A_{16}$ code for LF causes an ASCII display to move the cursor straight down, or a printer to roll the paper up one line, in both cases without going to the beginning of a new line. To display a message and move to the beginning of a new line, it is necessary to send the message characters plus CR and LF characters to the screen or printer.

Lesser-used control characters include form feed ($0C_{16}$), which causes many printers to eject a page; horizontal tab (09_{16}), which is generated by the Tab key on the keyboard; back space (08_{16}), generated by the Backspace key; and delete ($7F_{16}$), generated by the Delete key. Notice that the Backspace and Delete keys do not generate the same codes. The bell character (07_{16}) causes an audible signal when output to the display.

Many large computers represent characters using Extended Binary Coded Decimal Information Code (abbreviated EBCDIC and pronounced "ib-SEE-dick" or "eb-SEE-dick"). The EBCDIC system is only used in this book as an example of another coding scheme when translation from one coding system to another is discussed.

Exercises 1.2

1. Each of the following hexadecimal numbers can be interpreted as representing a decimal number or a pair of ASCII codes. Give both interpretations.

   (a) 2A45   *(b) 7352   (c) 2036   (d) 106E

2. Find the ASCII codes for the characters in each of the following strings. Don't forget spaces and punctuation. Carriage return and line feed are shown by CR and LF, respectively, written together as CRLF so that it will be clear that there is no space character between them.

   (a) January 1 is New Year's Day.CRLF

   *(b) George said, "Ouch!"

   (c) R2D2 was C3P0's friend.CRLF[0 is the numeral zero]

   (d) Your name?

   (e) Enter value:

3. What would be displayed if you output each of the following sequences of ASCII codes to a computer's screen?

   (a) 62 6C 6F 6F 64 2C 20 73 77 65 61 74 20 61 6E 64 20 74 65 61 72 73

   (b) 6E 61 6D 65 0D 0A 61 64 64 72 65 73 73 0D 0A 63 69 74 79 0D 0A

   *(c) 4A 75 6E 65 20 31 31 2C 20 31 39 34 37 0D 0A

   (d) 24 33 38 39 2E 34 35

   (e) 49 44 23 3A 20 20 31 32 33 2D 34 35 2D 36 37 38 39

1.3   Unsigned and Signed Integers

It is now time to look more carefully at how numbers are actually represented in a computer. We have looked at two schemes to represent numbers—by using ASCII codes or by using binary integers (often expressed in hex). However, there are two problems with these methods: (1) the number of bits available for representing a number is limited, and (2) it is not clear how to represent a negative number.

Chapter 2 discusses computer hardware, but for now you need to know that memory is divided into **bytes**, each byte containing 8 **bits**[1]. Suppose you want to use ASCII codes to represent a number in memory. A single ASCII code is normally stored in a byte. Recall that ASCII codes are 7 bits long; the extra (left-hand, or high-order) bit is set to 0. To solve the second representation problem mentioned earlier, you can simply include the code for a minus sign. For example, the ASCII codes for the four characters −817 are 2D, 38, 31, and 37. To solve the first problem, you could always agree to use a fixed number of bytes, perhaps padding on the left with ASCII codes for zeros or spaces. Alternatively, you could use a variable number of bytes, but agree that the number ends with the last ASCII code for a digit; that is, terminating the string with a nondigit. (A **null byte** 00 is often used for this purpose.)

Suppose you want to use internal representations for numbers corresponding to their binary values. Then you must choose a fixed number of bits for the representation. Most central processing units can do arithmetic on binary numbers having a few specific lengths. For the Intel 80x86 family, these lengths are 8 bits, a byte; 16 bits, a **word**[2]; 32 bits, a **doubleword**; and 64 bits, a **quadword**.

As an example, look at the word-length binary representation of 697.

$$697_{10} = 1010111001_2 = 0000001010111001_2$$

Leading zeros have been added to make 16 bits. Writing this in hex in a word, you have

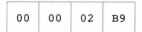

This illustrates a convention that is followed in many places in this book. Strips of boxes will represent sequences of bytes. The contents of a single byte will be represented in hex, with two hex digits in each byte, because a single hex digit corresponds to 4 bits. The doubleword representation of 697 simply has more leading zeros.

00	00	02	B9

---

1 Some early computer systems used byte sizes different than 8 bits.

2 Some other computer architectures use a word size different than 16 bits.

What we now have is a good system of representing nonnegative, or **unsigned** numbers—a predetermined length holding a binary representation padded with leading 0 bits, if needed. This system cannot represent negative numbers. Also, for any given length, there is a largest unsigned number that can be represented, for example FF_{16} or 255_{10} for byte length.

The **2's complement** system is similar to the above scheme for unsigned numbers, but it allows representation of negative numbers. Numbers will be a fixed length, so that you might refer to the "doubleword-length 2's complement representation" of a number. The 2's complement representation for a nonnegative number is almost identical to the unsigned representation, that is, you represent the number in binary with enough leading zeros to fill up the desired length. There is one additional restriction—*for a positive number, the leftmost bit must be zero*. This means, for example, that the most positive number that can be represented in word-size 2's complement form is 0111111111111111_2 or $7FFF_{16}$ or $32,767_{10}$.

As you have probably already guessed, the leftmost bit is always 1 in the 2's complement representation of a negative number. You might also guess that the rest of the representation is just the same as for the corresponding positive number, but unfortunately the situation is more complicated than that. That is, you *cannot* simply change the leading bit from 0 to 1 to get the negative version of a number.

A hex calculator makes it easy to convert a negative decimal number to 2's complement form. For instance, with the Windows calculator, if the decimal display shows -200 and the Hex radio button is clicked when Qword length is also selected, the display will show FFFFFFFFFFFFFF38. Note that this number has a leading 1 bit since the leading hex digit is F (1111). If the Dword, Word, or Byte lengths are selected, the result will be FFFFFF38, FF38, or 38, respectively. Notice that these are the same except for the number of leading 1 bits (hex F digits). Unfortunately, 38 is not a correct answer because the magnitude of -200 is too large to represent as a byte-size 2's complement number. One way you can tell that the answer is incorrect is that $38_{16} = 00111000_2$, a *positive* number. Later in this section we take a closer look at how big a number can be for word-size representations, and the exercises ask about other sizes.

Let's concentrate on word-length representations for a while. We just looked at converting -200 to 2's complement. If you use the Windows calculator with Word length selected, the Hex display gives FF38. Now click the Dec radio button. Instead of going back to -200, the display shows 65336! The reason is simple—the word FF38 has two interpretations: the unsigned number equivalent to 65336_{10}, and the signed (2's complement) number equivalent to -200_{10}. Neither the Windows calculator nor an 80x86 CPU can determine which is intended; it is up to the user to select the correct interpretation for the context.

Here is a way you can get the correct decimal interpretation for a negative 2's complement number using the Windows calculator. Assume that the calculator is in Hex mode, Word length, with FF38 on the display. If you click the +/− key, the calculator performs a **2's complement operation** and displays C8. Now click Dec, and the calculator displays 200. If you click +/− again, then you see −200.

The 2's complement operation is equivalent to finding the negative of a number; that is, it is the negation operation. If you start with the representation for a negative number, you will get its positive counterpart. If you start with a positive number, you will get its negative counterpart. (*Note:* The +/− key triggers the 2's complement operation with many handheld calculators in Hex mode, but not all.)

The 2's complement representation of a negative number can also be found without a calculator. One method is to first express the unsigned number in hex, and then subtract this hex number from 10000_{16} to get the word-length representation. The number you subtract from is, in hex, a 1 followed by the number of 0's in the length of the representation, for example, 100000000_{16} to get the doubleword-length representation. (What would you use for a byte-length 2's complement representation? For a quadword-length 2's complement representation?) In binary, the number of zeros is the length in binary digits. This binary number is a power of 2, and subtraction is sometimes called "taking the complement," so this operation is the source of the term "2's complement."

Example

The word-length 2's complement representation of the decimal number −76 is found by first converting the unsigned number 76 to its hex equivalent 4C, then by subtracting 4C from 10000.

```
  1  0  0  0  0
       −  4  C
```

Since you cannot subtract C from 0, you have to borrow 1 from 1000, leaving FFF.

```
  F  F  F  ¹0
     −  4   C
  ─────────────
  F  F  B   4
```

After borrowing, the subtraction is easy. The units digit is

$$10_{16} - C_{16} = 16_{10} - 12_{10} = 4 \text{ (in decimal or hex),}$$

and the 16's position is

$$F_{16} - 4 = 15_{10} - 4_{10} = 11_{10} = B_{16}$$

It is not necessary to convert the hex digits to decimal to subtract them if you learn the addition and subtraction tables for single hex digits.

The process of subtracting a number from 1 followed by an appropriate number of 0's is the manual version of the 2's complement operation. It is equivalent to the operation that the Windows calculator performs when you press the +/− key. It is a little confusing that "2's complement" refers both to a representation system and to an operation on numbers in that system. (*Note:* If you actually do the arithmetic 10000 − 4C with the Windows calculator, you will have to select Dword or Qword length first because 10000 is too large to fit in a word.)

Note that any time you take the 2's complement of a number and then take the 2's complement of the result, you get back to the original number. For a word-size number N, ordinary algebra gives you

$$N = 10000 - (10000 - N)$$

For example, using the word-length 2's complement value F39E,

$$10000 - (10000 - F39E) = 10000 - C62 = F39E$$

This says again that the 2's complement operation corresponds to negation. Because of this, if you start with a bit pattern representing a negative number, the 2's complement operation can be used to find the positive (unsigned) number corresponding to it.

Example

The word-length 2's complement number E973 represents a negative value since the sign bit (leading bit) is 1 (E = 1110). Taking the 2's complement finds the corresponding positive number.

$$10000 - E973 = 168D = 5773_{10}$$

This means that the decimal number represented by E973 is −5773.

Since a given 2's complement representation is a fixed length, obviously there is a maximum size number that can be stored in it. For a word, the largest positive number stored is 7FFF, since this is the largest 16-bit-long number that has a high-order bit of 0 when written in binary. The hex number 7FFF is 32767 in decimal. Positive numbers written in hex can be identified by a leading hex digit of 0 through 7.

Negative numbers are distinguished by a leading bit of 1, corresponding to hex digits of 8 through F. The word-length 2's complement representations range from 8000 to FFFF. The two extreme values convert to decimal as follows:

$$10000 \ - \ 8000 \ = \ 8000 \ = \ 32768_{10},$$

so 8000 is the representation of -32768. Similarly,

$$10000 \ - \ FFFF \ = \ 1,$$

so FFFF is the word-length 2's complement representation of -1. Recall that the largest positive decimal integer that can be represented as a word-length 2's complement number is 32767; the range of decimal numbers that can be represented in word-length 2's complement form is -32768 to 32767.

Exercises 1.3

1. Find the doubleword-length 2's complement representation of each of the following decimal numbers:
   *(a) 3874
   (b) 1000000
   (c) -100
   (d) -55555

2. Find the word-length 2's complement representation of each of the following decimal numbers:
   (a) 845
   (b) 15000
   (c) 100
   *(d) -10
   (e) -923

3. Find the byte-length 2's complement representation of each of the following decimal numbers:
   (a) 23
   *(b) 111

    (c) −100

    (d) −55

4. Each of these 32-bit doublewords can be interpreted as either a 2's complement number or an unsigned number. Find the decimal integer that corresponds to each interpretation.

    (a) 00 00 F3 E1

  *(b) FF FF FE 03

    (c) 98 C2 41 7D

    (d) FF FF FF 78

5. Each of these 16-bit words can be interpreted as either a 2's complement number or an unsigned number. Find the decimal integer that corresponds to each interpretation.

    (a) 00 A3

    (b) FF FE

  *(c) 6F 20

    (d) B6 4A

6. Each of these 8-bit bytes can be interpreted as either a 2's complement number or an unsigned number. Find the decimal integer that corresponds to each interpretation.

  *(a) E1

    (b) 7C

    (c) FF

    (d) 3E

7. (a) Find the range of signed decimal integers (smallest to largest) that can be stored in 2's complement form in a byte.

   (b) Find the range of unsigned decimal integers that can be stored in a byte.

*8. (a) Find the range of signed decimal integers (smallest to largest) that can be stored in 2's complement form in a word.

   (b) Find the range of unsigned decimal integers that can be stored in a word.

9. (a) Find the range of signed decimal integers (smallest to largest) that can be stored in 2's complement form in a doubleword.

   (b) Find the range of unsigned decimal integers that can be stored in a doubleword.

10. This section showed how to take the 2's complement of a number by subtracting it from an appropriate power of 2. An alternative method is to write the number in binary (using the correct number of bits for the length of the representation), change each 0 bit to 1 and each 1 bit to 0 (this is called "taking the 1's complement"), and then adding 1 to the result (discarding any carry into an extra bit). Show that these two methods are equivalent.

1.4 Integer Addition and Subtraction

One of the reasons that the 2's complement representation scheme is commonly used to store signed integers in computers is that addition and subtraction operations for signed integers are identical to the corresponding operations for unsigned integers. This means that the CPU does not need separate circuitry for signed and unsigned addition or subtraction operations. This section discusses addition and subtraction of integers, and introduces the concepts of carry and overflow, which can be used to determine if the results of an operation are "correct."

We first give several examples of addition operations. The 80x86 architecture uses the same addition instructions for unsigned and signed numbers. Although 32 bits (doubleword) is the preferred integer size in the 80x86 architecture, these examples use word-size numbers in the interest of brevity. The concepts illustrated are exactly the same for byte-size, word-size, doubleword-size or quadword-size operands.

First, 0A07 and 01D3 are added. These numbers are positive whether they are interpreted as unsigned numbers or as 2's complement numbers. The decimal version of the addition problem is given on the right.

```
  0A07          2567
+ 01D3        +  467
  0BDA          3034
```

The answer is correct since $BDA_{16} = 3034_{10}$.

Next, 0206 and FFB0 are added. These are, of course, positive as unsigned numbers, but interpreted as 2's complement signed numbers, 0206 is a positive number and FFB0 is negative. This means that there are two decimal versions of the addition problem. The signed one is given first, then the unsigned version.

```
   0206          518            518
 + FFB0        + (−80)       + 65456
  101B6          438          65974
```

There certainly appears to be a problem because the result will not even fit in a word. In fact, since 101B6 is the hex version of 65974, there is no way to represent the correct sum of unsigned numbers in a word. However, if the numbers are interpreted as signed and you ignore the extra 1 on the left, then the word 01B6 is the 2's complement representation of the decimal number 438.

Now FFE7 and FFF6 are added, both negative numbers in a signed interpretation. Again, both signed and unsigned decimal interpretations are shown.

```
   FFE7          (-25)           65511
+  FFF6        + (-10)         +  65526
  1FFDD          -35           131037
```

Again the sum in hex is too large to fit in 2 bytes, but if you throw away the extra 1, then FFDD is the correct word-length 2's complement representation of −35.

Each of the last two additions has a **carry** out of the usual high-order bit position into an extra bit. The remaining bits do not give the correct unsigned result. In fact, carry always indicates that the answer is wrong if the operands are interpreted as unsigned. Although in these examples the remaining bits gave the correct 2's complement representation, this is not always the case, even for signed numbers. Consider the addition of the following two positive numbers:

```
   483F           18495
+  645A         + 25690
   AC99           44185
```

There was no carry out of the high-order bit, but the signed interpretation is plainly incorrect since AC99 represents the *negative* number −21351. Intuitively what went wrong is that the decimal sum 44185 is bigger than the maximum value 32767 that can be stored in the 2 bytes of a word. (See Exercise 1.3.8.) However, when these numbers are interpreted as unsigned, the sum is correct.

Here is another example showing a "wrong" answer, this time resulting from adding two numbers that are negative in their signed interpretation.

```
   E9FF          (-5633)          59903
+  8CF0        + (-29456)       + 36080
  176EF          -35089          95983
```

This time there is a carry, but the remaining four hex digits 76 EF cannot be the correct signed answer since they represent the *positive* number 30447. Again, intuition tells you that something had to go wrong because −32768 is the most negative number that can be stored in a word.

In the previous examples with "incorrect" signed interpretations, **overflow** occurred. Computer hardware can detect overflow as it performs addition, and the signed sum will be correct if there is no overflow. The computer actually performs addition in binary, of course, and the process is logically a right-to-left pairwise addition of bits, very similar to the procedure that humans use for decimal addition. As the computer adds a pair of bits, sometimes there is a carry (of 1) into the next column to the left. This carry is added to the sum of these 2 bits, and so on. The column of particular interest is the leftmost one; the sign position. There may be a carry *into* this position and/or a carry *out of* this position into the "extra" bit. This "carry out" (into the extra bit) is what was called just "carry" earlier and was seen as the extra hex 1. Figure 1.4 identifies when overflow does or does not occur. The table can be summarized by saying that *overflow occurs when the number of carries into the sign position is different from the number of carries out of the sign position.*

Each of the previous addition examples is now shown again, this time in binary. Carries are written above the two numbers.

```
                       111
    0000 1010 0000 0111              0A07
  + 0000 0001 1101 0011            + 01D3
    0000 1011 1101 1010              0BDA
```

This example has no carry into the sign position (bit 15) and no carry out, so there is no overflow. The carries into bits 1, 2, and 3 have no significance with respect to overflow.

```
  1 1111 11
    0000 0010 0000 0110              0206
  + 1111 1111 1011 0000            + FFB0
  1 0000 0001 1011 0110              101B6
```

Carry into sign bit?	Carry out of sign bit?	Overflow?
no	no	no
no	yes	yes
yes	no	yes
yes	yes	no

Figure 1.4 Overflow in addition

This example has a carry into the sign position and a carry out, so there is no overflow.

```
1 1111 1111 11   11
  1111 1111 1110 0111        FFE7
+ 1111 1111 1111 0110      +  FFF6
1 1111 1111 1101 1101        1FFDD
```

Again, there is both a carry into the sign position and a carry out, so there is no overflow.

```
1           1111 11
  0100 1000 0011 1111        483F
+ 0110 0100 0101 1010      +  645A
  1010 1100 1001 1001        AC99
```

Overflow does occur in this addition since there is a carry into the sign position, but no carry out.

```
1    1   11 111
  1110 1001 1111 1111        E9FF
+ 1000 1100 1111 0000      +  8CF0
1 0111 0110 1110 1111        176EF
```

There is also overflow in this addition since there is a carry out of the sign bit, but no carry in.

In a computer, subtraction $a - b$ of numbers a and b is usually performed by taking the 2's complement of b and adding the result to a. This corresponds to adding the negation of b. For example, for the decimal subtraction $195 - 618 = -423$,

```
  00C3
- 026A
```

is changed to addition of FD96, the 2's complement of 026A.

```
  00C3
+ FD96
  FE59
```

The hex digits FE59 represent −423. Looking at the previous addition in binary, you have

```
        11        11
    0000 0000 1100 0011
  + 1111 1101 1001 0110
    1111 1110 0101 1001
```

Notice that there was no carry in the addition. However, this subtraction did involve a **borrow**. A borrow occurs in the subtraction $a - b$ when b is larger than a as *unsigned* numbers. Computer hardware can detect a borrow in subtraction by looking at whether a carry occurred in the corresponding addition. If there is *no* carry in the addition, then there *is* a borrow in the subtraction. If there is a carry in the addition, then there is *no* borrow in the subtraction. (Remember that "carry" by itself means "carry out.")

Here is one more example. Doing the decimal subtraction $985 - 411 = 574$ using word-length 2's complement representations,

```
    03D9
  - 019B
```

is changed to addition of FE65, the 2's complement of 019B.

```
            1 1111 1111 1        1
    03D9      0000 0011 1101 1001
  + FE65    + 1111 1110 0110 0101
    1023E   1 0000 0010 0011 1110
```

Discarding the extra 1, the hex digits 023E represent 574. This addition has a carry, so there is no borrow in the corresponding subtraction.

Overflow is also defined for subtraction. When you think like a person, you can detect it by the wrong answer that you expect when you know the difference is going to be outside of the range that can be represented in the chosen length for the representation. A computer detects overflow in subtraction by determining whether overflow occurs in the corresponding addition problem. If overflow occurs in the addition problem, then it occurs in the original subtraction problem; if it does not occur in the addition, then it does not occur in the original subtraction. There was no overflow in either of the previous subtraction examples. Overflow occurs if you use word-length 2's complement representations to attempt the subtraction $-29123 - 15447$. As a human, you know that the correct answer -44570 is outside the range $-32{,}768$ to $+32{,}767$. In the computer hardware

```
    8E3D
  - 3C57
```

is changed to addition of C3A9, the 2's complement of 3C57.

```
                1    1   11   111    1
    8E3D            1000 1110 0011 1101
  + C3A9          + 1100 0011 1010 1001
  151E6          1 0101 0001 1110 0110
```

There is a carry out of the sign position, but no carry in, so overflow occurs.

Although examples in this section used word-size 2's complement representations, the same techniques apply when performing addition or subtraction with byte-size, doubleword-size, or quadword-size 2's complement numbers.

Exercises 1.4

Perform each of the following operations on word-size numbers. For each, find the specified sum or difference, giving the answer as a word-size number. Determine whether overflow occurs. For a sum, determine whether there is a carry. For a difference, determine whether there is a borrow. Check your answers by converting the problem to both decimal interpretations (unsigned and 2's complement); show that the unsigned interpretation is correct when there is no carry (borrow for subtraction), and the signed interpretation is correct when there is no overflow.

*1. 003F + 02A4   2. 1B48 + 39E1

 3. 6C34 + 5028   4. 7FFE + 0002

*5. FF07 + 06BD   6. 2A44 + D9CC

 7. FFE3 + FC70   8. FE00 + FD2D

*9. FFF1 + 8005   10. 8AD0 + EC78

11. 9E58 − EBBC   12. EBBC − 9E58

*13. EBBC − 791C   14. 791C − EBBC

1.5 Other Systems for Representing Numbers

Sections 1.2 and 1.3 presented commonly used systems for representing numbers in computers, strings of character codes (often ASCII), binary representation for unsigned integers, and 2's complement representation for signed integers. This section introduces three additional schemes: 1's complement, binary coded decimal (BCD), and floating point. The 1's complement system is an alternative scheme for representing signed integers; it is used in a few computer systems, but not the Intel 80x86 family. Binary coded decimal can be thought of as halfway from ASCII to binary; while there are a few 80x86 instructions designed to operate on BCD representations, they are not covered in this book. Floating point forms are used to represent noninteger values; they are discussed more fully in Chapter 9. The primary reason for introducing 1's complement, BCD, and floating point here is to illustrate that there are many alternative representations for numeric data, each valid when used in the correct context.

The **1's complement** system is similar to 2's complement. A fixed length is chosen for the representation and a positive integer is simply the binary form of the number, padded with one or more leading zeros on the left to get the desired length. To take the negative of the number, each bit is "complemented"—each zero is changed to one and each one is changed to zero. This operation is sometimes referred to as taking the 1's complement of a number. Although it is easier to negate an integer using 1's complement than 2's complement, the 1's complement system has several disadvantages, the most significant being that it is harder to design circuitry to add or subtract numbers in this form. There are two representations for zero (Why?); an awkward situation. Also, a slightly smaller range of values can be represented; for example, -127 to 127 for an 8 bit length, instead of -128 to 127 in a 2's complement system.

The byte length 1's complement representation of the decimal number 97 is just the value 0110 0001 in binary (61 in hex). Changing each 0 to 1 and each 1 to 0 gives 1001 1110 (9E in hex), the byte length 1's complement representation of -97.

There is a useful connection between taking the 1's complement and taking the 2's complement of a binary number. If you take the 1's complement of a number and then add 1, you get the 2's complement. This is sometimes easier to do by hand than the subtraction method presented in Section 1.3. You were asked to verify the equivalence of these methods in Exercise 1.3.10.

In **binary coded decimal** (BCD) schemes, each decimal digit is coded with a string of bits with fixed length, and these strings are pieced together to form the representation. Most frequently 4 bits are used for each decimal digit; the choices for bit patterns are shown in Figure 1.5. Only these 10-bit patterns are used.

Decimal	BCD Bit Pattern
0	0000
1	0001
2	0010
3	0011
4	0100
5	0101
6	0110
7	0111
8	1000
9	1001

Figure 1.5   Binary coded decimal representation

One BCD representation of the decimal number 926708 is 1001 0010 0110 0111 0000 1000. Using one hex digit as shorthand for 4 bits, and grouping two hex digits per byte, this BCD representation can be expressed in three bytes as

92	67	08

Notice that the BCD representation in hex looks just like the decimal number.

Often BCD numbers are encoded using some fixed number of bytes. For purposes of illustration, assume a 4-byte representation. For now, the question of how to represent a sign will be ignored; without leaving room for a sign, eight binary coded decimal digits can be stored in four bytes. Given these choices, the decimal number 3691 has the BCD representation

00	00	36	91

Notice that the doubleword 2's complement representation for the same number would be 00 00 0E 6B, and that the ASCII codes for the four numerals are 33 36 39 31.

It is not as efficient for a computer to do arithmetic with numbers in a BCD format as with 2's complement numbers. It is usually very inefficient to do arithmetic on numbers represented using ASCII codes. However, ASCII codes are the only method so far for representing a number that is not an integer. For example, 78.375 can be stored as 37 38 2E 33 37 35. **Floating point** representation systems allow for nonintegers to be represented, or at least closely approximated.

Floating point schemes store numbers in a form that corresponds to scientific notation. The example below shows how to convert the decimal number 78.375 into **IEEE single precision format** which is 32 bits long. (IEEE is the abbreviation for the Institute of Electrical and Electronics Engineers.) This format was one of several sponsored by the Standards Committee of the IEEE Computer Society and approved by the IEEE Standards Board and the American National Standards Institute (ANSI). It is one of the floating point formats used by 80x86 processors.

First 78.375 must be converted to binary. In binary, the positions to the right of the binary point (it is not appropriate to say *decimal* point for the "." in a binary number) correspond to negative powers of 2 (1/2, 1/4, 1/8, etc.), just as they correspond to negative powers of 10 (1/10, 1/100, etc.) in a decimal number. Since $0.375 = 3/8 = 1/4 + 1/8 = .01_2 + .001_2$, $0.375_{10} = 0.011_2$. The whole part 78 is 1001110 in binary, so

$$78.375_{10} = 1001110.011_2$$

Next this is expressed in binary scientific notation with the mantissa written with 1 before the binary point.

$$1001110.011_2 = 1.001110011 \times 2^6$$

The exponent is found exactly as it is in decimal scientific notation by counting the number of positions the point must be moved to the right or left to produce the mantissa. The notation here is really mixed; it would be more proper to write 2^6 as 10^{110}, but it is more convenient to use the decimal form. Now the floating point number can be pieced together:

- left bit 0 for a positive number (1 means negative)
- 1000 0101 for the exponent. This is the actual exponent of 6, plus a **bias** of 127, with the sum, 133, in 8 bits.
- 00111001100000000000000, the fraction expressed with the leading 1 removed and padded with zeros on the right to make 23 bits

The entire number is then 0 10000101 00111001100000000000000. Regrouping gives 0100 0010 1001 1100 1100 0000 0000 0000, or, in hex

| 42 | 9C | C0 | 00 |

This example worked out easily because 0.375, the noninteger part of the decimal number 78.375, is a sum of negative powers of 2. Most numbers are not as nice, and usually a binary fraction is chosen to closely approximate the decimal fraction. Techniques for choosing such an approximation are not covered in this book.

To summarize, the following steps are used to convert a decimal number to IEEE single format:

- The leading bit of the floating point format is 0 for a positive number and 1 for a negative number.
- Write the unsigned number in binary.
- Write the binary number in binary scientific notation $f_{23}.f_{22} \ldots f_0 \times 2^e$, where $f_{23} = 1$. There are 24 fraction bits, but it is not necessary to write trailing 0's.
- Add a bias of 127_{10} to the exponent e. This sum, in binary form, is the next 8 bits of the answer, following the sign bit. (Adding a bias is an alternative to storing the exponent as a signed number.)
- The fraction bits $f_{22}f_{21} \ldots f_0$ form the last 23 bits of the floating point number. The leading bit f_{23} (that is always 1) is dropped.

Computer arithmetic on floating point numbers is usually much slower than with 2's complement integers. However, the advantages of being able to represent nonintegral values or very large or small values often outweigh the relative inefficiency of computing with them.

Exercises 1.5

Express each of the following decimal numbers as a word-length 1's complement number.

  *1. 175   *2. −175
   3. −43   4. 43

Use BCD to encode each of the following decimal numbers in 4 bytes. Express each answer in hex digits, grouped two per byte.

*5. 230   6. 1

 7. 12348765   8. 17195

Use IEEE single format to encode each of the following decimal numbers in single-precision floating point.

 9. 175.5   10. −1.25

*11. −11.75   12. 45.5

1.6 Chapter Summary

All data are represented in a computer using electronic signals. These can be interpreted as patterns of binary digits (bits). These bit patterns can be thought of as binary numbers. Numbers can be written in decimal, hexadecimal, or binary forms.

For representing characters, most microcomputers use ASCII codes. One code is assigned for each character, including nonprintable control characters.

Integer values are represented in a predetermined number of bits. An unsigned integer is simply the number in binary. Signed integers are stored in 2's complement form; a positive number is stored as a binary number (with at least one leading zero to make the required length), and the pattern for a negative number can be obtained by subtracting the positive form from a 1 followed by as many 0's as are used in the length. A 2's complement negative number always has a leading 1 bit. A hex calculator, used with care, can simplify working with 2's complement numbers.

Addition and subtraction are easy with 2's complement numbers. Since the length of a 2's complement number is limited, there is the possibility of a carry, a borrow, or overflow.

Other formats in which numbers are stored are 1's complement, binary coded decimal (BCD), and floating point.

CHAPTER 2

Parts of a Computer System

A practical computer system consists of hardware and software. The major hardware components of a typical microcomputer system are a central processing unit (CPU), memory circuits, a keyboard for input, a visual display, specialized input/output devices like a mouse or a network card, and one or more disk drives to store programs and data. Software refers to the programs that the hardware executes, including system software and application software.

These basic components vary from one computer system to another. This chapter discusses how the memory and CPU look to the assembly language programmer for a particular class of microcomputers, those using 80x86 microprocessors, where 80x86 refers to the series of products that began with the Intel 8086 and 8088 and continues through current processors such as the Intel Core 2. It also refers to most Advanced Micro Devices (AMD) processors since these execute essentially the same instruction set. This book assumes a computer that has an 80386 or higher processor and a Microsoft Windows operating system such as XP or

Vista. The bulk of this book is concerned with using assembly language to program these systems, with the intent of showing how such systems work at the hardware level. Some of the differences between 32-bit and 64-bit architectures and operating environments are covered.

2.1   PC Hardware: Memory

The memory in a computer is logically a collection of "slots," each of which can store 1 byte of instructions or data. Each memory byte has a numeric label called its **physical address**. The 32-bit processors such as the Pentium use 32-bit labels, each of which can be expressed as eight hex digits. The first address is 00000000_{16} and the last address can be as large as the unsigned number $FFFFFFFF_{16}$. Figure 2.1 shows a logical picture of the possible memory in a 32-bit PC. Since $FFFFFFFF_{16} = 4,294,967,295$, a 32-bit PC can contain up to 4,294,967,296 bytes of memory, or 4 GB. Remember that $2^{10} = 1$ KB (kilobyte), $2^{20} = 1$ MB (megabyte), $2^{30} = 1$ GB (gigabyte), and $2^{40} = 1$ TB (terabyte).

Prior to the 80386 chip, the 80x86 family of processors could only directly address 2^{20} bytes of memory. They used 20-bit physical addresses, often expressed as 5-hex-digit addresses ranging from 00000 to FFFFF.

The 64-bit 80x86 processors such as the Core 2 can operate in either 32-bit or 64-bit mode. When in 32-bit mode, they use 32-bit addresses just like 32-bit processors. In 64-bit mode they internally store 64-bit addresses. However, at the time this book is being written, processors use at most 48 bits of the possible 64. Even with this limitation, a 64-bit processor running with a 64-bit operating system could address up to 2^{48}

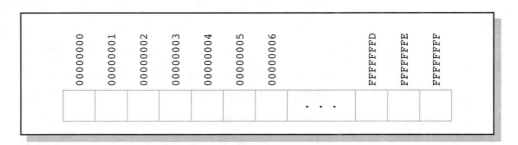

Figure 2.1 Logical picture of PC memory

bytes of physical memory (256 TB), 65,536 times the maximum in a 32-bit system. Current PC systems are not designed to hold this much memory.

Physically a PC's memory consists of integrated circuits (ICs). Many of these chips provide **random access memory (RAM)** that can be written to or read from by program instructions. The contents of RAM chips are lost when the computer's power is turned off. Other ICs are **read only memory (ROM)** chips that permanently retain their contents, and which can be read from but not written to.

The assembly language programs in this book use a **flat memory** model. This means that the programs actually encode 32-bit addresses to logically reference locations in a single memory space where data and instructions are stored.

The Intel 80x86 architecture also provides for a **segmented memory** model. In the 8086/8088 CPU, this is the only memory model available. With the 8086/8088, the PC's memory is visualized as a collection of segments, each segment 64-KB long, starting on an address that is a multiple of 16. This means that one segment starts at address 00000, another (overlapping the first) starts at address 16 (00010_{16}), another starts at address 32 (00020_{16}), and so on. Notice that the starting address of a segment ends in 0 when written in hex. The **segment number** of a segment consists of the first four hex digits of its physical address.

A program written for the 8086/8088 does not encode a five-hex-digit address. Instead, each memory reference depends on its segment number and a 16-bit **offset** from the beginning of the segment. Normally only the offset is encoded, and the segment number is deduced from context. The offset is the distance from the first byte of the segment to the byte being addressed. In hex an offset is between 0000 and $FFFF_{16}$. The notation for a segment–offset address is the four-hex-digit segment number followed by a colon (:) followed by the four-hex-digit offset.

As an example, 18A3:5B27 refers to the byte that is 5B27 bytes from the beginning of the segment starting at address 18A30. Add the starting address and the offset to get the five-hex-digit address.

```
18A30      starting address of segment 18A3
+ 5B27     offset
1E557      five-hex-digit address
```

From the 80386 on, 80x86 processors have had both 16-bit and 32-bit segmented memory models available. Segment numbers are still 16-bits long, but they do not directly reference a segment in memory. Instead, a segment number is used as an index into a table that contains the actual 32-bit starting address of the segment. In the

32-bit segmented model, a 32-bit offset is added to that starting address to compute the actual address of the memory operand. Segments can be logically useful to a programmer—in the segmented Intel model, the programmer normally assigns different memory segments to code, data, and a system stack. The 80x86 flat memory model is really a 32-bit segmented model with all segment registers containing the same value.

When a 64-bit processor is in 32-bit mode, it operates as described in the previous paragraph. However, segmented memory is not used in 64-bit mode.

In reality, the address generated by a program is not necessarily the physical address at which an operand is stored as the program executes. There is an additional layer of memory management performed by the operating system and the 80x86 CPU. A **paging** mechanism is used to map the program's addresses into physical addresses. Paging is useful when a logical address generated by a program exceeds the maximum address in the physical memory actually installed in a computer. It can also be used to swap parts of a program from disk as needed when the program is too large to fit into physical memory. The memory management mechanism will be transparent to us as we program in assembly language.

Exercises 2.1

1. Suppose that you buy a 32-bit PC with 512 MB of RAM. What is the eight-hex-digit address of the "last" byte of installed memory?

*2. Suppose that you buy a 64-bit PC with 2 GB of RAM. What is the 16-hex-digit of the "last" byte of installed memory?

3. Suppose that you discover that RAM addresses 000C0000 to 000C7FFF are reserved for a PC's video adapter in a 32-bit computer. How many bytes of memory is this?

4. Suppose that you have an Intel 8086. Find the five-hex-digit address that corresponds to each of these segment:offset pairs:
   *(a) 2B8C:8D21   (b) 059A:7A04   (c) 1234:5678

2.2   PC Hardware: The CPU

The 8086/8088 CPU can execute over 200 different instructions. This instruction set has been expanded significantly as the 80x86 processor family has grown. Much of this book is concerned with using these instructions to implement programs so that you understand machine-level computer capabilities. There are other processor families that execute different instruction sets. However, many have a similar architecture, so that the basic principles you learn about 80x86 CPUs also apply to these systems.

An 80x86 CPU contains **registers**, each an internal storage location that can be accessed much more rapidly than a location in RAM. The **application registers** are of most concern to the programmer. These are the basic program execution registers, as well as floating point registers, MMX, and XMM registers in some of the processors. A 32-bit 80x86 CPU (from 80386 on) has 16 **basic program execution** registers. Typical instructions transfer data between these registers and memory or perform operations on data stored in the registers or in memory. All of these registers have names, and some of them have special purposes. Their names are given below and some of the special purposes are described. You will learn additional special purposes later.

The EAX, EBX, ECX, and EDX registers are called **data registers** or **general registers**. The EAX register is sometimes known as the **accumulator** because it is the destination for many arithmetic results. An example of an instruction using the EAX register is

```
add   eax, 158
```

that adds the decimal number 158 (converted to doubleword-length 2's complement form) to the number already in EAX, replacing the number originally in EAX by the sum. (Full descriptions of the **add** instruction and others mentioned here are in Chapter 4.)

Each of EAX, EBX, ECX, and EDX is 32 bits long. The Intel convention is to number bits right to left starting with 0 for the low-order bit, so that if you view one of these registers as 4 bytes, then the bits are numbered like this:

```
        31    24 23   16 15    8 7       0
      ┌──────┬──────┬──────┬──────┐
EAX   │      │      │      │      │
      └──────┴──────┴──────┴──────┘
```

Parts of the EAX register can be addressed separately from the whole. The low-order word, bits 0–15, is known as AX.

```
        31    24 23   16 15              0
      ┌──────┬──────┬──────────────────┐
EAX   │      │      │        AX         │
      └──────┴──────┴──────────────────┘
```

The instruction

```
sub   ax, 10
```

subtracts 10 from the word stored in AX without changing any of the high-order bits (16–31) of EAX.

Similarly, the low-order byte (bits 0–7) and the high-order byte (bits 8–15) of AX are known as AL and AH, respectively.

	31	24	23	16	15	8	7	0
EAX					AH		AL	

The instruction

```
mov   ah, '*'
```

copies 2A, the ASCII code for an asterisk, to bits 8–15, without changing any of the other bits of EAX.

The EBX, ECX, and EDX registers also have low-order words BX, CX, and DX, which are divided into high-order and low-order bytes BH and BL, CH and CL, and DH and DL. Each of these parts can be changed without altering other bits. It may be a surprise that there are *no* comparable names for the high-order words in EAX, EBX, ECX, and EDX—you cannot reference bits 16–31 independently by name.

The 8086 through 80286 processors have four 16-bit general registers called AX, BX, CX, and DX. The "E" was added for "extended" with the 32-bit 80386 registers. The 80386 and later architectures effectively include the original 16-bit architecture.

There are four additional 32-bit registers that Intel also calls general registers: ESI, EDI, ESP, and EBP. In fact, you can use these registers for operations like arithmetic, but normally you should save them for their special purposes. The ESI and EDI registers are **index registers**, where SI stands for "source index" and DI stands for "destination index." One of their uses is to indicate memory addresses of the source and destination when strings of characters are copied from one place to another in memory. They can also be used to implement array indexes. The names SI and DI can be used for the low-order words of ESI and EDI, respectively, but we have no occasion to do this.

The ESP register is the **stack pointer** for the system stack. It is sometimes changed directly by a program, but is more frequently changed automatically when data is pushed onto the stack or popped from the stack. One use for the stack is in procedure (subroutine) calls. The address of the instruction following the procedure call instruction is stored on the stack. When it is time to return, this address is retrieved from the stack. You will learn much more about the stack and the stack pointer register in Chapter 6.

The EBP register is the **base pointer** register. Normally the only data item accessed in the stack is the one at the top of the stack. However, the EBP register is often used to mark a fixed point in the stack other than the stack top, so that data near this point can be accessed. This is especially important with procedure calls and will be discussed in Chapter 6.

In addition to the eight general-purpose registers, 32-bit 80x86 CPUs have six 16-bit **segment registers**: CS, DS, ES, FS, GS, and SS. In the older 16-bit segmented memory model, the CS register contains the segment number of the code segment, the area of memory storing instructions currently being executed. Since a segment is 64 KB long, the length of a program's collection of instructions is often limited to 64 KB; a longer program requires that the contents of CS be changed while the program is running. Similarly, DS contains the segment number of the data segment, the area of memory storing most data. The SS register contains the segment number of the stack segment, where the stack is maintained. The ES register contains the segment number of the extra data segment that could have multiple uses. The FS and GS registers were added with the 80386, and make possible easy access to two additional data segments.

With the flat 32-bit memory model we use, the segment registers become essentially irrelevant to the programmer. The operating system gives each of CS, DS, ES, and SS values. Recall that each value is a pointer to a table entry that includes the actual starting address of the segment. That table also includes the size of your program, so that the operating system can indicate an error if your program accidentally or deliberately attempts to write in another area. However, all of this is transparent to the programmer who can just think in terms of 32-bit addresses.

The 32-bit **instruction pointer**, or EIP register, cannot be directly accessed by an assembly language programmer. The CPU has to fetch instructions to be executed from memory, and EIP keeps track of the address of the next instruction to be fetched. If this were an older, simpler computer architecture, the next instruction to be fetched would also be the next instruction to be executed. However, an 80x86 CPU actually fetches instructions to be executed later while it is still executing prior instructions, making the assumption (usually correct) that the instructions to be executed next will follow sequentially in memory. If this assumption turns out to be wrong, for example, if a procedure call is executed, then the CPU throws out the instructions it has stored, sets EIP to contain the address of the procedure, and then fetches its next instruction from the new address.

In addition to prefetching instructions, an 80x86 CPU actually starts execution of an instruction before it finishes execution of prior instructions. This use of **pipelining** increases effective processor speed.

Bit	Mnemonic	Usage
0	CF	carry flag
2	PF	parity flag
6	ZF	zero flag
7	SF	sign flag
10	DF	direction flag
11	OF	overflow flag

Figure 2.2 Selected EFLAGS bits

The final register is called the **flags register**. The name EFLAGS refers to this register, but this mnemonic is not used in instructions. Some of its 32 bits are used to set some characteristic of the 80x86 processor. Other bits, called **status flags**, indicate the outcome of execution of an instruction. Some of the flag register's 32 bits are named, and the names we use most frequently are given in Figure 2.2.

Bit 11 is the overflow flag (OF). It is set to 0 following an addition in which no overflow occurred and to 1 if overflow did occur. Similarly, bit 0, the carry flag (CF), indicates the absence or presence of a carry out from the sign position after an addition. Bit 7, the sign flag, contains the left bit of the result after some operations. Since the left bit is 0 for a non-negative 2's complement number and 1 for a negative number, SF indicates the sign. Bit 6, the zero flag (ZF) is set to 1 if the result of an operation is zero, and to 0 if the result is non-zero. Bit 2, the parity flag, is based only on the low-order 8 bits of a result; it is set to 1 if an even number of these bits are 1's and to 0 if an odd number of these bits are 1's. Other flags will be described later when their uses are clearer.

As an example of how flags are set by instructions, consider again the instruction

```
add eax, 158
```

This instruction affects CF, OF, PF, SF, and ZF. Suppose that EAX contains the word FF FF FF F3 prior to execution of the instruction. Since 158_{10} corresponds to the word 00 00 00 9E, this instruction adds FF FF FF F3 and 00 00 00 9E, putting the sum 00 00 00 91 in the EAX register. It sets the carry flag CF to 1 since there is a carry, the overflow flag OF to 0 since there is no overflow, the sign flag SF to 0 (the leftmost bit of the sum 00 00 00 91), and the zero flag ZF to 0 since the sum is not zero. The parity flag PF is set to 0 since 1001 0001 contains three 1 bits, an odd number.

Name	Length (Bits)	Use/Comments
EAX	32	accumulator, general use; low-order word AX, divided into bytes AH and AL
EBX	32	general use; low-order word BX, divided into bytes BH and BL
ECX	32	general use; low-order word CX, divided into bytes CH and CL
EDX	32	general use; low-order word DX, divided into bytes DH and DL
ESI	32	source index; source address in string moves, array index
EDI	32	destination index; address of destination, array index
ESP	32	stack pointer; address of top of stack
EBP	32	base pointer; address of reference point in the stack
CS	16	holds selector for code segment
DS	16	holds selector for data segment
ES	16	holds selector for extra segment
SS	16	holds selector for stack segment
FS	16	holds selector for additional segment
GS	16	holds selector for additional segment
EIP	32	instruction pointer; address of next instruction to be fetched
EFLAGS	32	collection of flags, or status bits

Figure 2.3 32-bit 80x86 application registers

The 32-bit 80x86 application registers are summarized in Figure 2.3. All but the earliest 32-bit 80x86 processors also contain a collection of registers for floating point operations. These are discussed in Chapter 9. In addition, many 80x86 processors have MMX and XMM registers; these are also discussed further in Chapter 9.

In the evolution of the 80x86 family, just as the 32-bit architecture effectively extended the 16-bit architecture, the 64-bit architecture extends the 32-bit architecture.

There are sixteen 64-bit general registers. The 64-bit register RAX extends the 32-bit register EAX, RBX extends EBX, and so forth up to EBP. However, there are eight new 64-bit general registers named R8, R9, R10, R11, R12, R13, R14, and R15. Just as you can refer to the low-order word of EAX as AX in a 32-bit environment, you can refer to the low-order doubleword of RAX as EAX in a 32-bit environment. For the new registers R8–R15, you append a D to refer to the low-order doubleword. For example, R9D refers to the low-order 32 bits of R9. Similarly, R11W refers to the low-order word (16 bits) of R11, and R15B refers to the low-order byte of R15.

Recall that in the 32-bit architecture, you can also access bits 8–16 of EAX, EBX, ECX, and EDX using names AH, BH, CH, and DH, respectively. These bytes cannot be accessed by name with some 64-bit instructions.

Index registers ESI and EDI are extended to 64-bit registers RSI and RDI, respectively. Low-order doublewords can be referenced as ESI and EDI, low-order words as SI and DI, and low-order bytes as SIL and DIL. ESP and EBP are extended to 64-bit registers RSP and RBP, respectively.

Segment registers have not changed in the 64-bit architecture. However, recall that they are essentially unused when the processor is operating in 64-bit mode.

In the 64-bit environment, the instruction pointer is the 64-bit register RIP. The flags are stored in the 64-bit register RFLAGS. The low-order 32-bits correspond exactly to EFLAGS. Intel documentation says that the high-order 32-bits of RFLAGS are "reserved."

Here is an example of an instruction that is legal in a 64-bit program, but not in a 32-bit program:

```
add   rax, r12
```

This adds the quadword in R12 to the quadword in RAX, replacing the value in RAX.

Figure 2.4 summarizes the basic program execution registers in the 64-bit architecture. It does not list floating point, MMX, and XMM registers, the other application registers.

Exercises 2.2

1. Draw a diagram showing the relationship between the ECX, CX, CH, and CL registers.
2. Draw a diagram showing the relationship between the RBX, EBX, BX, and BL registers.
*3. Draw a diagram showing the relationship between the R12, R12D, R12W, and R12B registers.

Name	Length (Bits)	Use/Comments
RAX	64	accumulator, general use; low-order doubleword EAX low-order word AX low-order byte AL
RBX, RCX, RDX, RSI, RDI	64	general use; low-order doubleword EBX, ECX, EDX, ESI, EDI low-order word EBX, ECX, EDX, SI, DI low-order byte BL, CL, DL, SIL, DIL
R8–R15	64	general use; low-order doubleword R8D–R15D low-order word R8W–R15W low-order byte R8B–R15B[1]
RSP	64	stack pointer; address of top of stack low-order doubleword ESP; word SP; byte SPL
RBP	64	base pointer; address of reference point in the stack low-order doubleword EBP; word BP; byte BPL
CS, DS, ES, SS, FS, GS	16	segment registers, not used in 64-bit mode
RIP	64	instruction pointer; address of next instruction to be fetched
RFLAGS	64	collection of flags, or status bits

[1]Intel documentation uses R8L–R15L, but these are not recognized by the Microsoft assembler.

Figure 2.4 64-bit 80x86 application registers

4. For each add instruction in this problem, assume that EAX contains the given contents before the instruction is executed, and give the contents of EAX as well as the values of the CF, OF, SF, and ZF flags after the instruction is executed:

	EAX Before	**Instruction**
(a)	00 00 00 45	add eax, 45
*(b)	FF FF FF 45	add eax, 45
(c)	00 00 00 45	add eax, -45
(d)	FF FF FF 45	add eax, -45
*(e)	FF FF FF FF	add eax, 1
(f)	7F FF FF FF	add eax, 100

2.3   PC Hardware: Input/Output Devices

A CPU and memory make a computer, but without input devices to get data or output devices to display or write data the computer is not usable for many purposes. Typical **I/O devices** include a keyboard and a mouse for input, a monitor to display output, and a disk drive for data and program storage.

An assembly language programmer has multiple ways to look at I/O devices. At the lowest level, each device uses a collection of addresses or **ports** in the I/O address space. There are 64-KB port addresses in the 80x86 architecture, and a typical I/O device uses three to eight ports. These addresses are distinct from ordinary memory addresses. The programmer uses instructions that output data or commands to these ports, or input data or status information from them. Such programming is very tedious and the resulting programs are difficult to reuse with different computer systems.

Instead of using separate port addresses, a computer system can be designed to use addresses in the regular memory address space for I/O device access. Such a design is said to use **memory-mapped input/output**. Although memory-mapped I/O is possible with the 80x86, it is not used with most PCs.

Many operating systems, including Windows XP and Vista, put the CPU in a protected mode that does not allow ordinary application programs to directly access I/O ports. They provide a variety of input and output procedures that are much easier to use than is port-level I/O.

▬▬▬ **Exercises 2.3**

It was stated in this section that there are 64-KB port addresses.

1. How many addresses is this (in decimal)?
*2. Assuming that the first address is 0, what is the last address?
3. Express the range of port addresses in hex.

2.4   PC Software

Without software, computer hardware is virtually useless. **Software** refers to the programs or procedures that are executed by the hardware. This section discusses different types of software.

PC Software: The Operating System

A general-purpose computer system needs an operating system to enable it to run other programs. The original IBM PC usually ran the operating system known as PC-DOS; compatible systems used the very similar operating systems called MS-DOS. DOS stands for **disk operating system**. All of these operating systems were developed by Microsoft Corporation; PC-DOS was customized by IBM to work on the IBM PC, and the versions of MS-DOS that ran on other computer systems were sometimes customized by their hardware manufacturers. Later versions of PC-DOS were produced solely by IBM.

The DOS operating systems provide the user a **command line interface**. DOS displays a prompt (such as `C:\>`) and waits for the user to type a command. When the user presses the Enter (or Return) key, DOS interprets the command. The command may be to perform a function that DOS knows how to do (such as displaying the directory of file names on a disk), or it may be the name of a program to be loaded and executed.

Many users prefer a **graphical user interface** that displays icons representing tasks or files, so that the user can make a selection by clicking on an icon with a mouse. Microsoft Windows provides a graphical user interface for PCs. The versions through Windows 3.1 enhanced the operating environment, but still required DOS to run. Windows 95 included a major revision of the operating system, which was no longer sold separately from the graphical user interface. In Windows 95 the graphical user interface became the primary user interface, although a command line interface was still available. The Windows operating system has continued to evolve and is currently available in many versions.

PC Software: Text Editors

A **text editor** is a program that allows the user to create or modify text files that are stored on secondary storage like a hard disk. A text file is a collection of ASCII codes. The text files of most interest in this book are assembly language source code files—files that contain assembly language statements. A text editor is sometimes used to prepare a data file.

Microsoft Windows includes a text editor called *Notepad*. This full-screen editor uses all or part of the monitor display as a window into the file. The user can move the window up or down (or left or right when the window is narrow) to display different portions of the file. To make changes to the file, cursor control keys or the mouse are used to move the cursor to the place to be modified, and the changes are entered. Notepad can be used to write or modify assembly language source programs, but we do most editing in an integrated development environment, discussed below.

Word processors are text editors that provide extra services for formatting and printing documents. For example, when one uses a text editor, usually the Enter key must be pressed at the end of each line. However, a word processor usually wraps words automatically to the next line as they are typed, so that Enter or some other key is used only at the end of a paragraph. The word processor takes care of putting the words on each line within specified margins. A word processor can sometimes be used as an editor to prepare an assembly language source code file, but some word processors store formatting information with the file along with the ASCII codes for the text. Such extra information may make the file unsuitable as an assembly language source code file, so it is safest to avoid a word processor when editing an assembly language source program.

PC Software: Language Translators and the Linker

Language translators are programs that translate a programmer's source code into a form that can be executed by the computer. These are usually not provided with an operating system. Language translators can be classified as interpreters, compilers, or assemblers.

Interpreters directly decipher a source program. To execute a program, an interpreter looks at a line of source code and follows the instructions of that line. Programs written in the Basic or Lisp languages are often executed by an interpreter. Although the interpreter itself may be a very efficient program, interpreted programs often execute relatively slowly. An interpreter is generally convenient because it allows a program to be quickly changed and run. The interpreter itself is sometimes a large program.

Compilers start with source code and produce object code that consists mostly of instructions to be executed by the intended CPU. High-level languages such as Fortran, Cobol, C, and C++ are commonly compiled. The object code produced by a compiler must often be linked or combined with other object code to make a program that can be loaded and executed. This requires a utility called a **linker**, usually provided with a compiler. Instead of producing code for a particular CPU, some compilers produce an intermediate code that can be very efficiently interpreted; this is common with Java compilers.

An **assembler** is used much like a compiler, but translates assembly language rather than a high-level language into machine code. The resulting files must normally be linked to prepare them for execution. Because assembly language is closer to machine code than a high-level language, the job of an assembler is somewhat simpler than the job of a compiler. Assemblers historically existed before compilers.

Using again the assembly language instruction cited in Section 2.2,

```
add eax, 158
```

is translated by the assembler into the 5 **object code** bytes 05 00 00 00 9E. The first byte 05 is the **op code** (operation code) that says to add the number contained in the next 4 bytes to the doubleword already in the EAX register. The doubleword 00 00 00 9E is the 2's complement representation of 158_{10}.

A **debugger** allows a programmer to control execution of a program, stepping through instructions one at a time, or pausing at a preset breakpoint. When the program is temporarily stopped, the programmer can examine the contents of variables in a high-level language, or registers or memory in assembly language. A debugger is useful both to find errors and to "see inside" a computer to find out how it executes programs.

Integrated development environments use a single interface to access an editor, a compiler, an assembler, and a linker. They also initiate execution of the program being developed, and frequently provide other utilities, such as a debugger. An integrated development environment is convenient, but may not always be available for a particular programming language. You will learn how to use Microsoft's Visual Studio integrated development environment for assembly language programs in Chapter 3.

2.5 Chapter Summary

This chapter discussed the hardware and software components that make up a PC microcomputer system.

The major hardware components are the CPU and memory. The CPU executes instructions and uses its internal registers for instruction operands and results, and to determine addresses of data and instructions stored in memory. Objects in memory can be addressed by 32-bit addresses with a 32-bit CPU and by 64-bit addresses with a 64-bit CPU. In a flat memory model, such addresses are effectively actual addresses. In a segmented memory model, addresses are calculated from a starting address determined from a segment number, and an offset within the segment.

Input/output at the hardware level uses a separate collection of addresses called "ports." Input/output is usually done through operating systems procedure calls.

An operating system is a vital software component. Through a command line or a graphical user interface, it interprets the user's requests to carry out commands, or to load and execute programs.

A text editor, an assembler, and a linker are necessary software tools for the assembly language programmer. These may be separate programs or available as part of an integrated development environment. A debugger is also a useful programmer's tool.

CHAPTER 3

Elements of Assembly Language

This chapter tells how to write and execute assembly language programs in the Visual Studio 2008 environment. The first section describes the statements that are accepted by Visual Studio's assembler. Then there is an example of a complete assembly language program, with instructions on how to assemble, link, and execute this program using the Visual Studio's debugger. Sections 3.3 and 3.4 provide additional information about operands for data definition directives and executable instructions, respectively. Section 3.5 gives an example of an assembly language program that employs input and output, and Section 3.6 describes in more detail the I/O macros used in this book. Section 3.7 presents examples of programs that use 64-bit registers and describes how to use Visual Studio for assembly language in a 64-bit operating system.

3.1 Assembly Language Statements

An assembly language source code file consists of a collection of **statements**. Most statements fit easily on an 80-character line, a good limit to observe so that source code can easily be printed or displayed in a window. However, the assembler allows much longer statements; these can be extended over more than one physical line using back-slash (\) characters at the end of each line except the last.

Figure 3.1 shows a short but complete assembly language. This example is used here and in the next section of this chapter to illustrate basic assembly statements and the mechanics of editing, assembling, linking, and executing a program with execution under the control of the debugger.

```
; Example assembly language program
; adds 158 to number in memory
; Author: R. Detmer
; Date:  1/2008

.586
.MODEL FLAT

.STACK 4096                     ; reserve 4096-byte stack

.DATA                           ; reserve storage for data
number DWORD  -105
sum    DWORD  ?

.CODE                           ; start of main program code
main   PROC
       mov    eax, number       ; first number to EAX
       add    eax, 158          ; add 158
       mov    sum, eax          ; sum to memory

       mov    eax, 0            ; exit with return code 0
       ret
main   ENDP

END
```

Figure 3.1 Example assembly language program

Because assembly language programs are far from self-documenting, it is important to use an adequate number of **comments**. A comment can be used on any line. A semicolon (;) begins the comment, and the comment then extends until the end of the line. An entire line is a comment if the semicolon is in column 1, or a comment can follow working parts of a statement. Our example has comments on most lines. As important as they are for the human reader, comments are ignored by the assembler.

There are three types of functional assembly language statements: instructions, directives, and macros. An **instruction** is translated by the assembler into one or more bytes of object code (machine code) which is executed at run time. Each instruction corresponds to one of the operations that the 80x86 CPU can perform. Our program has five instructions:

```
mov     eax, number
add     eax, 158
mov     sum, eax
mov     eax, 0
ret
```

The first of these instructions copies the doubleword in memory at the location identified by *number* to the EAX register in the CPU. The second adds a doubleword representation of 158 to the current doubleword in the EAX register. The third copies the doubleword in the EAX register to the doubleword in memory identified by *sum*. The last two instructions exit to the operating system. Much of this book describes the formats and uses of 80x86 instructions.

A **directive** tells the assembler to take some action. Such an action generally does not result in machine instructions and may or may not cause object code to be generated. In our example program, the directive

```
.586
```

tells the assembler to recognize 80x86 instructions that use 32-bit operands. The directive

```
.MODEL FLAT
```

tells the assembler to generate code for flat memory model execution. These directives and many others start with a period, but others do not.

Our example program contains several other directives. The directive `.STACK 4096` tells the assembler to generate a request to the operating system to reserve 4096 bytes for the system stack. The system stack is used at execution time for procedure calls and local storage. A stack containing 4096 bytes is large enough for most programs.

The `.DATA` directive tells the assembler that data items are about to be defined in a **data segment**. Each `DWORD` directive tells the assembler to reserve a doubleword of memory for data, the first identified with the label *number* and initialized to FFFFFF97 (-105_{10}), the second identified with the label *sum* and given the default initial value of 00000000. Section 3.3 provides additional information about data definition directives.

The `.CODE` directive tells the assembler that the next statements are executable instructions in a **code section**. The `PROC` directive marks the beginning of a procedure and the `ENDP` directive the end of a procedure. The `END` directive on the last line tells the assembler to stop assembling statements.

A **macro** is "shorthand" for a sequence of other statements—instructions, directives, or even other macros. The assembler expands a macro to the statements it represents, and then assembles the resulting statements. Our example program uses no macro. You will see several examples of macros in Sections 3.5 and 3.6.

A statement that is more than just a comment almost always contains a mnemonic that identifies the purpose of the statement, and may have three other fields: name, operand, and comment. These components must be in the following order:

```
name      mnemonic      operand(s)      ; comment
```

For example, a program might contain the statement

```
zeroCount: mov ecx, 0  ; initialize count to zero
```

The name field ends with a colon (:) when used with an instruction. However, when used with a directive, the name field has no colon. The mnemonic in a statement indicates a specific instruction, directive, or macro. Some statements have no operand, others have one, others have more. If there is more than one, operands are separated by commas; spaces can also be added. Sometimes a single operand has components with spaces between them, making it look like more than one operand.

One use for the name field is to symbolically reference an instruction's address in memory. Other instructions can then easily refer to the labeled instruction. If the **add** instruction in the sample program needed to be repeatedly executed in a program loop, then it could be coded

```
addLoop:  add eax, 158
```

The instruction can then be the destination of a **jmp** (jump) instruction, the assembly language version of a *goto*:

```
jmp   addLoop   ; repeat addition
```

Notice that the colon does not appear at the end of the name *addLoop* in the **jmp** instruction.

High-level language loop structures like *while* or *for* are not available in machine language. However, they can be implemented using **jmp** or other instructions. You will learn how this is done in Chapter 5.

It is sometimes useful to have a line of source code consisting of just a name, for example

```
endWhile1:
```

Such a label might mark the end of a while loop. Technically it references the address of whatever instruction follows the loop, but you don't have to know what that next statement is to complete coding of the while loop.

Names and other identifiers used in assembly language are formed from letters, digits, and special characters. The allowable special characters are underscore (_), question mark (?), dollar sign ($), and at sign (@). The special characters are rarely used in this book. A name may not begin with a digit. An identifier may have up to 247 characters, so that it is easy to form meaningful names. The assembler does not allow instruction mnemonics, directive mnemonics, register designations, and other words that have a special meaning to the assembler to be used as names. Appendix B contains a list of reserved identifiers.

Assembly language statements can be entered using either uppercase or lowercase letters. Normally the assembler does not distinguish between uppercase and lowercase. It can be instructed to distinguish within identifiers, but this is only needed when you are linking to a program written in a language that is case-sensitive. Mixed-case code is easier for people to read than code written in all uppercase or lowercase. All uppercase code is especially difficult to read. The convention followed for programs in this book is to use mostly lowercase source code except for uppercase directives.

The assembler accepts code that is almost impossible for a person to read. However, since your programs will also be read by other people, you should make your code as readable as possible. Good program formatting and use of lowercase letters will help.

Recall that assembly language statements can contain name, mnemonic, operand, and comment fields. A well-formatted program has these fields aligned as you read down the program. Always put names in column 1. Mnemonics might all start in column 12, operands might all start in column 18, and comments might all start in column 30—the particular columns are not as important as being consistent. Blank lines are allowed in an assembly language source file; they visually separate sections of assembly language code, just like breaking a written narrative into paragraphs.

Exercises 3.1

1. Name and describe the three types of assembly language statements.
2. For each combination of characters in this problem, determine whether it is an allowable label (name). If not, give a reason.

   (a) repeat   (b) exit

   *(c) more   (d) EndIf

   *(e) 2much   (f) add

   (g) if   (h) add2

   (i) EndOfProcessLoop

3.2   A Complete 32-Bit Example Using the Debugger

This section describes how to actually run the example shown in Figure 3.1 in the Microsoft Visual Studio 2008 environment. It assumes that you already have Visual Studio 2008 installed on your computer. The easiest way to generate a new project is to start with the *console32* project folder from the *Software* folder in the software provided for this book. Copy the *console32* folder to a convenient location on your computer. You may rename the folder to describe the particular project, perhaps *example1*.

Open the project folder by double-clicking on it. Inside you will see a file named *console32.sln* and a folder named *console32*. *Do not* rename this inner folder even if you renamed the folder that contains it. Double-click *console32.sln* to start Visual Studio 2008. You will see a screen similar to the one shown in Figure 3.2. Visual Studio 2008 is highly configurable so you may not see exactly the same window arrangement.

Look in the *Solution Explorer* window and click the symbol ⊞ to the left of *console32*. This opens up a list showing folders *Header Files*, *Resource Files*, and *Source Files*, each empty since this project does not yet have user files associated with it. We now want to add our program as a source file. Right-click *Source Files*, click *Add*, then *New Item* . . . . Be sure that *Code* is selected under *Categories*. Type a name for the file in the *Name* box. Figure 3.3 shows the name entered as *example1.asm*. You can choose a

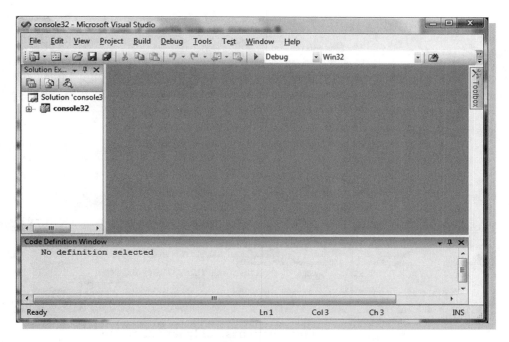

Figure 3.2 Project newly opened in Visual Studio 2008

different name, but be sure that it ends with the *.asm* extension. Finally, click the *Add* button. A text editor window named *example1.asm* opens.

You now have a choice. You can *carefully* type the code from Figure 3.1 into the *example1.asm* text editor window, or you can use Notepad to open *fig3-1.asm* from the *Code* folder of this book's software, select the entire contents (using control-A, for example), copy the text (control-C), click in the *example1.asm* window, and paste the text (control-V). The copy-and-paste method is definitely easier than typing the file!

You are now ready to execute the program. When you drop down the *Debug* menu in Visual Studio, you see *Start Debugging* as the second option, with F5 given as the shortcut key. You can either click on *Start Debugging* or just press F5 without opening the *Debug* menu. You will get a message that says "This project is out of date" and you click *Yes* to assemble, link, and initiate execution of the program. There are other options in the *Build* menu to do this, but just pressing F5 and clicking *Yes* for a new program or after any change is usually the fastest method to launch your program.

After clicking *Yes* you will see text in an *Output* window indicating progress of the assembly and linking process, and a console window will briefly open and close as the program executes. The bottom line in the output window will read "The program

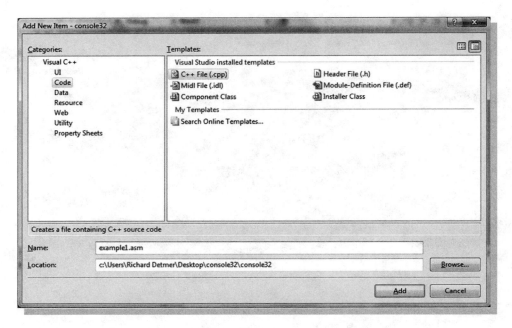

Figure 3.3 Adding a new assembly language file

'[1916] console32.exe: Native' has exited with code 0 (0x0)." (You will probably see a number different than 1916.)

What happened? The answer is that the computer followed our instructions exactly, but the program has no input or output and it executed in an instant. What we need to do now is to slow down program execution and "look inside" the computer to see what is going on as the program executes.

If necessary, scroll down in the *example1.asm* code window until the **mov** instruction is visible. Click next to this statement in the bar at the left of the window. You will then see a red dot marking a **breakpoint**, a place at which program execution will halt. Your Visual Studio display should then look something like the one shown in Figure 3.4. (*Note:* A breakpoint can be removed by clicking the red dot.)

Launch program execution by pressing F5. This time you may see the console window, or it may be hidden behind your Visual Studio window. Our program isn't going to use the console window, but you must not close it since technically the program is a console application. However, you can minimize it to reduce screen clutter. Execution is halted at the breakpoint, at the beginning of our program.

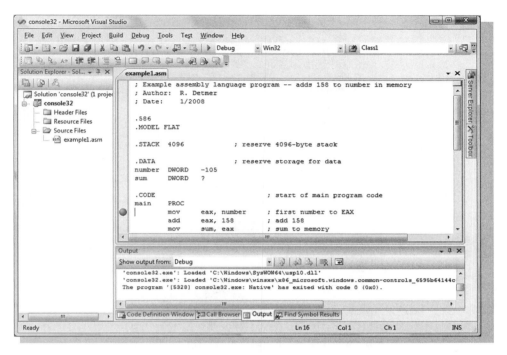

Figure 3.4 Program ready for execution with breakpoint set

We now want to arrange windows so that we can see contents of registers and relevant memory. In the drop-down *Debug* menu select the first option (*Windows*) and then *Registers*. Repeat the *Debug-Windows* option, selecting *Memory* and then *Memory 1*. You should have two collections of tabbed windows at the bottom of your screen. Drag the *Registers* tab to the right-hand collection, dropping it to the right of the existing tabs. (If you need to start over at any point, you can select the top-level *Window* option, and *Reset Window Layout*.)

Select the tab for the *Memory 1* window and type *&number* in the Address box. The C/C++ "address-of" operator is used here to select memory starting at the address of the variable *number*. You should now see a display similar to the one in Figure 3.5.

The *Memory 1* window shows in hex what is stored in memory starting at *number*. In this display, *number* is stored at address 00DF4000, but it may be different with a different system or at a different time. For each byte having an interpretation as a printable ASCII character, that character is shown to the right of the hex listing. An extended ASCII set is used, so unusual characters may appear. Control characters are displayed as periods on the right.

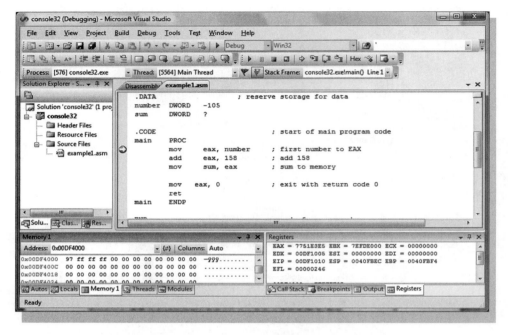

Figure 3.5 Program halted at first instruction

Here we see that the 4 bytes at *number* contain 97 ff ff ff. This is slightly surprising, since -105_{10} is FF FF FF 97 in 2's complement form. The reason for this is that the Intel architecture stores multi-byte integers in **little endian** form, that is, the bytes are reversed from the order you would usually expect, with the low-order bytes stored before the high-order bytes. We only have to think about little endian representation when looking at a memory display.

Look at the *Registers* window. Most of the register contents aren't meaningful—the registers simply contain whatever is left over from other usage. However, EIP contains the address of the first **mov** instruction since it is the instruction about to be executed. Press F10 to execute this instruction. (This is *Step Over* in the *Debug* menu.) In the *Registers* window, the contents of EAX and of EIP both become red to indicate that they have changed. EIP now contains the address of the **add** instruction, the next instruction to be executed. The yellow arrow on the left also points at the next instruction to be executed. EAX contains FFFFFF97, the value from number shown in high-order byte first order. The computer did exactly what we told it to—it copied the doubleword in memory at the address referenced by *number* into EAX.

Press F10 again. Now EAX, EIP, and EFL are in red. EIP has changed to be the address of the third instruction. EAX contains the sum of FFFFFF97 and 0000009E, or 00000035. The low-order word of EFLAGS is 0217_{16} = 0000 0010 0001 0111_2, where bits 0, 6, 7, and 11 have been highlighted. Recall that bit 0 is the carry flag, so CF=1 says there was a carry in this addition. Bit 11 is the overflow flag, so OF=0 says there was no overflow. Bit 6 is the zero flag and ZF=0 says that the result is not zero. Finally, bit 7 is the sign flag, and SF=0 says that the result is not negative.

Press F10 again. This time the *Memory 1* display changes as the 00000035 from EAX is copied to the second doubleword of the memory display. Since doublewords are stored in little endian form, you will see 35 00 00 00. Notice that EFL didn't change—more on which instructions actually affect flags is discussed in Chapter 4.

The program is now ready to execute the code

```
mov     eax, 0          ; exit with return code 0
ret
```

that exits to the calling program (in this case the operating system), returning a 0 value that indicates no errors. You should not use F10 to step through this code because no debug code is available. Just push F5 or click the continue button ▶ to exit the program. The console window closes, and your *Registers* and *Memory 1* windows also close. You can run the program again by pressing F5, and the *Registers* and *Memory 1* windows will reopen—you don't have to arrange windows again. If you ever need to terminate execution early, you can click the stop debugging button ■ on the toolbar, or select the stop debugging option from the *Debug* menu.

The *console32* Visual Studio project has an assembly option set that causes a **listing file** to be generated when your program is assembled. This file shows the source and the object code generated by the assembler. It is sometimes helpful to locate an assembly error (although double-clicking on the error message in the output window usually puts the cursor on the offending line of code). However, it is invaluable in understanding the assembly process.

In our example, the listing file is named *example1.lst*. (If you chose a different name than *example1.asm*, the listing file will have the name you chose with an extension of *.lst*.) You can open it by clicking the *Open File* icon in the toolbar, and then double-clicking *example1.lst*. It appears in an editor window with a new tab. The first part of the listing file is displayed in Figure 3.6. Sections 3.3 and 3.4 describe some listing file entries.

```
Microsoft (R) Macro Assembler Version 9.00.21022.08          07/05/08 20:28:05
.\example1.asm                              Page 1 - 1

                    ; Example assembly language program -- adds 158 to number in memory
                    ; Author:  R. Detmer
                    ; Date:    1/2008

                    .586
                    .MODEL FLAT

                    .STACK  4096           ; reserve 4096-byte stack

00000000            .DATA                  ; reserve storage for data
00000000 FFFFFF97      number  DWORD   -105
00000004 00000000      sum     DWORD   ?

00000000            .CODE                       ; start of main program code
00000000            main    PROC
00000000 A1 00000000 R         mov     eax, number   ; first number to EAX
00000005 05 0000009E           add     eax, 158      ; add 158
0000000A A3 00000004 R         mov     sum, eax      ; sum to memory

0000000F B8 00000000           mov     eax, 0        ; exit with return code 0
00000014 C3                    ret
00000015            main    ENDP

            END                                ; end of source code
```

Figure 3.6 Listing file

Programming Exercises 3.2

1. Modify the sample program to change the value of *number* to −253, and the second instruction to add 74 to the number in EAX. Assemble, link, and execute the program. Explain the changes that are displayed in registers and memory after execution of each instruction.

2. Modify the sample program to add two numbers stored in memory at *number1* and *number2*, respectively. (*Hint:* Copy *number1* to EAX, and then use add eax, *number2* to add the second number.) Continue to store the total in memory at *sum*. Assemble, link, and execute the program. Explain the changes that are displayed in registers and memory after execution of each instruction.

3.3   Data Declarations

This section explains the formats of operands used in **BYTE, WORD, DWORD,** and **QWORD** directives. Most of the information also applies to constant operands in instructions since simple constants are written the same way in directives and in instructions.

Numeric operands can be expressed in decimal, hexadecimal, binary, or octal notations. The assembler assumes that a number is decimal unless the number has a suffix indicating another base or a **.RADIX** directive (not used in this book) changes the default number base. The suffixes that may be used are

Suffix	Base	Number System
H	16	hexadecimal
B	2	binary
O or Q	8	octal
none	10	decimal

Any of these suffixes can be coded in uppercase or lowercase. The letter Q is easier to read than O on the rare occasions when you might need to code a constant in octal.

A hexadecimal value must start with a digit. You must, for example, code **0a8h** instead of **a8h** to get a constant with value $A8_{16}$. The assembler will interpret **a8h** as a name.

Now for some examples: The directive

```
byte0   BYTE   01111101b
```

reserves one byte of memory and initializes it to 7D. This is equivalent to any of the following directives

```
byte0   BYTE   7dh
byte0   BYTE   125
byte0   BYTE   175q
byte0   BYTE   '{'
```

since $1111101_2 = 7D_{16} = 125_{10} = 175_8$ and $7D_{16}$ is the ASCII code for a left brace. The choice of number systems should depend on the use planned for the constant. A binary value is appropriate when you need to think of the value as a sequence of eight separate bits, as in one of the logical operations covered in Chapter 7. A character in apostrophes is appropriate if you are using the value as a character.

A **BYTE** directive reserves storage for one or more bytes of data. If a data value is numeric, it can be thought of as signed or unsigned. The decimal range of unsigned values that can be stored in a single byte is 0 to 255. The decimal range of signed values that can be stored in a single byte is −128 to 127. The assembler will generate an error message for a **BYTE** directive with a numeric operand outside the range −128 to 255. Here are several examples. The comments in the examples indicate the initial values of the bytes that are reserved.

```
byte1    BYTE    255    ; value is FF
byte2    BYTE    127    ; value is 7F
byte3    BYTE    91     ; value is 5B
byte4    BYTE    0      ; value is 00
byte5    BYTE    -1     ; value is FF
byte6    BYTE    -91    ; value is A5
byte7    BYTE    -128   ; value is 80
```

The situation for **WORD**, **DWORD**, and **QWORD** directives is similar. Each operand of a **WORD** directive is stored in a doubleword, **DWORD** in a doubleword, or **QWORD** in a quadword. Doublewords are usually the best choice for integers. Since 4 bytes can store a signed number in the range −2,147,483,648 to 2,147,483,647 or an unsigned number from 0 to 4,294,967,295, you must restrict operand values to the range −2,147,483,648 to 4,294,967,295. Similarly, each operand for a **WORD** directive should be restricted to the range −32,768 to 65,535. The following examples give the initial values reserved for a few doublewords and words. Quadwords are used primarily in a 64-bit environment, but the assembler recognizes the **QWORD** directive in a 32-bit environment.

```
double1   DWORD   4294967295   ; value is FFFFFFFF
double2   DWORD   4294966296   ; value is FFFFFC18
double3   DWORD   0            ; value is 00000000
double4   DWORD   -1           ; value is FFFFFFFF
double5   DWORD   -1000        ; value is FFFFFC18
double6   DWORD   -2147483648  ; value is 80000000

word1     WORD    65535        ; value is FFFF
word2     WORD    32767        ; value is 7FFF
word3     WORD    1000         ; value is 03E8
word4     WORD    0            ; value is 0000
```

```
word5   WORD   -1              ; value is FFFF
word6   WORD   -1000           ; value is FC18
word7   WORD   -32768          ; value is 8000


quad1   QWORD -1               ; value is FFFFFFFFFFFFFFFF
quad2   QWORD 1000             ; value is 00000000000003E8
```

One of the points of these examples is that different operands can result in the same stored value. For instance, note that the **DWORD** directives with operands **4294967295** and **-1** both generate words containing FFFFFFFF. This value can be thought of as either the unsigned number 4,294,967,295 or the signed number -1, depending on the context in which it is used.

In addition to numeric operands, the **BYTE** directive allows character operands with a single character or string operands with many characters. Either apostrophes (') or quotation marks (") can be used to designate characters or delimit strings. They must be in pairs; you cannot put an apostrophe on the left and a quotation mark on the right. A string delimited with apostrophes can contain quotation marks, and one delimited with quotation marks can contain apostrophes, making it possible to have strings containing these special characters. Unless there is reason to do otherwise, this book follows the convention of putting single characters between apostrophes and strings of characters between quotation marks.

Each of the following **BYTE** directives is allowable.

```
char1   BYTE   'm'       ; value is 6D
char2   BYTE   6dh       ; value is 6D
string1 BYTE   "Joe"     ; value is 4A 6F 65
string2 BYTE   "Joe's"   ; value is 4A 6F 65 27 73
```

The same values are stored for *char1* and *char2*. As noted before, the directive you use should depend on the context of the code. If you are trying to store the letter *m*, it is wasted effort to look up the ASCII code $6D_{16}$—the assembler has a built-in ASCII chart! Notice that the delimiters, the apostrophes or quotation marks on the ends of the character or string, are not themselves stored.

BYTE, **WORD**, **DWORD**, and **QWORD** directives may have multiple operands separated by commas. The directive

```
dwords   DWORD  10, 20, 30, 40
```

reserves four doublewords of storage with initial values 0000000A, 00000014, 0000001E, and 00000028. The directives

```
string1   BYTE   "Joe"
string1   BYTE   'J', 'o', 'e'
```

result in the same 3 bytes being reserved.

The **DUP** operator can be used to generate multiple uninitialized values data fields as well as fields with known values. Its use is limited to **BYTE**, **WORD**, **DWORD**, **QWORD**, and other directives that reserve storage. The directive

```
DblArray   DWORD   100 DUP(999)
```

reserves 100 doublewords of storage, each initialized to 000003E7. This is an effective way to initialize elements of an array. If one needs a string of 50 asterisks, then

```
stars   BYTE   50 DUP('*')
```

will do the job. If one wants 25 asterisks separated by spaces, then

```
starsAndSpaces BYTE 24 DUP("* "), '*'
```

reserves these 49 bytes and assigns the desired initial values.

To reserve space without assigning any particular initial value, use the operand **?**. This reserves the appropriate number of bytes for the directive. These bytes are logically undefined; in fact the assembler assigns 00 to each byte. The **?** operand may be used with **DUP**, for example,

```
wordArray   DWORD   100 DUP (?)
```

to reserve 100 "undefined" doublewords, each actually containing 00000000.

An operand of a **BYTE**, **WORD**, **DWORD**, **QWORD**, or other statement can be an expression involving arithmetic or other operators. These expressions are evaluated by the assembler at assembly time, not at run time, with the resulting value used for assembly. It is rarely helpful to use an expression instead of the equivalent value, but sometimes it can contribute to clearer code. The following directives are equivalent, each reserving a word with an initial hex value of 00000090.

```
gross   DWORD   144
gross   DWORD   12*12
gross   DWORD   10*15 - 7 + 1
```

Each symbol defined by a **BYTE**, **WORD**, **DWORD**, or **QWORD**, directive is associated with a length. The assembler notes this length and checks to be sure that symbols are used appropriately in instructions. For example, the assembler will generate an error message if

```
char    BYTE    'x'
```

is used in the data segment and

```
mov EAX, char    ; illegal, different sizes
```

is used in the code segment—the EAX register is a doubleword long, but *char* is associated with a single byte of storage.

The Microsoft assembler recognizes several additional directives for reserving storage. These include **TBYTE** for a 10-byte integer, **REAL4**, for reserving a 4-byte floating point number, **REAL8** for an 8-byte floating point number, and **REAL10** for a 10-byte floating point number. It also has directives to distinguish signed bytes, words, and doublewords from unsigned. We use a few of these directives in Chapter 9.

Let us look again at three data section lines from the listing file in Figure 3.6 (slightly edited to save space):

```
00000000                .DATA            ; reserve storage
00000000 FFFFFF97        number  DWORD    -105
00000004 00000000        sum     DWORD    ?
```

The first **DWORD** directive generates a doubleword containing FFFFFF97. The second **DWORD** directive generates a doubleword containing 00000000. These values are shown in the second column of numbers. The first column of numbers contains addresses. The assembler assumes that the data segment starts at address 00000000. (This is adjusted when the program is linked and loaded.) Therefore, the assembly time address associated with *number* is 00000000. Since number is 4 bytes long starting at 00000000, the next available space is at address 00000004. This becomes the assembly time address of *sum*. Notice that the length of *sum* isn't needed to tell its starting address, but we know if there were a third data item, it would be at address 00000008. The next section looks at how these assembly time data locations are used in machine code.

Although data definition directives are often coded with a label, this is not required. For example, you might code

```
value1  DWORD   ?
        DWORD   ?
```

Since there are two DWORD directives, each with a single operand, two doublewords are reserved in the data segment. The first can be referenced by *value1*. The second can be referenced by *value1+4* as it is assembled 4 bytes after the first doubleword.

▨▨▨▨ Exercises 3.3

Find the initial values that the assembler will generate for each directive below. Write your answer using two hex digits for each byte generated. (*Hint:* You can check an answer by putting the directive in the data section of the sample program, and then looking at the listing file after assembly.)

```
 *1. byte1    BYTE   10110111b
  2. byte2    BYTE   33q
 *3. byte3    BYTE   0B7h
  4. byte4    BYTE   253
  5. byte5    BYTE   108
  6. byte6    BYTE   -73
 *7. byte7    BYTE   'D'
  8. byte8    BYTE   'd'
  9. byte9    BYTE   "Mary's program"
*10. byte10   BYTE   5 DUP("<>")
 11. byte11   BYTE   61 + 1
 12. byte12   BYTE   'c' - 1
 13. dword1   DWORD  1000000
 14. dword2   DWORD  1000000b
 15. dword3   DWORD  1000000h
 16. dword4   DWORD  1000000q
*17. dword5   DWORD  -1000000
 18. dword6   DWORD  -2
 19. dword7   DWORD  -10
 20. dword8   DWORD  23B8C9A5h
*21. dword9   DWORD  0, 1, 2, 3
 22. dword10  DWORD  5 DUP(0)
 23. word1    WORD   1010001001011001b
 24. word2    WORD   2274q
 25. word3    WORD   2274h
 26. word4    WORD   0ffffh
 27. word5    WORD   5000
```

```
   28. word6    WORD   -5000
   29. word7    WORD   -5, -4, -3, -2, -1
  *30. word8    WORD   8 DUP(1)
   31. word9    WORD   6 DUP(-999)
   32. word10   WORD   100/2
  *33. quad1    QWORD  -10
   34. quad2    QWORD  0ffffffffffffffffh
```

3.4   Instruction Operands

There are three basic types of instruction operands: (1) constants; (2) CPU register designations; and (3) references to memory locations. There are several ways of referencing
memory; two of the simpler ways are discussed in this section, and more complex methods will be explained later in this book.

Many instructions have two operands. In general, the first operand gives the
destination of the operation, although it may also designate a source that will be
replaced by the result of the operation. The second operand identifies a source for the
operation, never the destination. For example, when

```
    mov   al, '/'
```

is executed, the byte 2F (the ASCII code for the slash /) will be loaded into the AL register,
replacing the previous byte. The second operand '/' specifies the constant source. When

```
    add   eax, number1
```

is executed, EAX gets the sum of the doubleword in memory referenced by *number1*
and the old contents of EAX. The first operand EAX specifies the source for one doubleword as well as the destination for the sum; the second operand *number1* identifies the
memory location for the other of the two doublewords that are added together.

Figure 3.7 lists the addressing modes used by Intel 80x86 microprocessors, giving the location of the data for each mode. For an **immediate mode** operand, the data
to be used is built into the instruction before it is executed; once there it is constant.[1]
Normally the data is placed in the instruction by the assembler, although it can be

---

[1]One can write **self-modifying code**, that is, code that changes its own instructions as it executes. This is
considered a very poor programming practice.

Mode	Location of Data
immediate	in the instruction itself
register	in a register
memory	at some address in memory

Figure 3.7 80x86 addressing modes

inserted by the linker or loader, depending on the stage at which the value can be determined. The programmer writes an instruction including an actual value, or a symbol standing for a constant value. For a **register mode** operand, the data to be used is in a register. To indicate a register mode operand, the programmer simply codes the name of the register. A register mode operand can be coded as a source or as a destination, but an immediate mode operand cannot be a destination.

Here is a line from the code section of the Figure 3.6 listing file:

```
00000005   05 0000009E        add      eax, 158     ; add 158
```

The instruction mnemonic is **add**, the first operand EAX is obviously a register operand, and the second operand 158 is immediate. The number 00000005 is the assembly-time address of this instruction. The assembler starts assembling instructions at address 00000000 so whatever was assembled before this instruction took 5 bytes. This instruction also takes 5 bytes, an **opcode** 05 (in this case saying to add a doubleword built into the instruction to EAX), and the 4 bytes 0000009E of the doubleword representation of 158. Collectively, these 5 bytes are called the **object code** for this instruction. The listing file shows this object code, and since there is no address to be modified it is exactly the machine code that will be executed.

Here is another example where the first operand is register mode and the second operand is immediate mode. The object code (taken from an assembler listing file) is shown as a comment.

```
mov   al, '/'  ; B0 2F
```

The opcode B0 says to copy the next byte into AL, and the byte after the opcode contains the ASCII code 2F for a slash.

Memory addresses can be calculated several ways; Figure 3.8 lists the two most common in a 32-bit 80x86 environment. Any memory mode operand specifies a source of data in memory, or specifies a destination address in memory. A **direct mode** operand

✳ Memory Mode	Location of Data
direct	at a memory location whose address is built into the instruction
register indirect	at a memory location whose address is in a register

Figure 3.8 Two 80x86 memory addressing modes

has its 32-bit address built into the instruction. Generally the programmer will code a name that appears on a directive that reserves space in the data segment, and the assembler will translate this into the address.

Here is the third code segment line from the Figure 3.6 listing file:

```
0000000A  A3 00000004 R    mov   sum, eax  ; sum to memory
```

In this instruction, the second operand EAX is obviously register mode. The operand *sum* clearly references memory. In assembly language written for a 32-bit environment any memory reference coded as just a name will be direct. Here we can see exactly how the instruction is assembled. It starts with opcode A3, which says to copy a doubleword from EAX to the memory location specified in the instruction. The next 4 bytes 00000004 give the assembly time location of that destination. (Recall that *sum* appears in the data segment at assembly time address 00000004.) The value of *sum* is not stored at address 00000004 at execution time. The R following the address in the assembly listing says that this address is **relocatable**—it will be adjusted to the run-time address by the linker and loader.

Our example program has no instruction with a register indirect memory operand. Here is what one looks like. The comment gives the object code you would see in a listing file.

```
add   eax, [edx]   ; 03 02
```

The first operand EAX obviously is register mode, and the second operand is **register indirect mode**. Notice that there only 2 bytes of object code, not enough to contain a 32-bit memory address. Instead, the second byte contains bits that say to use the address in the EDX register to locate the second doubleword operand. In other words, the second number is not in EDX, but its address is. The square bracket notation ([ ]) indicates indirect addressing in assembly language. Figure 3.9 illustrates how register indirect addressing works in this example.

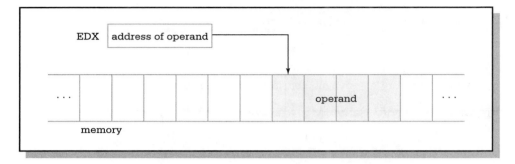

Figure 3.9 Register indirect addressing

Any of the general registers EAX, EBX, ECX, and EDX or the index registers ESI and EDI can be used for register indirect addressing. The base pointer EBP can also be used, but for an address in the stack rather than for an address in the data segment; this is used for procedure parameters. Although the stack pointer ESP can be used for register indirect addressing in special circumstances, we have no need to do so in 32-bit code.

With register indirect mode, the register serves like a pointer variable in a high-level language. The register contains the location of the data to be used in the instruction, not the data itself. When the size of the memory operand is ambiguous, the PTR operator must be used to give the size to the assembler. For example, the assembler will give an error message for

```
mov [ebx], 0     ; ambiguous destination size
```

because it cannot tell whether the destination is a byte, word, doubleword, or quadword. If it is a byte, you can use

```
mov BYTE PTR [ebx], 0    ; store 00 byte in memory
```

For a word, doubleword, or quadword destination, use **WORD PTR**, **DWORD PTR**, or **QWORD PTR**, respectively. In an instruction like

```
add    eax, [edx]
```

it is not necessary to use **DWORD PTR [edx]** because the assembler assumes that the source will be a doubleword, the size of the destination EAX.

A few instructions have no operand. Many have a single operand. Sometimes an instruction with no operand requires no data to operate on or an instruction with one operand needs only one value. Other times the location of one or more operands is implied by the instruction and is not coded. For example, one 80x86 instruction for multiplication is `mul`—it might be coded

```
mul   bh
```

Only one operand is given for this instruction; the other value to be multiplied is always in the AL register. The `mul` instructions are fully explained in the next chapter.

Exercises 3.4

Assuming a 32-bit operating environment, identify the mode of each operand in the following instructions. (*Note:* There are two operands in each instruction; identify both modes.) For a memory operand, specify whether it is direct memory mode or register indirect memory mode. Assume that the instructions are in a program also containing the code

```
.DATA
value   DWORD    ?
char    BYTE     ?

*1. mov   value, 100
 2. mov   ecx, value
 3. mov   ah, 0ah
*4. mov   eax, [esi]
 5. mov   [ebx], ecx
 6. mov   char, '*'
*7. add   value, 1
 8. add   DWORD PTR [ecx], 10
```

3.5   A Complete 32-Bit Example Using Windows Input/Output

The example program presented in Figure 3.1 includes no input or output. To see what it actually does, we traced the execution one instruction at a time using the debugger and looked at the state of memory and registers while execution was paused. While this is very helpful to understand how a computer works on the inside, our primary objective in this book, we are accustomed to programs that input data, do some computations, and output results. This section presents a simple example that does I/O using macros developed for this book. They are described more completely in Section 3.6.

In addition to adding I/O, this new example serves to emphasize the fact that data is represented in multiple forms—we use ASCII characters for input and output and 2's complement doubleword integers for computation. Obviously something is necessary to do the conversions from one format to another. We use macros developed for this book to do these tasks, too. These macros are introduced here, described more fully in Section 3.6, and have their internal workings explained in later chapters.

Here is a design for the program:

> prompt for the first number;
>
> input ASCII characters representing the first number;
>
> convert the characters to a 2's complement doubleword;
>
> store the first number in memory;
>
> prompt for the second number;
>
> input ASCII characters representing the second number;
>
> convert the characters to a 2's complement doubleword;
>
> store the second number in memory;
>
> add the two numbers;
>
> convert the sum to a string of ASCII characters;
>
> display a label and the characters representing the sum;

This design is implemented by the complete program shown in Figure 3.10. The parts are explained below. This program is already built into the *windows32* Visual Studio project included with the software for this book.

There are many similarities between this program and the simpler program in Figure 3.1. It starts with opening comments and the **.586** and **.MODEL FLAT** directives. The first new statement is the directive **INCLUDE io.h** that says to process the header file *io.h* just as if its lines were physically in the source code at this point. The header file *io.h* contains descriptions of the macros that are used for I/O and for conversions between ASCII and integer formats.

The data segment is longer than for our earlier example. It has two doublewords to store the 2's complement versions of our two numbers, two character strings to prompt for the numbers, and a string to label the output. In addition, there is a 40-byte-long undefined string used to input ASCII characters that will be converted to 2's complement form for computation, and an 11-byte-long string that will be used for holding

```
; Example assembly language program -- adds two numbers
; Author:  R. Detmer
; Date:    1/2008

.586
.MODEL FLAT

INCLUDE io.h              ; header file for input/output

.STACK 4096

.DATA
number1 DWORD    ?
number2 DWORD    ?
prompt1 BYTE     "Enter first number", 0
prompt2 BYTE     "Enter second number", 0
string  BYTE     40 DUP (?)
resultLbl BYTE   "The sum is", 0
sum     BYTE     11 DUP (?), 0

.CODE
_MainProc PROC
        input   prompt1, string, 40      ; read ASCII characters
        atod    string           ; convert to integer
        mov     number1, eax     ; store in memory

        input   prompt2, string, 40      ; repeat for second number
        atod    string
        mov     number2, eax

        mov     eax, number1     ; first number to EAX
        add     eax, number2     ; add second number
        dtoa    sum, eax         ; convert to ASCII characters
        output  resultLbl, sum   ; output label and sum

        mov     eax, 0  ; exit with return code 0
        ret
_MainProc ENDP
END                              ; end of source code
```

Figure 3.10 Assembly language program with I/O

the ASCII version of the sum. Note that each of the strings used for output is null-terminated, that is, with a final 0 operand that will be stored as a 00 byte.

The code segment contains one **PROC** named _MainProc_. The code framework we are using is actually a C program whose execution starts with function _main_. This framework is designed to always call _MainProc_, so this must be the name of our assembly language procedure. Chapter 6 carefully examines procedure calls.

The statement

```
input    prompt1, string, 40    ; read ASCII characters
```

is a macro with three operands. It expands to instructions that call a procedure to display a Windows dialog box that looks like

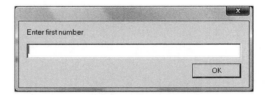

The first operand specifies the label that appears in the dialog box for this program the string in memory referenced by _prompt1_. This serves to prompt the user for what is expected in the text box. The user should enter a number in the text box and then click OK. After OK is clicked, the ASCII codes for whatever has been entered in the text box are copied to the destination specified by the second operand here, _string_. _The third operand must always be the length of the destination string_—40 in this case because 40 bytes are reserved for _string_ in the data segment. There is nothing special about the choice of 40 in this example other than the fact that it provides a longer string than you would expect a user to enter. In general, you want to be somewhat generous with the size of an input area—you might be expecting the user to enter 7, but the user might type several leading spaces before 7, or might type the numerically equivalent 000000000007.

The next statement in _MainProc_

```
atod     string          ; convert to integer
```

is a macro with a single operand. Its name stands for "ASCII to double" and it expands to instructions that call a procedure to scan memory starting at the location specified by the operand looking for the ASCII representation for a number. It converts the ASCII representation to the corresponding 2's complement doubleword integer. This doubleword is always stored in EAX—no destination operand is allowed.

The third statement requires little explanation. This **mov** instruction copies the doubleword in EAX to a doubleword in memory at *number1*.

Obviously, statements 4 through 6 of *_MainProc* repeat the task just for the second number. One thing to notice is that although the final result is copied to a separate doubleword, the same 40-byte input area is reused—we need each ASCII representation only long enough to convert it to a 2's complement doubleword.

The two instructions

```
mov     eax, number1    ; first number to EAX
add     eax, number2    ; add second number
```

just add the two doublewords. This is similar to the addition done in the first example program, the difference being that the second number added is stored in memory instead of as an immediate operand built into the instruction. You might notice that the second number is already in EAX following the **atod** macro, so we could have simply added the first number. This code implements the design element "add the two numbers" in the way that is done most often, even though this isn't the most efficient implementation for this particular situation.

The sum in EAX is in 2's complement form. It must be converted to an ASCII representation for display purposes. This is the job of the macro

```
dtoa    sum, eax     ; convert to ASCII characters
```

The "double to ASCII" macro has two operands, specifying a destination string and a doubleword source, respectively. The destination string *must* be exactly 11 bytes long because the procedure called by the **dtoa** code *always* stores exactly 11 ASCII code bytes at the destination. The destination will often be terminated with a null byte in the data segment, but the **dtoa** macro does not generate a trailing null byte.

The statement

```
output  resultLbl, sum          ; output label and sum
```

is a macro that expands to statements calling a procedure to display a Windows message box. The string specified by the first operand is used as a label, and the string specified by the second operand is the message. It might look like

To terminate the program, the last two instructions put a value of 0 in EAX to indicate no error, and execute a **ret** (return) instruction. This returns control to the C program that called *_MainProc*. The reader familiar with C or C++ will recognize the similarity to the **return** 0 statement that usually terminates function *main* written in C/C++.

Although this program doesn't require the debugger to see results, it is still very instructive to run it under the debugger to see what is actually happening in registers and memory. Set a breakpoint at the first statement, start the program, and arrange memory and register windows as done in Section 3.2. Start the memory display at the address of *number1*. Your display should be similar to the one shown in Figure 3.11.

Notice that the memory display is more interesting this time. The first 8 bytes are undefined memory (actually null bytes) for *number1* and *number2*, but next you see the ASCII codes for the strings defined in *prompt1* and *prompt2*. Because they are ASCII codes, the corresponding characters appear in the display. The 40 bytes of *string* resulted in null bytes, but then you see the ASCII codes for *resultLbl*.

Now press F10 to execute the code associated with the **input** macro, type −5247 in the dialog box and click OK. The memory display will then be similar to the one in Figure 3.12.

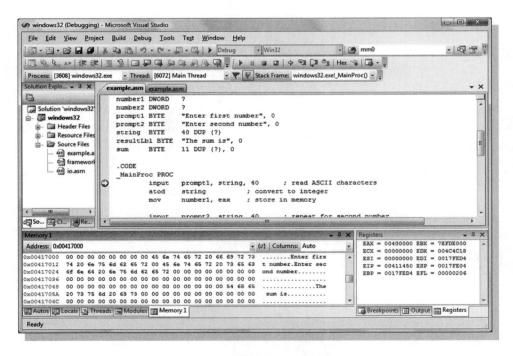

Figure 3.11 Program halted at first instruction

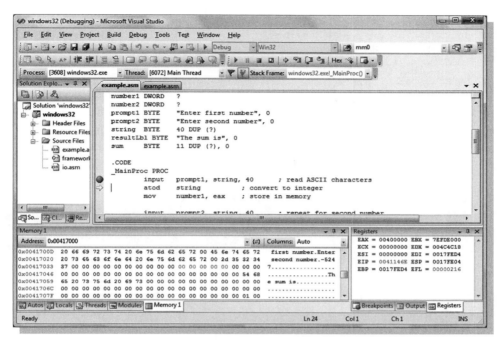

Figure 3.12 Text from dialog box stored in string

Notice that the ASCII codes 2D, 35, 32, 34, and 37 have now been added to the memory display in the area associated with *string*.

Now press F10 to execute the code to which the **atod** macro expands. The register display changes to show FFFFEB81 in EAX. The macro has done its job of converting the ASCII representation of −5247 to the doubleword 2's complement representation. One more press of F10 copies FFFFEB81 from EAX to memory at *number1*, where you can see it in little endian form in Figure 3.13.

Step through the next three statements, this time entering 486 in the dialog box. The resulting display is shown in Figure 3.14. One small thing to notice is that the memory at *string* starts with 34 38 36 00 37, the ASCII codes for 4, 8, and 6, respectively, followed by a null byte, followed by the 37 code left over from the 7 in −5247. The input macro provided the null byte to terminate its string, and this ensures that **atod** doesn't pick up extra characters from prior input when scanning memory for digits of an integer.

After executing the next three statements, the display looks like the one shown in Figure 3.15. EAX still contains FFFFED67, the sum of −5247 and 486 as a 2's complement doubleword. Memory starting at sum has 20 20 20 20 20 20 2d 34 37 36 31, ASCII

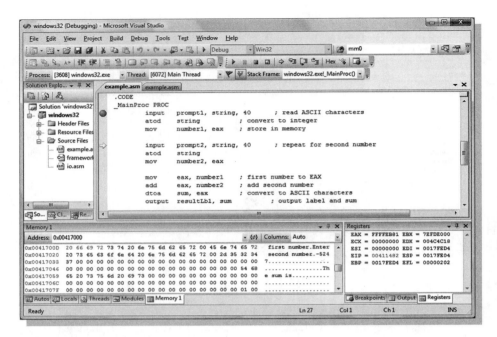

Figure 3.13 ASCII codes converted to 2's complement

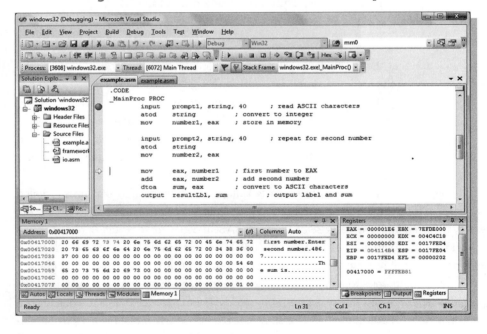

Figure 3.14 Program ready to add numbers

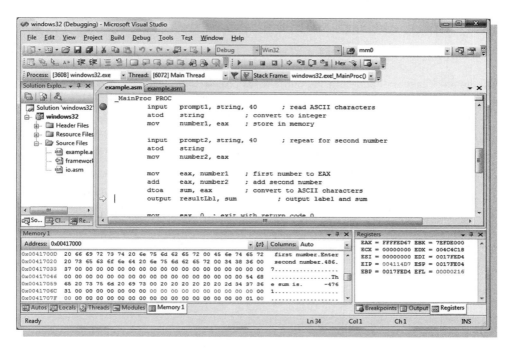

Figure 3.15 Program ready to output sum

codes for six spaces, a minus sign, 4, 7, 6, and 1, that is, the ASCII representation for the sum −4761 padded with leading spaces.

Programming Exercises 3.5

1. Starting with the *windows32* project, modify the example program given in this section to prompt for, input and add three numbers, and display the sum. Run the program several times with different data. Trace execution using the debugger.

2. The instruction sub eax, *label* will subtract the doubleword at *label* from the doubleword already in the EAX register. Starting with the *windows32* project, modify the example program given in this section to prompt for and input two numbers, subtract the second number from the first, and finally, display the result. Run the program several times with different data. Trace execution using the debugger.

3.6 Input/Output and Data Conversion Macros Defined in IO.H

The header file *io.h* included in the *windows32* project defines six macros; one for input, one for output, and four for conversions between ASCII and 2's complement formats. The I/O macros facilitate input and output in a Windows environment, and the conversion macros can be used whenever ASCII/integer conversions are needed. Both doubleword-size and word-size conversions are available, but recall that doubleword integers are the preferred size. The six macros are summarized in Figure 3.16.

The job of the *input* macro is to prompt for and input a string of characters. It causes a Windows dialog box to open. The label of the dialog box will be the string in

Name	Parameter(s)	Action
atod	*source*	Scans the string starting at *source* for + or − followed by digits, interpreting these characters as an integer. The corresponding 2's complement number is put in EAX.
dtoa	*destination, source*	Converts the doubleword at *source* (register or memory) to an 11-byte-long ASCII string at *destination*.
atow	*source*	Similar to **atod**, except that the resulting number is placed in AX.
wtoa	*destination, source*	Converts the word at *source* (register or memory) to a 6-byte-long ASCII string at *destination*.
input	*prompt, destination, length*	Generates a dialog box with label specified by *prompt*, where *prompt* references a string in the data segment. When OK is pressed, up to *length* characters are copied from the dialog box to memory at *destination*.
output	*labelMsg, valueMsg*	Generates a message box with the label *labelMsg*, and *valueMsg* in the message area. Each of *labelMsg* and *valueMsg* references a string in the data segment.

Figure 3.16 Macros in IO.H

memory referenced by the first operand. The dialog box has an OK button. If no entry is made in the dialog box and OK is pressed, a message box appears with "Warning—Nothing entered." Otherwise, characters that have been entered in the dialog box are copied to memory when OK is pressed. These characters are followed in memory by a null (00) byte. The second operand references the destination address, and the third operand is a constant that gives the number of bytes reserved at the destination. If too many characters are entered in the dialog box, the extra characters are truncated.

The *output* macro generates a Windows message box displaying two strings. The first string provides a label for the message box and the second string appears in the main message area. These strings are referenced by the first and second parameters, respectively. Each must be null-terminated.

The output message box *valueMsg* string will appear on multiple lines if it contains newline characters. For example, if the data segment contains

```
addrLbl BYTE    "address", 0
strCity BYTE    "123 Main Street", 0dh, 0ah, "Bigtown, NY", 0
```

and

```
output  addrLbl, strCity
```

is executed, then the following message box is displayed.

The street and city lines of the message are separated in the *strCity* operand by 0D and 0A bytes, carriage return and linefeed characters. Actually, either of these separators will work by itself, but we followed the "MS-DOS" convention for separating text lines.

Although the *input* macro can be used to input any string, commonly we use it to input a string that is the ASCII representation of an integer. To use this number for arithmetic, it is necessary to convert it to "internal" form. This is the job done by the *atod* ("ASCII to double") or *atow* ("ASCII to word") macro. They work the same way except that *atod* produces a doubleword-length 2's complement number in EAX, while *atow* produces a word-length 2's complement number in AX. Each has a single operand referencing an address in the data segment at which to start scanning memory. The scan process skips leading spaces. After spaces, if any, there can be a plus (+) or minus (−) character. Immediately following the sign, if any, there must be ASCII codes 30 to 39; that is, characters '0' through '9.' The value that corresponds to the aggregate of these digits is computed, negated if there was a minus sign, and returned in EAX or AX.

The *atod* or *atow* macro code stops scanning memory when it comes to a nondigit (except for optional leading spaces and sign, of course). Often this nondigit is a null byte. In the event that there is no digit, 0 is returned. In the event that there are too many digits so that the resulting number is too large for the destination register, the return value is undefined, but there is no way to detect this error other than unexpected results.

The *dtoa* ("double to ASCII") and *wtoa* ("word to ASCII") macros perform conversions from 2's complement to ASCII representations. They are very similar except that *dtoa* starts with a doubleword source and produces an 11-byte-long string, while *wtoa* starts with a word source and produces a 6-byte-long string. In both cases, the second operand specifies the source; it can be in a register or in memory. The first operand specifies the destination address in memory. The *dtoa* macro always produces 11 ASCII codes, so the destination area will be 11 bytes long. Similarly, the *wtoa* macro always produces six ASCII codes, so the destination area will be 6 bytes long.

Let's look at an example. If EBX contains the 2's complement number FFFFC9D3, the corresponding decimal value is −13869, so the statement

```
dtoa    dest, ebx
```

will produce ASCII codes 20 20 20 20 20 2D 31 33 38 36 39 starting at *dest*. Similarly, if EBX contains 000000F4, the corresponding decimal value is 244 and the *dtoa* macro will produce 20 20 20 20 20 20 20 20 32 34 34, padding with leading spaces. Notice that no trailing null byte is generated—often a destination area in the data segment will have a trailing extra null byte defined, for instance

```
dest    BYTE 11 DUP(?), 0
```

Sometimes the 11-byte destination area is much longer than necessary for the size of the source number. This is particularly true for doubleword values. The extra bytes are always filled on the left with 20 (space) codes. Why is the *dtoa* macro written to always generate 11 ASCII codes? The answer is to keep it simple. In decimal the range of integers that can be stored in 2's complement form in a word is −4,294,967,296 to 4,294,967,295, so for a big negative number 11 bytes are actually needed, but never more. Exercise 3.6.1 asks you to explain why 6 bytes are used for *wtoa*.

Except for *atod* and *atow*, each of the macros defined in IO.H is designed to leave general registers unchanged. The macros *atod* and *atow* obviously change EAX and AX, respectively, since this is their job. However, these macros change no other general register.

Exercises 3.6

1. Why wasn't the *wtoa* macro designed to produce a smaller number of ASCII codes? Explain what is important about the number 6.

*2. Given the data segment definitions

```
response1 BYTE    20 DUP(?)
askLbl    BYTE    "Please enter a number", 0
```

and the code segment macro

```
input   askLbl, response1, 20
```

   (a) What bytes will be stored in the data segment at *response1* if −578 is entered in the dialog box and OK is pressed?

   (b) If the macro

```
atod    response1
```

   follows the above input macro, what will be stored in the EAX register?

3. Suppose a program contains the data segment definitions

```
value1    DWORD   ?
sumLbl    BYTE    "The result is", 0
result1   BYTE    11 DUP(?), " total", 0
```

and the code segment macro

```
dtoa    result1, value1
```

   (a) Assuming that at run time the doubleword referenced by *value1* contains FFFFFF1A, what bytes will be placed in memory at *result1* by the *dtoa* macro?

   (b) If the *dtoa* macro is followed by

```
output  sumLbl, result1
```

   draw a picture that shows what the resulting message box will look like.

3.7   64-Bit Examples

When Visual Studio 2008 is installed on a 64-bit 80x86 CPU using a 64-bit operating system, 64-bit assembly language programs can be assembled and executed using steps

```
; Example assembly language program
; adds 158 to number in memory
; Author:   R. Detmer
; Date:     1/2008

.DATA
number   QWORD    -105
sum      QWORD    ?

.CODE
main     PROC
         mov     rax, number      ; first number to EAX
         add     rax, 158         ; add 158
         mov     sum, rax         ; sum to memory

         mov     rax, 0           ; return code
         ret                      ; exit to operating system
main     ENDP
END
```

Figure 3.17 Example assembly language program

similar to those described in Sections 3.2 and 3.5 for 32-bit programs. These steps are described in this section.

Figure 3.17 displays a 64-bit version of the simple program shown in Figure 3.1 and discussed in Section 3.2. The first difference to note is that the 64-bit version has no **.586**, **.MODEL FLAT**, or **.STACK** directives; these are not needed nor are they recognized in the 64-bit environment. (Stack size can be adjusted using a Visual Studio project property.) The data segment reserves quadwords for *number* and *sum* instead of doublewords, and the code segment uses the 64-bit register RAX instead of the 32-bit register EAX. It exits by putting 0 in RAX and executing a **ret** instruction.

This project is put together much as described in Section 3.2 for the 32-bit example. Copy the *console64* project folder from this book's source files. As with the *console32* project, you can rename the outer folder, but not the inner folder. Double-click on the *console64.sln* file to start Visual Studio and open the project. Look in the *Solution Explorer* window and click the symbol ⊞ to the left of *console64*. Right-click *Source Files*, click *Add*, then *New Item...*. Check that *Code* is selected under *Categories*. Type a name for the file in the *Name* box, being sure it ends with the *.asm* extension. Finally, click the *Add* button. Copy the file *fig3-17.asm* into the text editor window.

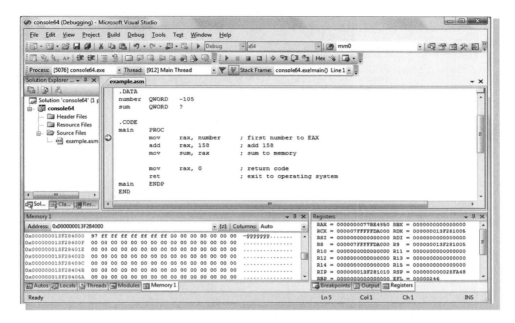

Figure 3.18 Program stopped at breakpoint

Put a breakpoint at the first **mov** instruction. Launch the program by pressing F5. When the program stops at the breakpoint, open a memory window to display memory starting at *&number* and open the registers window. The resulting display will look similar to the one in Figure 3.18.

Several things are different about this display. The *Registers* window shows 64-bit registers, including the new general registers R8 to R15. The *Memory1* window shows 64-bit addresses and you can see the quadword representation of −105 at the beginning of the block of memory. As in the 32-bit environment, the program is traced by repeatedly pressing F10; to terminate the program you should press F5 or the Continue button when you come to the **ret** statement.

Figure 3.19 shows part of the listing file. It is somewhat surprising that assembly time addresses are shown as only 32 bits. However, the data segment reserves two quadwords, as expected. In the code segment, the immediate operand 158 for the **add** instruction is encoded as a doubleword, even though it will be added to a quadword. Each of the two **mov** instructions references memory, but there is only 4 bytes built into the instruction for an address. The reason for this is that "direct" memory references are encoded using **RIP-relative addressing**, a memory addressing mode not even available in 32-bit mode. With RIP-relative addressing the memory operand is located as a

```
Microsoft (R) Macro Assembler (x64) Version 9.00.21022.08    02/04/08 18:01:00
.\example.asm                           Page 1 - 1

                    ; Example assembly language program
                    ; adds 158 to number in memory
                    ; Author:  R. Detmer
                    ; Date:    1/2008

00000000            .DATA
00000000            number  QWORD   -105
     FFFFFFFFFFFFFF97
00000008            sum     QWORD   ?
        0000000000000000

00000000            .CODE
00000000            main    PROC
00000000  48/ 8B 05         mov     rax, number    ; first number to EAX
          00000000 R
00000007  48/ 05            add     rax, 158       ; add 158
          0000009E
0000000D  48/ 89 05         mov     sum, rax       ; sum to memory
          00000008 R

00000014  48/ C7 C0         mov     rax, 0         ; return code
          00000000
0000001B  C3                ret                    ; exit to operating system

0000001C            main    ENDP
          END
```

Figure 3.19 Listing file for 64-bit program

displacement from the address in the code segment of the next instruction. A 32-bit displacement locates memory 2^{31} bytes before or after the instruction, and it is not difficult for the linker and loader to place the data and code segments within 2 GB of each other! It is left as an exercise to verify that. For this example, the 4 bytes in the first **mov** instruction at execution time are actually the displacement from the **add** instruction to number in the data segment.

The project *windows64* in this book's source files contains a 64-bit version of the *windows32* program that first appeared in Figure 3.10. It appears now in Figure 3.20. It has the same omissions as the 64-bit console application, namely the **.586**, **.MODEL**

```
; Example assembly language program -- adds two numbers
; Author:  R. Detmer
; Date:    1/2008

INCLUDE io.h                ; header file for input/output

.DATA                       ; reserve storage for data
number1   DWORD   ?
number2   DWORD   ?
prompt1   BYTE    "Enter first number", 0
prompt2   BYTE    "Enter second number", 0
string    BYTE    40 DUP (?)
resultLbl BYTE    "The sum is", 0
sum       BYTE    11 DUP(?), 0

.CODE
MainProc  PROC
          sub    rsp, 120          ; reserve stack space for MainProc
          input  prompt1, string, 40    ; read ASCII characters
          atod   string            ; convert to integer
          mov    number1, eax      ; store in memory

          input  prompt2, string, 40    ; repeat for second number
          atod   string
          mov    number2, eax

          mov    eax, number1      ; first number to EAX
          add    eax, number2      ; add second number
          dtoa   sum, eax          ; convert to ASCII characters
          output resultLbl, sum    ; output label and sum

          add    rsp, 120          ; restore stack
          mov    rax, 0            ; value to return (0)
          ret
MainProc  ENDP
END
```

Figure 3.20 64-bit program using Windows I/O

FLAT and **.STACK** directives. The only other changes are the statements that appear at the beginning and end of the code:

```
sub     rsp, 120       ; reserve stack space for MainProc
        . . .
add     rsp, 120       ; restore stack
```

The first of these statements reserves stack space for the use of this procedure, and the second statement releases it. They are required because *MainProc* calls other procedures inside the macro code for the *input* and *output* macros. This is explained more fully when 64-bit procedure protocol is discussed in Chapter 6.

Although the underlying code is different, exactly the same six macros are defined in the 64-bit version of *io.h* as are defined in the 32-bit version. These were described in Section 3.6. In particular, there are *not* new "atoq" or "qtoa" macros. This may seem like an omission since there are quadword registers in the 64-bit environment. However, it turns out that 32-bit integers are still the default size in most 64-bit environments. There is also no educational advantage to adding more conversion routines. The reader who misses "atoq" and "qtoa" is invited to write them as the various pieces of *atod* and *dtoa* are explained in later chapters.

The *windows64* project is built and executed identically to the *windows32* project. Of course, if you set breakpoints and examine memory and registers, you will see 64-bit memory addresses and 64-bit registers.

Exercise 3.7

1. Assemble and run the *console64* program in Figure 3.17, stopping at the add instruction. Note the run-time address of *number* (the address at which the *Memory1* display begins). Note the address of the add instruction (the value in the RIP register). Open a *Memory2* window that starts at the address *main*, and find the displacement in the first mov instruction (the 4 bytes following 48 8b 05, stored in little endian order). Verify that the address of the add instruction plus the displacement equals the address of *number*.

Programming Exercises 3.7

These exercises are identical to those in Section 3.5.

1. Starting with the *windows64* project, modify the example program given in this section to prompt for, input and add three numbers,

and display the sum. Run the program several times with different data. Trace execution using the debugger.

2. The instruction sub eax, *label* will subtract the doubleword at *label* from the doubleword already in the EAX register. Starting with the *windows64* project, modify the example program given in this section to prompt for and input two numbers, subtract the second number from the first, and finally, display the result. Run the program several times with different data. Trace execution using the debugger.

3.8 Chapter Summary

This chapter introduced 80x86 assembly language as translated by the Visual Studio 2008 assembler.

Assembly language comments start with a semicolon. Other statements have the format

```
name mnemonic operand(s) ; comment
```

where some of these fields may be optional.

The three types of assembly language statements are

- instructions—each corresponds to a CPU instruction
- directives—tell the assembler what to do
- macros—expand into additional statements

An assembly language program consists mainly of a data segment in which variables are defined and a code segment that contains statements to be executed at run time. To get an executable program, one must translate the program to object code using an assembler and then link the program using a linker. An executable program can be traced with a debugger. All of these tools are integrated in Visual Studio 2008.

BYTE, WORD, DWORD, and QWORD directives reserve bytes, words, doublewords, and quadwords of storage, respectively, and optionally assign initial values.

Instruction operands have three modes:

- immediate—data built into the instruction

- register—data in a register
- memory—data in storage

Memory mode operands come in several formats, two of which are

- direct—at an address in the instruction
- register indirect—data at an address in a register

The 64-bit environment uses RIP-relative addressing instead of direct memory addressing.

Several macros for input and output are defined in the file *io.h*. They call procedures with source code in the file *io.asm*. The macros are

- *output*—to display a label and a result string in a message box
- *input*—to input a string using a dialog box
- *atod*—to convert a string to a doubleword-length 2's complement number
- *dtoa*—to convert a doubleword-length 2's complement number to a string
- *atow*—to convert a string to a word-length 2's complement number
- *wtoa*—to convert a word-length 2's complement number to a string

There are minor differences in the steps for building a 32-bit Visual Studio project and a 64-bit Visual Studio project. There are also minor differences in the assembly language code.

CHAPTER 4

Basic Instructions

This chapter covers instructions used to copy data from one location to another and instructions used for integer arithmetic. It specifies what types of operands are allowed for the various instructions. After studying this chapter you will know how to copy data between memory and CPU registers, and between two registers. You will also know how to use 80x86 addition, subtraction, multiplication, and division instructions, and how execution of these instructions affects flags. You will know some of the details of how the assembler encodes 80x86 instructions for execution.

4.1 Copying Data

Most computer programs copy data from one location to another. With a high-level language, this is the job of a simple assignment statement. With 80x86 machine language, copying is done by **mov** ("move") instructions. Each **mov** instruction has the form

        mov   *destination, source*

and copies a single byte, word, doubleword, or (in 64-bit mode) quadword value from the source operand location to the destination operand location. The value stored at the source location is not changed. The destination location is the same size as the source. No **mov** instruction changes any 80x86 flag.

The C++ or Java assignment statement

        count = number;

might correspond directly to the assembly language instruction

        mov   count, ecx   ; count := number

assuming that the ECX register contains the value of *number* and that *count* references a doubleword in memory. The analogy between high-level language assignment statements and **mov** instructions cannot be carried too far. For example, the assignment statement

        count = 3*number + 1;

cannot be coded with a single **mov** instruction. Several instructions are required to evaluate the right-hand expression and place the resulting value in the destination location.

One limitation of the 80x86 architecture is that not all "logical" combinations of source and destination operands are allowed. In particular, *you cannot have both source and destination in memory*. The instruction

        mov   count, number   ; illegal for two memory operands

is not allowed if both *count* and *number* reference memory locations. In fact, no 80x86 instruction encodes two memory operands.

All 80x86 **mov** instructions are coded with the same mnemonic. The assembler selects the correct opcode and other bytes of the object code by looking at the operands as well as the mnemonic.

As was discussed in Chapter 2, instructions sometimes affect various flag bits in the flags register. In general, an instruction may have one of three effects:

- no flags are altered
- specific flags are given values depending on the results of the instruction
- some flags may be altered, but their settings cannot be predicted

All **mov** instructions fall in the first category—no **mov** instruction changes any flag.

Figure 4.1 lists **mov** instructions that have a byte-size destination. Since the source and destination sizes must match, this means that the source is also a byte. This

Destination	Source	Opcode	Bytes of Object Code
AL	immediate byte	B0	2
CL	immediate byte	B1	2
DL	immediate byte	B2	2
BL	immediate byte	B3	2
AH	immediate byte	B4	2
CH	immediate byte	B5	2
DH	immediate byte	B6	2
BH	immediate byte	B7	2
register 8 (AL, AH, BL, BH, CL, CH, DL, DH)	register 8	8A	2
AL	memory byte direct address mode	A0	5
register 8	memory byte	8A	2+
memory byte	immediate byte	C6	3+
memory byte (direct mode)	AL	A2	5
memory byte	register 8	88	2+
64-bit mode			
R8B	immediate byte	*41* B0	3
R9B	immediate byte	*41* B1	3
R10B	immediate byte	*41* B2	3
R11B	immediate byte	*41* B3	3
R12B	immediate byte	*41* B4	3
R13B	immediate byte	*41* B5	3
R14B	immediate byte	*41* B6	3
R15B	immediate byte	*41* B7	3
R8B–R15B	R8B–R15B	*45* 8A	3
R8B–R15B	AL, BL, CL, DL	*44* 8A	3
AL, BL, CL, DL	R8B–R15B	*41* 8A	3
memory byte	R8B-R15B	*44* 88	3+

Figure 4.1 mov instructions with byte destination

table shows the opcode and the total number of object code bytes for each instruction. Except as noted, operand formats and object code are the same for 32-bit and 64-bit mode. The operand patterns shown in Figure 4.1 include most of the possibilities that appear for all 80x86 instructions, so we take time to explain them carefully before showing **mov** instruction formats for other size operands.

Look at the first group of instructions in Figure 4.1. These are a bit unusual in that there is a distinct opcode for each destination register. However, when you consider that **mov** instructions are probably the most commonly used instructions, it makes sense that the designers of the 80x86 architecture would make these take as few bytes of object code as possible. For these instructions, the first byte of the object code is the opcode and the second byte is the immediate operand. For instance, the instruction

```
mov     dl, 10     ; object code B2 0A
```

has the decimal value 10 stored as the byte-size hex value 0A. The opcode code and immediate value complete the 2 bytes of object code promised in the last column of the table.

Now look at the row of the table where the source and destination both say *register 8*. This row actually stands for **mov** instructions with 64 possible operand combinations—any of AL, AH, BL, BH, CL, CH, DL, or DH for the source or for the destination. The opcode for any of these possibilities is always 8A, and the second object code byte identifies the registers. This byte, which Intel documentation refers to as the **ModR/M** byte, has many uses in encoding instructions. The *ModR/M* byte always has three fields, the first of which is a 2-bit **Mod** ("mode") field in bits 7 and 6. The other two fields are each 3 bits long, and these fields have different meanings in different instructions. However, for instructions with two register operands, *Mod*=11 and the next field (called **Reg** for "register") in bits 5, 4, and 3 encodes the destination, while the final field (called **R/M** for "register/memory") in bits 2, 1, and 0 encodes the source register. The 8-bit register encodings used are shown in Figure 4.2.

As an example, the instruction **mov ch, bl** will have object code 8A EB, where the *ModR/M* byte EB is pieced together from 11 101 011; 11 for register to register, 101 for CH, and 011 for BL.

The next two rows of the table have a register destination and a memory source. Notice that the first row is redundant since AL is a *register 8*. Recall that EAX is known as the "accumulator." In older architectures, the accumulator was often the only register that could be used for arithmetic operations but as CPUs have been given more features, the ability to use other registers has been added. The accumulator is still the register of choice because the object code is sometimes slightly more compact (takes

Register Code	Register
000	AL
001	CL
010	DL
011	BL
100	AH
101	CH
110	DH
111	BH

Figure 4.2 80x86 8-bit register codes

fewer bytes) when the accumulator is used. AL is the 8-bit accumulator, and because it takes 5 bytes of object code instead of 6 to use the A0 opcode, this is the choice that the assembler makes for destination AL and memory direct source.

As an example, suppose that *memByte* references a byte in memory. Then the opcode for **mov al, memByte** will be A0. In 32-bit systems, the remaining 4 bytes are the address in memory of *memByte*. In 64-bit systems, the remaining 4 bytes are the displacement from RIP to the address of *memByte*.

Consider the instruction **mov bl, memByte**. Since BL is not the accumulator, the opcode is 8A and the number of object code bytes is "2+"; this notation means that there are at least 2 bytes of object code, but the number depends on the mode of the memory operand. The second byte of object code is a *ModR/M* byte. Direct memory addressing is always encoded with *Mod*=00 and *R/M*=101, while the *Reg* field encodes the destination. The source address takes 4 additional bytes. With direct memory mode, "2+" always means "2+4," so that the actual number of bytes of object code is 6.

However, for register indirect mode (the only other 32-bit memory addressing mode we have covered so far), *Mod*=00, *Reg* encodes the destination, and *R/M* encodes the register used as the "pointer." Figure 4.3 lists additional register encodings for 32-bit and 16-bit registers.

As an example, suppose **mov al, [ebx]** is assembled. The accumulator AL is not special except for direct memory addressing, so the opcode will be 8A, and the *ModR/M* byte will consist of *Mod*=00 for register indirect memory addressing, *Reg*=000 for AL, and *R/M*=011 for EBX, making 00 000 011 or 03. No other object code is needed,

Register Code	Register 32	Register 16
000	EAX	AX
001	ECX	CX
010	EDX	DX
011	EBX	BX
100	ESP	SP
101	EBP	BP
110	ESI	SI
111	EDI	DI

Figure 4.3 More 80x86 register codes

so the assembler generates 8A 03. In general, for register indirect mode, "2+" means "2+0" or just 2.

Continuing down Figure 4.1, the next row is for immediate-to-memory moves. Each of these instructions has opcode C6, a *ModR/M* byte, additional address bytes (if needed), and finally a byte containing the immediate operand. The address is encoded as described above for memory-to-register moves. If, for example, *smallCounter* references a byte in memory and the instruction **mov smallCounter, 100** is assembled, the assembler will generate 7 (3+4) bytes of object code, C6 05 xx xx xx xx 64, where xx xx xx xx represents the address in memory, and 64 is the byte-size hex version of 100. The *ModR/M* byte 05 is 00 000 101, *Mod*=00 and *R/M*=101 for direct memory addressing, with the *Reg* field not needed and set to 000.

As another example, consider **mov BYTE PTR [edx], -1** with the memory destination using register indirect mode. The opcode is still C6 and the immediate byte (which always comes last) is now FF for −1. The second byte is the *ModR/M* byte with *Mod*=00 for register indirect, *Reg*=000 (unused), and *R/M*=010 for EDX, making 00 000 010 or 02. The object code is therefore C6 02 FF.

The next two rows of Figure 4.1 are for register-to-memory **mov** instructions. These are encoded just like the memory-to-register **mov** instructions, but with different opcodes for different directions. Again, there is a special, slightly more compact version for use when AL is the source and direct memory addressing is used for the destination.

Finally we come to the instructions in Figure 4.1 that work only with a 64-bit processor. These are very similar to the instructions above, except that the opcode is preceded by an extra byte, here 41, 44, or 45, shown in italics because technically it is not part of the opcode. In 64-bit mode, this byte is a **REX prefix**. It is used only when the instruction uses one of the 64-bit registers or uses a 64-bit operand. The first 4 bits of any REX prefix are always 0100 (4_{16}). Recall that there are 16 general registers in a 64-bit 80x86 processor, but the *Reg* and *R/M* fields of the *ModR/M* byte each contain 3 bits, only enough to encode eight different registers. Bit 2 of the REX prefix is combined with the 3 *Reg* bits in the *ModR/M* byte, making 4 bits to encode 16 register possibilities. Similarly, bit 0 of the REX prefix is appended as the high-order bit of the *R/M* field to give 16 possibilities there, too. The idea is simple, but the details are messy, so we will not attempt to assemble 64-bit instructions by hand.

One thing to note is that AH, BH, CH, and DH may not be used in combination with R8B–R15B. There are 16 8-bit registers when you count these 12 plus AL, BL, CL, and DL, but the machine code designers chose to make DIL, SIL, BPL, and SPL available for 8-bit operations instead of AH, BH, CH, and DH. We have no occasion to code instructions with DIL, SIL, BPL, or SPL operands.

Each instruction in Figure 4.4 has a doubleword destination. They are very similar to the byte-destination instructions in Figure 4.1. The opcodes are different, and the instructions with immediate operands have more bytes of object code because a 4-byte immediate value rather than a 1-byte immediate value is assembled into the instruction. Let's look at how a few of these instructions are assembled.

First, **mov edx, 1000** will have opcode BA and the remaining bytes of the object code will be 000003E8, 1000 as a doubleword integer. Next, if *dblOp* references a doubleword in memory, **mov eax, dblOp** will have 5 bytes of object code, the opcode A1 followed by the 32-bit address of *dblOp*. Finally, **mov dblOp, esi** will have 6 bytes of object code, the opcode 89, the *ModR/M* byte, 4 bytes for the address of *dblOp*. The *ModR/M* byte will have *mod*=00 and *R/M*=101, the combination always used for direct memory addressing, and *reg*=110 for ESI (see Figure 4.3), combined to give 00 110 101. This makes the object code 89 35 xx xx xx xx, where the x's stand for the address bytes.

Figure 4.5 shows **mov** instructions that copy a word source to a word destination. This table is very similar to Figure 4.4, the major difference being a new prefix byte in front of each opcode. Instructions for 32-bit and 16-bit operands actually have the same opcodes. A 32-bit 80x86 processor maintains a **segment descriptor** for each active segment. One bit of this descriptor determines whether operands are 16-bit or 32-bit length by default. With the assembly and linking options used in this book, this bit is set to 1 to indicate 32-bit operands. Therefore, the B8 opcode means, for instance, to copy the immediate doubleword following the opcode to EAX, not an immediate word to

Destination	Source	Opcode	Bytes of Object Code
EAX	immediate doubleword	B8	5
ECX	immediate doubleword	B9	5
EDX	immediate doubleword	BA	5
EBX	immediate doubleword	BB	5
ESP	immediate doubleword	BC	5
EBP	immediate doubleword	BD	5
ESI	immediate doubleword	BE	5
EDI	immediate doubleword	BF	5
register 32 (listed above)	register 32	8B	2
EAX	memory doubleword (direct mode)	A1	5
register 32	memory doubleword	8B	2+
memory doubleword	immediate doubleword	C7	6+
memory doubleword (direct mode)	EAX	A3	5
memory doubleword	register 32	89	2+
64-bit mode			
R8D	immediate doubleword	*41* B8	6
R9D	immediate doubleword	*41* B9	6
R10D	immediate doubleword	*41* BA	6
R11D	immediate doubleword	*41* BB	6
R12D	immediate doubleword	*41* BC	6
R13D	immediate doubleword	*41* BD	6
R14D	immediate doubleword	*41* BE	6
R15D	immediate doubleword	*41* BF	6
R8D–R15D	R8D–R15D	*45* 8B	3
R8D–R15D	register 32	*44* 8B	3
register 32	R8D–R15D	*41* 8B	3
memory doubleword	R8D–R15D	*44* 89	3+

Figure 4.4 mov instructions with doubleword destination

Destination	Source	Opcode	Bytes of Object Code
AX	immediate word	*66* B8	4
CX	immediate word	*66* B9	4
DX	immediate word	*66* BA	4
BX	immediate word	*66* BB	4
SP	immediate word	*66* BC	4
BP	immediate word	*66* BD	4
SI	immediate word	*66* BE	4
DI	immediate word	*66* BF	4
register 16 (listed above)	register 16	*66* 8B	3
register 16	memory word	*66* 8B	3+
memory word	immediate word	*66* C7	4+
memory word	register 16	*66* 89	2+
64-bit mode			
R8B	immediate word	*66 41* B8	5
R9W	immediate word	*66 41* B9	5
R10W	immediate word	*66 41* BA	5
R11W	immediate word	*66 41* BB	5
R12W	immediate word	*66 41* BC	5
R13W	immediate word	*66 41* BD	5
R14W	immediate word	*66 41* BE	5
R15W	immediate word	*66 41* BF	5
R8W–R15W	R8W–R15W	*66 45* 8B	3
R8W–R15W	register 16	*66 44* 8B	3
register 16	R8W–R15W	*66 41* 8B	3
memory word	R8W–R15W	*66 44* 89	3+

Figure 4.5 mov instructions with word destination

AX. If you code a 16-bit instruction, then the assembler inserts the prefix byte 66 in front of the object code. In general, the prefix byte 66 tells the assembler to switch from the default operand size (32 bit or 16 bit) to the alternative size (16 bit or 32 bit) for the single instruction that follows the prefix byte.

To make this clearer, suppose you assemble a program containing the following three instructions.

```
mov     al, 155
mov     ax, 155
mov     eax, 155
```

The assembly listing shows the object code as follows.

```
B0 9B           mov   al, 155
66| B8 009B     mov   ax, 155
B8 0000009B     mov   eax, 155
```

Recall that an immediate operand is actually assembled into the object code. Each of these instructions contains 155 converted to binary in the appropriate length, 9B in the first instruction, 009B in the second, and 0000009B in the third. The first instruction has opcode B0, but both of the other instructions have opcode B8. The 66 byte shown in the second instruction is the prefix byte that tells the assembler to switch from 32-bit operand size to 16 bit for this instruction.

A 64-bit 80x86 processor runs in either legacy 32-bit mode, exactly as described previously, or in 64-bit mode. Different code segments can be in different modes at the same time. In 64-bit mode, the default operand size is still 32 bits.

Figure 4.6 shows the **mov** instructions with a quadword destination. Obviously these are only available in 64-bit processors. The first 16 rows are not surprising, showing separate instructions for loading a 64-bit immediate operand in a 64-bit register. Each consists only of a REX prefix, the opcode, and the 8 bytes of the immediate operand. The next two rows show a feature that we have not seen in previous instructions; the immediate value stored in the instruction is a doubleword even though the destination is a quadword. Storing a doubleword saves 4 bytes of object code. The immediate doubleword is **sign-extended** to a quadword as it is stored in the destination, that is, the sign bit (bit 31) in the source is copied to each of bits 32–63 in the destination. This ensures that 2's complement signed numbers are properly represented, but in rare instances could cause a large unsigned number to be incorrectly extended to 64 bits. Also, the REX prefix for each of the last five rows is shown as *4x* since there is more than one possible value in each row.

Particularly with older processors, instructions that access memory are slower than instructions that use data in registers. A programmer should plan to keep frequently used data in registers when possible.

When you first look at all the **mov** instructions in Figures 4.1, 4.4, 4.5, and 4.6 you may think that you can use them to copy any source value to any destination loca-

Destination	Source	Opcode	Bytes of Object Code
64-bit mode			
RAX	immediate quadword	*48* B8	10
RCX	immediate quadword	*48* B9	10
RDX	immediate quadword	*48* BA	10
RBX	immediate quadword	*48* BB	10
RSP	immediate quadword	*48* BC	10
RBP	immediate quadword	*48* BD	10
RSI	immediate quadword	*48* BE	10
RDI	immediate quadword	*48* BF	10
R8	immediate quadword	*49* B8	10
R9	immediate quadword	*49* B9	10
R10	immediate quadword	*49* BA	10
R11	immediate quadword	*49* BB	10
R12	immediate quadword	*49* BC	10
R13	immediate quadword	*49* BD	10
R14	immediate quadword	*49* BE	10
R15	immediate quadword	*49* BF	10
register 64	immediate doubleword	*4x* C7	7
memory quadword	immediate doubleword	*4x* C7	7+
register 64	register 64	*4x* 8B	3
register 64	memory quadword	*4x* 8B	3+
memory quadword	register 64	*4x* 89	3+

Figure 4.6 mov instructions with quadword destination

tion. However, there are many seemingly logical combinations that are not available. These include:

- a move with both source and destination in memory
- any move where the operands are not the same size
- a move of several objects

You may need to do some of these operations. We describe next how to accomplish some of them.

Although there is no **mov** instruction to copy from a memory source to a memory destination, two moves using an intermediate register can do the job. For doubleword-length data in memory referenced by *count* and *number* the illegal instruction

```
mov   count, number       ; illegal for two memory operands
```

can be replaced by

```
mov   eax, number         ; count := number
mov   count, eax
```

each using the accumulator EAX and one direct memory operand. Some register other than EAX could be used, but each of these instructions using the accumulator requires 5 bytes, while each of the corresponding instructions using some other register takes 6 bytes—EAX is chosen in the interest of compact code.

Suppose you have numeric data stored in a doubleword at *dblSize*, but you want the byte size version at *byteSize*. Assuming that the high-order 24 bits are not significant, you can do this with

```
mov   eax, dblSize
mov   byteSize, al
```

Going the other way, if an unsigned or positive value is stored at *byteSize* and we want the doubleword equivalent at *dblSize*, then

```
mov   eax, 0
mov   al, byteSize
mov   dblSize, eax
```

does the job. Notice that the first move ensures that each of the 3 high-order bytes in EAX contain 0 rather than unknown values left over from prior operations. Later we will see other instructions to extend the length of a number.

Suppose that you have source and destination locations declared as

```
source    DWORD 4 DUP(?)
dest      DWORD 4 DUP(?)
```

and that you want to copy all four doublewords from the source to the destination. One way to do this is with eight instructions

```
mov   eax, source        ; copy first doubleword
mov   dest, eax
mov   eax, source+4      ; copy second doubleword
```

```
mov   dest+4, eax
mov   eax, source+8        ; copy third doubleword
mov   dest+8, eax
mov   eax, source+12       ; copy fourth doubleword
mov   dest+12, eax
```

An address like *source+4* refers to the location 4 bytes (one doubleword) after the address of *source*. Since the four doublewords reserved at *source* are contiguous in memory, *source+4* refers to the second doubleword. This code clearly would not be space efficient if you needed to copy 40 or 400 doublewords. In Chapter 5 you will learn how to set up a loop to copy multiple objects.

The 80x86 has a very useful **xchg** instruction that exchanges data in one location with data in another location. It accomplishes in a single instruction the operation that often requires three high-level language instructions. Suppose *value1* and *value2* are being exchanged. In a design or a high-level language, this might be done using

```
temp := value1;     // swap value1 and value2
value1 := value2;
value2 := temp;
```

If *value1* is stored in the EAX register and *value2* is stored in EBX, we might use ECX for *temp* and directly implement this design with

```
mov    ecx, eax          ; swap value1 and value2
mov    eax, ebx
mov    ebx, ecx
```

The **xchg** instruction makes the code shorter and clearer.

```
xchg   eax, ebx          ; swap value1 and value2
```

It is much easier to write one instruction than three and the resulting code is easier to understand.

Figure 4.7 lists the various forms of the **xchg** instruction. Although the table does not show it, the first operand can be a memory operand when the second operand is a register; the assembler effectively reverses the order of the operands and uses the form shown in the table. The **xchg** instructions illustrate again that the accumulator sometimes plays a special role in a computer's architecture. The instructions that swap another register with the accumulator take 1 byte (plus prefix bytes) instead of 2. Notice again that the word, doubleword, and quadword instructions are the same except for prefix bytes. We will take advantage of this in future tables to make them more compact.

Operand 1	Operand 2	Opcode	Bytes of Object Code (excluding prefix bytes)
register 8	register 8	86	2
register 8	memory byte	86	2+
AX	CX	*66* 91	1
AX	DX	*66* 92	1
AX	BX	*66* 93	1
AX	SP	*66* 94	1
AX	BP	*66* 95	1
AX	SI	*66* 96	1
AX	DI	*66* 97	1
register 16 (except AX)	register 16 (except AX)	*66* 87	2
register 16	memory word	*66* 87	2+
EAX	ECX	91	1
EAX	EDX	92	1
EAX	EBX	93	1
EAX	ESP	94	1
EAX	EBP	95	1
EAX	ESI	96	1
EAX	EDI	97	1
register 32 (except AX)	register 32 (except EAX)	87	2
register 32	memory doubleword	87	2+
64-bit mode			
register 8, R8B–R15B	register 8, R8B–R15B	*4x* 86	2
R8B–R15B	memory byte	*4x* 86	2
AX	R8W	*66 41* 90	1
AX	R9W	*66 41* 91	1
AX	R10W	*66 41* 92	1
AX	R11W	*66 41* 93	1
AX	R12W	*66 41* 94	1
AX	R13W	*66 41* 95	1
AX	R14W	*66 41* 96	1
AX	R15W	*66 41* 97	1

Figure 4.7 xchg instructions

Operand 1	Operand 2	Opcode	Bytes of Object Code (excluding prefix bytes)
register 16, R8W–R15W	R8W–R15W	*66 4x* 87	2
memory word	R8W–R15W	*66 44* 87	2+
EAX	R8D	*66 41* 90	1
EAX	R9D	*66 41* 91	1
EAX	R10D	*66 41* 92	1
EAX	R11D	*66 41* 93	1
EAX	R12D	*66 41* 94	1
EAX	R13D	*66 41* 95	1
EAX	R14D	*66 41* 96	1
EAX	R15D	*66 41* 97	1
register 32, R8D–R15D	R8D–R15D	*66 4x* 87	2
memory word	R8D–R15D	*66 44* 87	2+
RAX	RCX	*48* 91	1
RAX	RDX	*48* 92	1
RAX	RBX	*48* 93	1
RAX	RSP	*48* 94	1
RAX	RBP	*48* 95	1
RAX	RSI	*48* 96	1
RAX	RDI	*48* 97	1
RAX	R8	*49* 90	1
RAX	R9	*49* 91	1
RAX	R10	*49* 92	1
RAX	R11	*49* 93	1
RAX	R12	*49* 94	1
RAX	R13	*49* 95	1
RAX	R14	*49* 96	1
RAX	R15	*49* 97	1
register 64 (except RAX)	register 64	*4x* 87	2
memory quadword	register 64	*4x* 87	2+

Figure 4.7 xchg instructions (continued)

Note that you *cannot* use an **xchg** instruction to swap two memory operands. In general, 80x86 instructions do not allow two memory operands to be encoded. Like **mov** instructions, **xchg** instructions do not alter any status flag. That is, after execution of an **xchg** instruction, the bits of the flags register remain the same as before execution of the instruction.

Exercises 4.1

1. For each part of this problem, assume the "before" values when the given mov instruction is executed. Give the requested "after" values.

Before	Instruction	After
*(a) EBX: 00 00 FF 75		
ECX: 00 00 01 A2	mov ebx, ecx	EBX, CEX
(b) EAX: 00 00 01 A2	mov eax, 100	EAX
(c) EDX: FF 75 4C 2E		
dValue: DWORD −1	mov edx, dValue	EDX, Value
*(d) AX: 01 4B	mov ah, 0	AX
(e) AL: 64	mov al, −1	AL
(f) EBX: 00 00 3A 4C		
dValue: DWORD ?	mov dValue, ebx	EBX, Value
(g) ECX: 00 00 00 00	mov ecx, 128	ECX
*(h) RAX: 00 00 00 00 00 00 00 00	mov rax, −1	RAX
(i) qValue: QWORD 0	mov qValue, 100	qValue

*2. Give the opcode and number of bytes of object code (including prefix bytes) for each instruction in Exercise 1.

*3. Include each instruction (a)–(g) from Exercise 1 in a short program. Assemble the program and examine the listing file. If the object code has a *ModR/M* byte, give the value for each of the three fields and, if possible from the discussion in this section, interpret the value of each field.

4. For each part of this problem, assume the "before" values when the given xchg instruction is executed. Give the requested "after" values.

Before	Instruction	After
*(a) EBX: 00 00 FF 75		
ECX: 00 00 01 A2	xchg ebx, ecx	EBX, ECX

(b) EAX: 01 A2

Temp: DWORD −1   xchg   Temp, eax   EAX, Temp

(c) DX: FF 75   xchg   dl, dh   DX

*(d) AX: 01 4B

BX: 5C D9   xchg   ah, bl   AX, BX

(e) EAX: 12 BC 9A 78

EDX: 56 DE 34 F0   xchg   eax, edx   EAX, EDX

*5. Give the opcode and number of bytes of object code (including prefix bytes) for each instruction in Exercise 4.

6. Note that xchg cannot swap two values in memory. Write a sequence of mov and/or xchg instructions to swap doublewords stored at *value1* and *value2*. Pick instructions that give the smallest possible total number of bytes of object code. Assume that any register 32 you want to use is available.

4.2   Integer Addition and Subtraction Instructions

The Intel 80x86 microprocessor has **add** and **sub** instructions to perform addition and subtraction using byte-, word-, doubleword-, or quadword-length operands. The operands can be interpreted as unsigned numbers or 2's complement signed numbers. The 80x86 architecture also has **inc** and **dec** instructions to increment (add 1 to) and decrement (subtract 1 from) a single operand, and a **neg** instruction that negates (takes the 2's complement of) a single operand.

One difference between the instructions covered in this section and the **mov** and **xchg** instructions of Section 4.1 is that **add**, **sub**, **inc**, **dec**, and **neg** instructions all update flags in the flags register. The SF, ZF, OF, PF, and AF flags are set according to the value of the result of the operation. For example, if the result is negative, then the sign flag SF will be set to one; if the result is zero, then the zero flag ZF will be set to one. The carry flag CF is also given a value by each of these instructions except **inc** and **dec**.

Each **add** instruction has the form

```
add    destination, source
```

When executed, the integer at *source* is added to the integer at *destination* and the sum replaces the original value at *destination*. Each **sub** instruction has the form

```
sub    destination, source
```

When a **sub** instruction is executed, the integer at *source* is subtracted from the integer at *destination* and the difference replaces the old value at *destination*. For subtraction, it is important to remember that the difference calculated is *destination − source* or "operand 1 minus operand 2." With both **add** and **sub** instructions the source (second) operand is unchanged. Here are some examples showing how these instructions function at execution time.

Example

Before	Instruction Executed	After

EAX: 00 00 00 75   add   eax, ecx

EAX	00	00	02	17
ECX	00	00	01	A2

SF 0 ZF 0 CF 0 OF 0

EAX: 00 00 00 75   sub   eax, ecx

EAX	FF	FF	FE	D3
ECX	00	00	01	A2

SF 1 ZF 0 CF 1 OF 0

AX: 77 AC   add   ax, cx

AX	C2	E1
CX	4B	35

SF 1 ZF 0 CF 0 OF 1

EAX: 00 00 00 75   sub   ecx, eax

EAX	00	00	00	75
ECX	00	00	01	2D

SF 0 ZF 0 CF 0 OF 0

BL: 4B	add bl, 4	BL	4F		

SF 0 ZF 0 CF 0 OF 0

DX: FF 20	sub dx, Value	DX	00	00

Value | FF | 20

SF 0 ZF 1 CF 0 OF 0

EAX: 00 00 00 09	add eax, 1	EAX	00	00	00	0A

SF 0 ZF 0 CF 0 OF 0

doubleword at Dbl:	sub Dbl, 1	Dbl	00	00	00	FF

SF 0 ZF 0 CF 0 OF 0

Addition and subtraction instructions set the sign flag SF to be the same as the high-order bit of the result. Thus, when these instructions are used to add or subtract 2's complement integers, SF=1 indicates a negative result. The zero flag ZF is 1 if the result is zero, and 0 if the result is nonzero. The carry flag CF records a carry out of the high-order bit with addition, or a borrow with subtraction. The overflow flag OF records overflow, discussed in Chapter 1.

One reason that 2's complement form is used to represent signed numbers is that it does not require special hardware for addition or subtraction—the same circuits can be used to add unsigned numbers and 2's complement numbers. The flag values have different interpretations, though, depending on the operand type. For instance, if you add two large unsigned numbers and the high-order bit of the result is 1, then SF will be set to 1, but this does not indicate a negative result, only a relatively large sum. For an **add** with unsigned operands, CF=1 would indicate that the result was too large to store in the destination, but with signed operands, OF=1 would indicate a size error.

Figure 4.8 gives information for both addition and subtraction instructions. For each **add** there is a corresponding **sub** instruction with exactly the same operand types and number of bytes of object code, so that it is redundant to make separate tables for **add** and **sub** instructions. Also, in the interest of more compact tables, prefix bytes are not shown with the opcode and are not counted in the number of bytes. Recall that 16-bit instructions will have a *66* prefix byte and instructions that only work in 64-bit mode will have a *4x* prefix. The 64-bit mode rows do not include entries for R8B–R15B because these are identical to the register 8 entries except for prefix bytes.

With the 80x86, one memory operand can be encoded. Many computer architectures have no instructions for arithmetic when the destination is a memory operand. Some other processors allow two memory operands for arithmetic operations.

With **add** and **sub**, as with **mov**, the accumulator again has special instructions, this time when RAX, EAX, AX, or AL is the destination and the source is immediate. These instructions take one less byte of object code than the corresponding instructions for other registers.

The total number of object code bytes for instructions with "+" entries in Figure 4.8 can be calculated once you know the memory operand type. In particular, for direct mode, there are 4 additional bytes for the 32-bit address. For register indirect mode, no additional object code is required.

Notice that an immediate source can be a single byte even when the destination is a word, doubleword, or quadword. Since immediate operands are often small, this makes the object code more compact. Byte-size operands are sign-extended to the destination size at run time before the addition or subtraction operation. If the original operand is negative (viewed as 2's complement number), then it is extended with FF bytes (1 bit) to get the corresponding word- or doubleword-length value. A nonnegative operand is simply extended with 00 bytes. In both cases this is equivalent to copying the original sign bit to the high-order bit positions.

A similar sign extension takes place in the instructions where the destination is a 64-bit register or a memory quadword and the source is an immediate doubleword. Addition and subtraction instructions do not permit 64-bit immediate operands. If you need to add or subtract a large immediate operand, you could use a **mov** instruction to put it in a register, and then use the register as the source for the **add** or **sub**.

It may be surprising that some **add** and **sub** instructions have the same opcode. In such cases, the *reg* field in the *ModR/M* byte distinguishes between addition and subtraction. In fact, these same opcodes are used for additional instructions, most of which are covered later in this book. Figure 4.9 shows how the *reg* field is encoded for these opcodes and some others.

Destination Operand	Source Operand	Opcode		Bytes of Object Code
		add	sub	
register 8	immediate byte	80	80	3
register 16	immediate byte	83	83	3
register 32	immediate byte	83	83	3
register 16	immediate word	81	81	4
register 32	immediate doubleword	81	81	6
AL	immediate byte	04	2C	2
AX	immediate word	05	2D	3
EAX	immediate doubleword	05	2D	5
memory byte	immediate byte	80	80	3+
memory word	immediate byte	83	83	3+
memory doubleword	immediate byte	83	83	3+
memory word	immediate word	81	81	4+
memory doubleword	immediate doubleword	81	81	6+
register 8	register 8	02	2A	2
register 16	register 16	03	2B	2
register 32	register 32	03	2B	2
register 8	memory byte	02	2A	2+
register 16	memory word	03	2B	2+
register 32	memory doubleword	03	2B	2+
memory byte	register 8	00	28	2+
memory word	register 16	01	29	2+
memory doubleword	register 32	01	29	2+
64-bit mode				
register 64	immediate byte	83	83	3
register 64	immediate doubleword	81	81	6
RAX	immediate doubleword	05	2D	5
memory quadword	immediate byte	83	83	3+
memory quadword	immediate doubleword	81	81	6+
register 64	register 64	03	2B	2
register 64	memory quadword	03	2B	2+
memory quadword	register 64	01	29	2+

Figure 4.8 add and sub instructions

				Reg Field				
Opcode	**000**	**001**	**010**	**011**	**100**	**101**	**110**	**111**
80, 81	ADD	OR	ADC	SBB	AND	SUB	XOR	CMP
D0, D1	ROL	ROR	RCL	RCR	SHL	SHR		SAR
F6, F7	TEST		NOT	NEG	MUL	IMUL	DIV	IDIV
FE, FF	INC	DEC					PUSH	

Figure 4.9 *reg* field for specified opcodes

Suppose a program has *dbl* at address 000001C8 in the data section and contains the following instructions:

```
add    ebx,  1000
sub    ebx,  1000
add    dbl,  1000
sub    dbl,  1000
add    ebx,  10
```

Then the assembly listing will contain

```
81 C3 000003E8      add    ebx,  1000
81 EB 000003E8      sub    ebx,  1000
81 05 000001C8 R    add    dbl,  1000
      000003E8
81 2D 000001C8 R    sub    dbl,  1000
      000003E8
83 C3 0A            add    ebx,  10
```

Notice the difference between the first and last instructions. Each has the register 32 destination operand EBX. The assembler could use the 81 opcode for both and encode the immediate operand 10 as 0000000A. However, it chooses the 83 opcode for the last instruction in order to generate more compact code. The immediate value 0A will be extended to 0000000A when the instruction is executed.

The immediate operand 1000 will not fit in a byte, so the first four instructions encode it as the doubleword 000003E8. Look at the *ModR/M* byte in each of the first two instructions; C3 in the **add** instruction breaks down into 11 000 011, and EB in the **sub** instruction breaks down into 11 101 011. Notice that the *reg* values of 000 and 101 are what Figure 4.9 shows for **add** and **sub** instructions with opcode 81. Also recall from Figure 4.3 that EBX is encoded as 011, the value in the *r/m* field of both instructions. The 11 in the *mod* field indicates an immediate operand.

Now look at the two instructions that have source *dbl*. You can see this direct memory operand's address encoded as 000001C8. The *ModR/M* bytes of 05 and 2D for the **add** and **sub** instructions, respectively, break down into 00 000 101 and 00 101 101. The *reg* fields again distinguish between addition and subtraction, and the combination of 00 in *mod* and 101 in *r/m* means direct memory addressing.

The **inc** (increment) and **dec** (decrement) instructions are special-purpose addition and subtraction instructions, always using 1 as an implied source. They have the forms

```
inc     destination
```

and

```
dec     destination
```

Like the **add** and **sub** instructions, these instructions are paired with respect to allowable operand types, clock cycles, and bytes of object code. They are summarized together in Figure 4.10. Prefix bytes are not shown and are not counted in the bytes of object code.

Notice the 4x opcodes used for single byte **inc** and **dec** instructions with register 16 and register 32 operands. These are exactly the bit patterns used for REX prefixes in 64-bit mode. In a 64-bit environment the assembler chooses the FF opcode, and uses the *reg* field of the *ModR/M* as shown in Figure 4.9 to distinguish between **inc** and **dec**, and the *R/M* field to identify the destination register. This 2-byte form could be used in 32-bit mode also, but the assembler normally chooses the more compact 1-byte form.

The **inc** and **dec** instructions treat the value of the destination operand as an unsigned integer. They affect the OF, SF, and ZF flags just like addition or subtraction of one, but they do not change the carry flag CF. Here are examples showing the execution of a few increment and decrement instructions:

Destination Operand	Opcode inc	Opcode dec	Bytes of Object Code
register 8	FE	FE	2
AX	40	48	1
CX	41	49	1
DX	42	4A	1
BX	43	4B	1
SP	44	4C	1
BP	45	4D	1
SI	46	4E	1
DI	47	4F	1
EAX	40	48	1
ECX	41	49	1
EDX	42	4A	1
EBX	43	4B	1
ESP	44	4C	1
EBP	45	4D	1
ESI	46	4E	1
EDI	47	4F	1
memory byte	FE	FE	2+
memory word	FF	FF	2+
memory doubleword	FF	FF	2+
64-bit mode			
register 8	FE	FE	2
register 16	FF	FF	2
register 32	FF	FF	2
register 16	FF	FF	2
memory quadword	FF	FF	2+

Figure 4.10 inc and dec instructions

Example

Before	Instruction Executed	After
ECX: 00 00 01 A2	inc ecx	ECX 00 00 01 A3
		SF 0 ZF 0 OF 0
AL: F5	dec al	AL F4
		SF 1 ZF 0 OF 0
word at *count*: 00 09	inc count	*count* 00 0A
		SF 0 ZF 0 OF 0
BX: 00 01	dec bx	BX 00 00
		SF 0 ZF 1 OF 0
EDX: 7F FF FF FF	inc edx	EDX 80 00 00 00
		SF 1 ZF 0 OF 1

The **inc** and **dec** instructions are especially useful for incrementing and decrementing counters. They sometimes take fewer bytes of code than corresponding addition or subtraction instructions. For example, the instructions

```
add    ecx, 1        ; increment loop counter
```

and

```
inc    ecx           ; increment loop counter
```

are functionally equivalent. The **add** instruction requires 3 bytes of object code (3 bytes instead of 6 because the immediate operand will fit in 1 byte), while the **inc** instruction uses only 1 byte. This example uses a register for a counter. In general, a register is the best place to keep a counter, if one can be reserved for this purpose.

A **neg** instruction negates, or finds the 2's complement of, its single operand. When a positive value is negated the result is negative; a negative value will become positive. Zero remains zero. Each **neg** instruction has the form

neg   *destination*

Figure 4.11 shows allowable operands for **neg** instructions.

Here are four examples illustrating how the **neg** instructions operate. In each case the "after" value is the 2's complement of the "before" value.

Example

Before	Instruction Executed	After
EBX: 00 00 01 A2	neg ebx	EBX FF FF FE 5E
		SF 1 ZF 0
DH: F5	neg dh	DH 0B
		SF 0 ZF 0
word at *flag*: 00 01	neg flag	*flag* FF FF
		SF 1 ZF 0
EAX: 00 00 00 00	neg eax	EAX 00 00 00 00
		SF 0 ZF 1

Destination Operand	Opcode	Bytes of Object Code
register 8	F6	2
register 16	F7	2
register 32	F7	2
memory byte	F6	2+
memory word	F7	2+
memory doubleword	F7	2+
64-bit mode		
register 64	F7	2
memory quadword	F7	2+

Figure 4.11 neg instructions

We now look at an example of a complete, if unexciting, program that uses these new instructions. The program starts with integer values for three numbers x, y, and z in memory doublewords, and evaluates the expression $-(x + y - 2z + 1)$, leaving the result in EAX. The design implemented is

```
result := x;
add y to result, giving x + y;
temp := z;
temp := temp + temp, to get 2*z;
subtract temp from result, giving x + y − 2*z;
add 1 to result, giving x + y − 2*z + 1;
negate result, giving − (x + y − 2*z + 1);
```

To write an assembly language program, you need to plan how registers and memory will be used. The problem specifies that the result will be in EAX, so the only decision is what to use for *temp*. Since the "next" general register EBX has no assigned use, it is a good choice.

Figure 4.12 shows the source program listing. This *console32* program closely follows the design, and the program's comments are taken from the design. Comments that simply repeat the instruction mnemonics are not useful. Notice that the value of $2*z$ is found by adding z to itself; multiplication will be covered in the next section, but it is more efficient to compute $2*z$ by addition anyway.

You should always test a program by predicting results for sample data. In this program there is only one set of data. Use a calculator to find that $-(35 + 47 - 2*26 + 1)$ has value -31, or FFFFFFE1 as a 2's complement doubleword. If you set a breakpoint at the first instruction, launch the debugger with F5, and step through the program to the end, the debugger shows the screen pictured in Figure 4.13. The correct result is in EAX.

The debugger memory display in Figure 4.13 shows memory starting at x, so that the first 12 bytes are the doublewords containing 35, 47, and 26. The debugger

```
; program to evaluate the expression - (x + y - 2z + 1) for
; doubleword values stored in memory, leaving the result in EAX
; author:  R. Detmer
; date:   revised 6/2008

.586
.MODEL  FLAT
.STACK  4096

.DATA
x               DWORD   35
y               DWORD   47
z               DWORD   26

.CODE
main    PROC
                mov     eax, x          ; result := x
                add     eax, y          ; result := x + y
                mov     ebx, z          ; temp := z
                add     ebx, ebx        ; temp := 2*z
                sub     eax, ebx        ; result := x + y - 2z
                inc     eax             ; result := x + y - 2*z + 1
                neg     eax             ; result := - (x + y - 2*z + 1)
                mov     eax, 0          ; exit with return code 0
                ret

main    ENDP
        END
```

Figure 4.12 Program to evaluate $-(x + y - 2z + 1)$

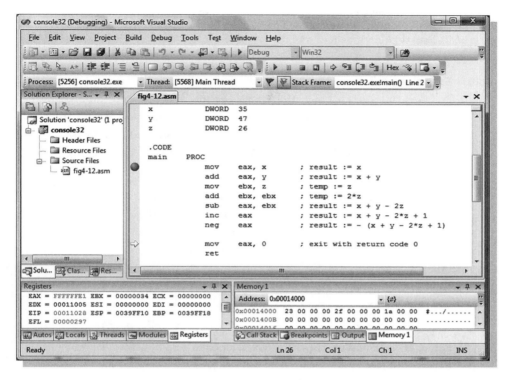

Figure 4.13 Execution of sample program

allows the user to change a value in memory or a register, but this can be confusing. One of the programming exercises at the end of this section asks you to modify this sample program to provide dialog box input for x, y, and z and message box output for the value of the expression.

You may wonder how an 80x86 CPU can add integers larger than doubleword size. Earlier CPUs only had instructions to add byte-size integers; how did they handle 16- or 32-bit numbers? The answer is that in addition to regular addition instructions, CPUs have *add with carry* instructions. These work just like regular addition instructions except that the current value (0 or 1) of the carry flag is added to the normal sum. To add large integers, break them down into whatever size parts the CPU will handle. Use ordinary addition on the rightmost part to get the low-order part of the sum. Then add the next pieces using *add with carry* instructions. This process is very similar to the procedure most students learn for addition of decimal numbers. It can be continued for as many parts as necessary since the *add with carry* instruction sets the carry flag just like an ordinary add instruction. The procedure for subtraction of large numbers is similar, using a *subtract with borrow* instruction.

▬▬▬ **Exercises 4.2**

1. For each instruction, give the 80x86 opcode and the total number of bytes of object code, *including* prefix bytes. Assume you are in 32-bit mode and that *wordOp* and *dblOp* reference a word and doubleword in data, respectively. You can check your answers by assembling the instructions in a short *console32* program.

   *(a) add   ax,wordOp   (b) sub   wordOp,ax
    (c) sub   eax,10   (d) add   dblOp,10
    (e) add   eax,[ebx]   (f) sub   [ebx],eax
   *(g) sub   dl,ch   (h) add   bl,5
    (i) inc   ebx   (j) dec   al
    (k) dec   dblOp   *(l) inc   BYTE PTR [esi]
    (m) neg   eax   (n) neg   bh
   *(o) neg   dblOp   (p) neg   DWORD PTR [ebx]

2. For each instruction, give the 80x86 opcode and the total number of bytes of object code, including prefix bytes. Assume you are in 64-bit mode and that *wordOp, dblOp*, and quadOp reference a word, double-word, and quadword in data, respectively. You can check your answers by assembling the instructions in a short *console64* program.

   (a) add   ax,wordOp   (b) sub   dblOp,ebx
   (c) sub   rax,10   *(d) add   quadOp,1000
  *(e) inc   r10b   (f) dec   wordOp
   (g) neg   rdx   (h) inc   QWORD PTR [rdx]

3. For each part of this problem, assume the "before" values when the given instruction is executed. Give the requested "after" values.

Before	Instruction	After
*(a) EBX: FF FF FF 75		
ECX: 00 00 01 A2	add ebx,ecx	EBX, ECX, SF, ZF, CF, OF
(b) EBX: FF FF FF 75		
ECX: 00 00 01 A2	sub ebx,ecx	EBX, ECX, SF, ZF, CF, OF

(c) BX: FF 75

   CX: 01 A2   sub   cx,bx   BX, CX, SF, ZF, CF, OF

(d) DX: 01 4B   add   dx,40h   DX, SF, ZF, CF, OF

*(e) EAX: 00 00 00 64   sub   eax,100   EAX, SF, ZF, CF, OF

 (f) AX: 0A 20   word at *wordOp*,

   word at *wordOp*: FF 20 add   ax,wordOp   AX, SF, ZF, CF, OF

(g) AX: 0A 20   word at *wordOp*,

   word at *wordOp*: FF 20 sub   wordOp,ax   AX, SF, ZF, CF, OF

(h) CX: 03 1A   inc   cx   CX, SF, ZF

*(i) EAX: 00 00 00 01   dec   eax   EAX, SF, ZF

 (j) word at *wordOp*: 00 99 inc   wordOp   word at *wordOp*, SF, ZF

(k) word at *wordOp*: 00 99 dec   wordOp   word at *wordOp*, SF, ZF

 (l) EBX: FF FF FF FF   neg   ebx   EBX, SF, ZF

(m) CL: 5F   neg   cl   CL, SF, ZF

(n) word at *wordOp*: FB 3C neg   wordOp   word at *wordOp*, SF, ZF

(o) RBX: FF FF FF FF FF FF FF FF

                                    add   rbx, r14   RBX, R14, SF, ZF, CF, OF

   R14: 00 00 00 00 00 00 00 01

(p) R12: FF FF FF FF FF FF FF FF

                                    dec   r12   R12, SF, ZF

*(q) R11: FF FF FF FF FF FF FF FC

                                    neg   r11   R11, SF, ZF

Programming Exercises 4.2

1. Using the *windows32* or *windows64* framework, modify the program in Figure 4.12 to use the *input* macro to prompt for and input values for *x*, *y*, and *z*, and the *output* macro to display an appropriate label and the value of the expression. You will also use the data conversion macros from IO.H as appropriate.

2. Using the *console32* or *console64* framework, write a complete assembly language program that computes in EAX the value of the expression $x - 2y + 4z$ for doublewords in memory at *x*, *y*, and *z*. Choose the current month (1–12), day (1–31), and year (all four digits) for the values of *x*, *y*, and *z*, and predict the result before building the program and executing it under control of the debugger. (*Hint:* You don't need a multiplication instruction for *4*z*.)

3. Using the *windows32* or *windows64* framework, modify the program in Programming Exercise 2 to use the *input* macro to prompt for and input

values for *x*, *y*, and *z*, and the *output* macro to display an appropriate label and the value of the expression. You will also use the data conversion macros from IO.H as appropriate.

4. Using the *console32* or *console64* framework, write a complete assembly language program that computes in EAX the value of the expression $2(-a + b - 1) + c$ for doublewords in memory at *a*, *b*, and *c*. Choose your area code for *a*, the first three digits of your local phone number for *b*, and the last four digits of your local phone number for *c*, and predict the result before building the program and executing it under control of the debugger.

5. Using the *windows32* or *windows64* framework, modify the program in Programming Exercise 4 to use the *input* macro to prompt for and input values for *a*, *b*, and *c*, and the *output* macro to display an appropriate label and the value of the expression. You will also use the data conversion macros from IO.H as appropriate.

6. Using the *console32* or *console64* framework, write a complete assembly language program that computes in EAX the perimeter *(2*length + 2*width)* of a rectangle where the length and width are in memory doublewords. Choose the dimensions of a racquetball court for the length and width, and predict the result before building the program and executing it under control of the debugger. (*Hint:* You can find the dimensions of a racquetball court at the USA Racquetball website.)

7. Using the *windows32* or *windows64* framework, modify the program in Programming Exercise 6 to use the *input* macro to prompt for and input values for *length* and *width*, and the *output* macro to display an appropriate label and the value of the perimeter. You will also use the data conversion macros from IO.H as appropriate.

4.3   Multiplication Instructions

The 80x86 architecture has two multiplication instruction mnemonics. Any `imul` instruction treats its operands as signed numbers; the sign of the product is determined by the usual rules for multiplying signed numbers. A `mul` instruction treats its operands as unsigned binary numbers; the product is also unsigned.

There are fewer variants of `mul` than of `imul`, so we consider it first. The `mul` instruction has a single operand; its format is

```
mul     source
```

The source operand can be byte-, word-, doubleword-, or quadword-length (quadword in 64-bit mode only). It can be in a register or in memory, but cannot be immediate. The location of the other number to be multiplied is always the accumulator—AL for a byte source, AX for a word source, EAX for a doubleword source, and RAX for a quadword source. If *source* has byte length, then it is multiplied by the byte in AL; the product is 16 bits long, with destination the AX register. If *source* has word length, then it is multiplied by the word in AX; the product is 32 bits long, with its low-order 16 bits going to the AX register and its high-order 16 bits going to the DX register. This is often written DX:AX. If *source* is a doubleword, then it is multiplied by the doubleword in EAX; the product is 64 bits long, with its low-order 32 bits in the EAX register and its high-order 32 bits in the EDX register, written EDX:EAX. If *source* is a quadword, then it is multiplied by the quadword in RAX; the product is 128 bits long, with its low-order 64 bits in the RAX register and its high-order 64 bits in the RDX register, written RDX:RAX. For byte multiplication, the original value in AX is replaced. For word multiplication the original values in AX and DX are both wiped out. For doubleword multiplication the values in EAX and EDX are replaced by the product. Similarly, for quadword multiplication the values in RAX and RDX are replaced by the product. In each case the source operand is unchanged unless it is half of the destination location.

At first glance, it may seem strange that the product is twice the length of each factor. However, this also occurs in ordinary decimal multiplication—if, for example, two 4-digit numbers are multiplied, the product will be 7 or 8 digits long. Computers that have multiplication operations often put the product in double-length locations so that there is no danger that the destination location will be too small.

You may also wonder why the 80x86 places a 32-bit product in DX and AX instead of EAX. This is because the `mul` instruction existed in the 8086, 8088, 80186, and 80286 processors with their 16-bit registers, and when the 80386 introduced 32-bit registers it was designed to extend the earlier architecture. Later processors continued the compatibility with earlier designs.

Figure 4.14 summarizes the allowable operand types for `mul` instructions. Notice that no immediate operand is allowed in a `mul`.

Operand	Opcode	Bytes of Object Code
register 8	F6	2
register 16	F7	2
register 32	F7	2
memory byte	F6	2+
memory word	F7	2+
memory doubleword	F7	2+
64-bit mode		
register 64	F7	2
memory quadword	F7	2+

Figure 4.14 mul instructions

Even when provision is made for double-length products, it is useful to be able to tell whether the product is the same size as the source, that is, if the high-order half is zero. With mul instructions, the carry flag CF, and overflow flag OF are cleared to 0 if the high-order half of the product is zero, but are set to 1 if the high-order half of the product is not zero. These are the only meaningful flag values following multiplication operations; previously set values of AF, PF, SF, and ZF flags may be destroyed. In Chapter 5 (Branching and Looping), instructions that check flag values will be covered; it is possible to check that the high-order half of the product can be safely ignored.

Here are some examples to illustrate how the mul instructions work.

Example

Before	Instruction Executed	After

EAX: 00 00 00 05   mul ebx

EBX: 00 00 00 02

EDX: ?? ?? ?? ??

EDX	00	00	00	00

EAX	00	00	00	0A

CF, OF 0

EAX: ?? ?? 00 05	`mul bx`	EDX	??	??	00	00		
EBX: ?? ?? 00 02								
EDX: ?? ?? ?? ??		EAX	??	??	00	0A		
		CF, OF 0						

EAX: 00 00 00 0A	`mul  eax`	EDX	00	00	00	00		
EDX: ?? ?? ?? ??								
		EAX	00	00	00	64		
		CF, OF 0						

AX: ?? 05	`mul  factor`	AX	04	FB
byte at *factor*: FF				
		CF, OF 1		

The first example shows multiplication of doublewords in EAX and EBX. The contents of EDX are not used in the multiplication but are replaced by the high-order 32 bits of the 64-bit product 000000000000000A. The carry and overflow flags are cleared to 0 since EDX contains 00000000. The second example is the same as the first, except that the operands are word size. The contents of DX are not used in the multiplication but are replaced by the high-order 16 bits of the 32-bit product 0000000A. The carry and overflow flags are cleared to 0 since DX contains 0000. The high-order 16 bits of each of EAX and EDX are unchanged. The third example shows multiplication of EAX by itself, illustrating that the explicit source for the multiplication can be the same as the other, implicit factor. The final example shows multiplication of the byte in AL by a byte at *factor* in memory with value equivalent to the unsigned number 255_{10}. The product is the unsigned 16-bit number $04FB_{16}$, and since the high-order half (AH) is not zero, both CF and OF are set to 1.

The signed multiplication instructions use mnemonic `imul`. There are three formats, each with a different number of operands. The first format is

        `imul    source`

the same as for `mul`, with *source* containing one factor and the accumulator the other. As with `mul` the source operand cannot be immediate. The destination is AX, DX:AX,

EDX:EAX, or RDX:RAX depending on the size of the source operand. The carry and over-flow flags are set to 1 if the bits in the high-order half are significant, and cleared to 0 otherwise. The high-order half will contain all 1 bits for a negative product, but this is *not* significant if the sign position of the low-order half is also 1. Similarly, all high-order bits of 0 are significant if the sign bit of the low-order half is 1. This can be summarized by saying that CF and OF are set to 1 if any bit in the high-order half is different from the sign bit in the low-order half.

Single-operand `imul` instructions are summarized in Figure 4.15. Notice that this table is identical to Figure 4.14. Even the opcodes are the same for `mul` and single-operand `imul` instructions, with the *reg* field in the *ModR/M* byte of the instruction distinguishing the two. Figure 4.9 shows *reg* = 100 for `mul` and *reg* = 101 for `imul`.

The second `imul` format is

`imul`   *destination register, source*

With this format the source operand can be in a register, in memory, or immediate. The other factor is in the destination register, so that this format is similar to those for **add** and **sub** instructions. Register and memory operands must be words, doublewords, or quadwords, not bytes. The product must fit in the destination register; if it does, CF and OF are cleared to 0; if not, they are set to 1.

Figure 4.16 summarizes two-operand `imul` instructions. Note that some of these instructions have 2-byte-long opcodes. Immediate operands for all size destinations can be a single byte that is sign-extended before multiplication. For word and dou-

Operand	Opcode	Bytes of Object Code
register 8	F6	2
register 16	F7	2
register 32	F7	2
memory byte	F6	2+
memory word	F7	2+
memory doubleword	F7	2+
64-bit mode		
register 64	F7	2
memory quadword	F7	2+

Figure 4.15 `imul` instructions (single-operand format)

Destination	Source	Opcode	Bytes of Object Code
register 16	register 16	0F AF	3
register 32	register 32	0F AF	3
register 16	memory word	0F AF	3+
register 32	memory doubleword	0F AF	3+
register 16	immediate byte	6B	3
register 16	immediate word	69	4
register 32	immediate byte	6B	3
register 32	immediate doubleword	69	6
64-bit mode			
register 64	register 64	0F AF	3
register 64	memory quadword	0F AF	3+
register 64	immediate byte	6B	3
register 64	immediate doubleword	69	6

Figure 4.16 `imul` instructions (two-operand format)

bleword operations, an immediate operand can also be a word or doubleword, respectively. However, for a quadword destination, only byte and doubleword immediate operands are available; either is sign-extended to 64 bits.

The third `imul` format is

```
imul    register, source, immediate
```

With this version, the first operand, a register, is only the destination for the product; the two factors are the contents of the register or memory location given by *source* and the immediate value. Operands *register* and *source* are the same size: 16-bit, 32-bit, or 64-bit. Immediate operands are treated the same as with the two-operand format—byte size if small enough, otherwise word or doubleword, in all cases sign-extended to the size of the source operand. If the product will fit in the destination register, then CF and OF are cleared to 0; if not, they are set to 1. The three-operand `imul` instructions are summarized in Figure 4.17.

RegDestination	Source	Immediate Operand	Opcode	Bytes of Object Code
register 16	register 16	byte	6B	3
register 16	register 16	word	69	4
register 16	memory word	byte	6B	3 +
register 16	memory word	word	69	4 +
register 32	register 32	byte	6B	3
register 32	register 32	doubleword	69	6
register 32	memory doubleword	byte	6B	3 +
register 32	memory doubleword	doubleword	69	6 +
64-bit mode				
register 64	register 64	byte	6B	3
register 64	register 64	doubleword	69	6
register 64	memory quadword	byte	6B	3 +
register 64	memory quadword	doubleword	69	6 +

Figure 4.17 `imul` **Instructions (three-operand format)**

Some examples will help show how the `imul` instructions work.

Example

Before	Instruction Executed	After
EAX: 00 00 00 05	`imul ebx`	EDX 00 00 00 00
EBX: 00 00 00 02		EAX 00 00 00 0A
		CF, OF 0
EAX: ?? ?? 00 05	`imul bx`	EDX ?? ?? 00 00
EBX: ?? ?? 00 02		EAX ?? ?? 00 0A
		CF, OF 0
AX: ?? 05	`imul factor`	AX FF FB
byte at *factor*: FF		CF, OF 0

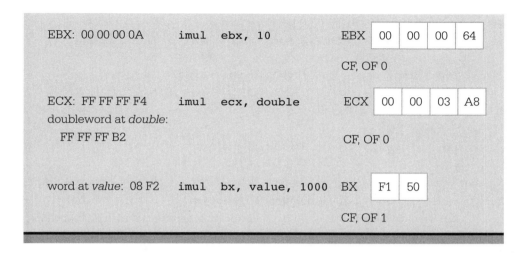

The first three examples are the single-operand format and the products are twice the length of the operands. The first example shows doublewords in EAX (the implied operand) and EBX being multiplied, with the result in EDX:EAX. The second example is the word-size version of the first, where only the values in AX and BX are multiplied and the result is in DX:AX. The third example shows 5 in AL being multiplied by -1 in the memory byte at *factor*, giving a word-size product equivalent to -5 in AX. In each case CF and OF are cleared to 0 since the high-order half of the product is not significant.

The fourth example shows the two-operand format, with 10 in EBX multiplied by the immediate operand 10, and the result of 100 in EBX. The EDX register is not used with the two-operand format unless it is specified as the destination. CF and OF are cleared to 0 since the product fits in EBX. In the next-to-last example, two negative numbers are multiplied, giving a positive result.

The last example shows the three-operand format, with $8F2_{16}$ multiplied by 1000_{10} to give $22F150_{16}$—too large to fit in BX. The flags CF and OF are set to 1 to indicate that the result is too large, and the low-order digits are saved in BX.

Earlier 80x86 CPUs processed each instruction in a fixed number of clock cycles. As the line developed, the same instruction would often take fewer clock cycles on a newer processor than on its predecessor. This, along with higher clock rates, contributes to faster speeds of newer computers. Current 80x86 processors use pipelining to effectively process more than one instruction at a time. This makes it difficult to determine the exact timing of any instruction. However, generally multiplication instructions are among the slowest 80x86 instructions to execute. If, for example, you want to multiply the value in EAX by 2, it is much more efficient to use

```
add    eax, eax      ; double the value
```

than

```
imul   eax, 2        ; double the value
```

Whether you are programming in assembly language or a high-level language, avoid using multiplication when a simple addition will do the job.

As you have seen in this section, the 80x86 architecture includes multiplication instructions in three formats. You may have noted that the destination of the product cannot be a memory operand. This may sound restrictive, but some processors have even greater limitations. In fact, most 8-bit microprocessors, including the Intel 8080, had no multiplication instruction; any multiplication had to be done using a software routine.

This section concludes with an example of a *windows32* program that will input the length and width of a rectangle in memory, calculate its area (length*width), and display the result. (Admittedly, this is a job much better suited for a hand calculator than for a computer program in assembly language or any other language.) Figure 4.18 shows the source code for the program. Note that the program uses **mul** rather than **imul** for finding the product—lengths and widths are positive numbers. You may wonder why the variables that hold the length and width are named *long* and *wide* rather than the more obvious choices of *length* and *width*. The reason is that *length* and *width* are reserved words for the assembler. If you get an unusual error when assembling a program, check Appendix B to see whether you accidentally used a reserved word as an identifier.

Figure 4.19 shows a sample run of the program. If you use the debugger to view registers right after the **mul** instruction you will see the product in EAX, but you will also see that EDX has been set to all zeros—the actual product computed by the **mul** instruction is 64 bits long.

```
; program to find the area of a rectangle
; author:  R. Detmer
; date:  revised 6/2008

.586
.MODEL FLAT
INCLUDE io.h
.STACK 4096

.DATA
long        DWORD   ?
wide        DWORD   ?
prompt1 BYTE     "Length of rectangle?", 0
prompt2 BYTE     "Width of rectangle?", 0
string  BYTE     30 DUP (?)
areaLbl BYTE     "The area is", 0
area    BYTE     11 DUP (?), 0

.CODE
_MainProc PROC
        input   prompt1, string, 30    ; get length
        atod    string         ; convert to integer
        mov     long, eax      ; store in memory

        input   prompt2, string, 40    ; repeat for width
        atod    string
        mov     wide, eax

        mov     eax, long      ; length to EAX
        mul     wide           ; length*width
        dtoa    area, eax       ; convert to ASCII
        output  areaLbl, area  ; output label and area

        mov     eax, 0 ; exit with return code 0
        ret
_MainProc ENDP
END
```

Figure 4.18 Program to find the area of a rectangle

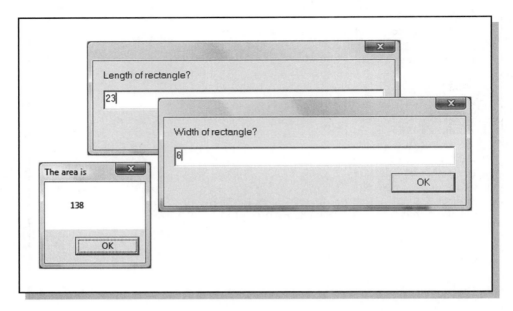

Figure 4.19 Execution of program to calculate area of rectangle

Exercises 4.3

1. For each part of this problem, assume the "before" values when the given instruction is executed. Give the requested "after" values.

Before		Instruction		After
(a) EAX: FF FF FF E4				
EBX: 00 00 00 02		mul	ebx	EAX, EDX, CF, OF
*(b) AX: FF FF FF E4				
doubleword at *value*:		mul	value	EAX, EDX, CF, OF
FF FF FF 3A				
(c) AX: FF FF		mul	ax	AX, DX, CF, OF
(d) AL: 0F				
BH: 4C		mul	bh	AX, CF, OF
(e) AL: F0				
BH: C4		mul	bh	AX, CF, OF
*(f) EAX: 00 00 00 17				
ECX: 00 00 00 B2		imul	ecx	EAX, EDX, CF, OF
(g) EAX: FF FF FF E4				
EBX: 00 00 04 C2		imul	ebx	EAX, EDX, CF, OF

(h) AX: FF FF FF E4
    doubleword at *value*:   imul   value   EAX, EDX, CF, OF
      FF FF FF 3A

  (i) EAX: FF FF FF FF   imul   eax   EAX, EDX, CF, OF

*(j) AL: 0F
    BH: 4C   imul   bh   AX, CF, OF

 (k) AL: F0
    BH: C4   imul   bh   AX, CF, OF

*2. Give the opcode and the number of bytes of object code (including prefix bytes) for each instruction in Exercise 1.

3. For each part of this problem, assume the "before" values when the given instruction is executed. Give the requested "after" values.

Before	*Instruction*	*After*
*(a) EBX: 00 00 00 17		
ECX: 00 00 00 B2	imul ebx, ecx	EBX, CF, OF
(b) EAX: FF FF FF E4		
EBX: 00 00 04 C2	imul eax, ebx	EAX, CF, OF
*(c) EAX: 00 00 0F B2	imul eax, 15	EAX, CF, OF
(d) ECX: 00 00 7C E4		
doubleword at *mult*:	imul ecx, mult	ECX, CF, OF
00 00 65 ED		
(e) DX: 7C E4		
BX: 49 30	imul dx, bx	DX, CF, OF
(f) DX: 0F E4		
word at *value*: 04 C2	imul dx, value	DX, CF, OF
(g) EBX: 00 00 04 C2	imul ebx, –10	EBX, CF, OF
*(h) ECX: FF FF FF E4	imul ebx, ecx, 5	EBX, CF, OF
(i) EDX: 00 00 00 64	imul eax, edx, 10	EAX, CF, OF

*4. Give the opcode and the number of bytes of object code (including prefix bytes) for each instruction in Exercise 3.

5. Suppose you need to evaluate the polynomial

$$p(x) = 5x^3 - 7x^2 + 3x - 10$$

for some value of x. If this is done in the obvious way, as

$$5*x*x*x - 7*x*x + 3*x - 10$$

there are six multiplications and three additions/subtractions. An equivalent form, based on Horner's scheme for evaluation of polynomials, is

$$((5*x - 7)*x + 3)*x - 10$$

This has only three multiplications.

Suppose that the value of x is in the EAX register.

(a) Write 80x86 assembly language statements that will evaluate $p(x)$ the "obvious" way, putting the result in EAX.

(b) Write 80x86 assembly language statements that will evaluate $p(x)$ using Horner's scheme, again putting the result in EAX.

(c) Compare the number of bytes of object code required for the code fragments in (a) and in (b) above.

6. The 80x86 architecture has distinct instructions for multiplication of signed and unsigned numbers. It does not have separate instructions for addition of signed and unsigned numbers. Why are different instructions needed for multiplication but not for addition?

Programming Exercises 4.3

1. Using the *windows32* or *windows64* framework, write a complete 80x86 assembly language program that prompts for and inputs the length, width, and height of a box and computes and displays its volume (length * width * height).

2. Using the *windows32* or *windows64* framework, write a complete 80x86 assembly language program that prompts for and inputs the length, width, and height of a box and calculates and displays its surface area

   2*(length*width + length*height + width*height).

3. Suppose that someone has a certain number of coins (pennies, nickels, dimes, quarters, 50-cent pieces, and dollar coins) and wants to know the total value of the coins, and how many coins there are. Using the *windows32* or *windows64* framework, write a program to help. Specifically, use the following design.

   prompt for and input the number of pennies;
   total := number of pennies;
   numberOfCoins := number of pennies;
   prompt for and input the number of nickels;

total := total + 5 * number of nickels;

add number of nickels to numberOfCoins;

prompt for and input the number of dimes;

total := total + 10 * number of dimes;

add number of dimes to numberOfCoins;

prompt for and input the number of quarters;

total := total + 25 * number of quarters;

add number of quarters to numberOfCoins;

prompt for and input the number of 50-cent pieces;

total := total + 50 * number of 50-cent pieces;

add number of 50-cent pieces to numberOfCoins;

prompt for and input the number of dollars;

total := total + 100 * number of dollars;

add number of dollars to numberOfCoins;

display the number of coins, the dollar value and the cents;

The final display will be in a single message box with a label that says "Coin Information" and three lines of message, the first saying "Number of coins" and giving the number, the second saying "Dollars" and giving the value of *total* div 100, and the third displaying "Cents" and the value of *total* mod 100. Assume that all values will fit in doublewords. (*Hint:* Convert the total to ASCII, and the last two characters are total *mod* 100, while the preceding characters are *total* div 100.)

4.4   Division Instructions

The Intel 80x86 instructions for division parallel those of the single-operand multiplication instructions; `idiv` is for division of signed 2's complement integers and `div` is for division of unsigned integers. Recall that the single-operand multiplication instructions start with a multiplier and multiplicand and produce a double-length product. Division instructions start with a double-length dividend and a single-length divisor, and produce a single-length quotient *and* a single-length remainder. The 80x86 has instructions that can be used to produce a double-length dividend prior to division.

The division instructions have formats

```
idiv    source
```

Source (divisor) Size	Implicit Operand (dividend)	Quotient	Remainder
byte	AX	AL	AH
word	DX:AX	AX	DX
doubleword	EDX:EAX	EAX	EDX
quadword	RDX:RAX	RAX	RDX

Figure 4.20 Operands and results for 80x86 division instructions

and

```
div     source
```

The source operand identifies the divisor. The divisor can be in a register or memory but not immediate. Both **div** and **idiv** use an implicit dividend (the operand you are dividing into). If *source* is byte length, then the double-length dividend is word size and it must be in the AX register. If *source* is word length, then the dividend is always the doubleword in DX:AX, that is, with its high-order 16 bits in the DX register and its low-order 16 bits in the AX register. If *source* is doubleword length, then the dividend is a quadword (64 bits) in EDX:EAX, that is, with its high-order 32 bits in the EDX register and its low-order 32 bits in the EAX register. If *source* is quadword length, then the dividend is the double quadword (128-bit number) in RDX:RAX, that is, with its high-order 64 bits in the RDX register and its low-order 64 bits in the RAX register.

The table in Figure 4.20 summarizes the locations of the dividend, divisor, quotient, and remainder for 80x86 division instructions.

The source operand (the divisor) is not changed by a division instruction. After a word in AX is divided by a byte-length divisor, the quotient will be in the AL register and the remainder will be in the AH register. After a doubleword in DX and AX is divided by a word-length divisor, the quotient will be in the AX register and the remainder will be in the DX register. After a quadword in EDX and EAX is divided by a doubleword-length divisor, the quotient will be in the EAX register and the remainder will be in the EDX register. After a 128-bit integer in RDX:RAX is divided by a quadword-length divisor, the quotient will be in the RAX register and the remainder will be in the RDX register.

For all division operations the dividend, divisor, quotient, and remainder are defined by the equation

```
dividend = quotient*divisor + remainder
```

For unsigned **div** operations the dividend, divisor, quotient, and remainder are all treated as nonnegative numbers. For signed **idiv** operations, the sign of the quotient is determined by the signs of the dividend and divisor using the ordinary rules of signs; the sign of the remainder is always the same as the sign of the dividend.

Division instructions do not set flags to any meaningful values. They may change previously set values of AF, CF, OF, PF, SF, or ZF flags.

Some examples show how the division instructions work.

Example

Before	*Instruction Executed*	*After*

EDX: 00 00 00 00   **div   ebx   ; 100/13**   EDX | 00 | 00 | 00 | 09

EAX: 00 00 00 64   EAX | 00 | 00 | 00 | 07

AX: 00 64   **div   divisor   ; 100/13**   AX | 09 | 07 |

In both of these examples, the decimal number 100 is divided by 13. Since

$$100 = 7 * 13 + 9$$

the quotient is 7 and the remainder is 9. For the doubleword-length divisor, the quotient is in EAX and the remainder is in EDX. For the byte-length divisor, the quotient is in AL and the remainder is in AH.

For operations where the dividend or divisor is negative, equations analogous to the one above are

$$100 = (-7) * (-13) + 9 \qquad (100/-13, \text{ quotient } -7, \text{ remainder } 9)$$
$$-100 = (-7) * 13 + (-9) \qquad (-100/13, \text{ quotient } -7, \text{ remainder } -9)$$
$$-100 = 7 * (-13) + (-9) \qquad (-100/-13, \text{ quotient } 7, \text{ remainder } -9)$$

Note that in each case the sign of the remainder is the same as the sign of the dividend. The following examples reflect these equations for doubleword-size divisors of 13 or −13. In the second and third examples, the dividend −100 is represented as the 64-bit number FF FF FF FF FF FF FF 9C in EDX:EAX.

Example

Before	Instruction Executed	After				
EDX: 00 00 00 00	idiv ecx ; 100/(-13)	EDX	00	00	00	09
EAX: 00 00 00 64		EAX	FF	FF	FF	F9
EDX: FF FF FF FF	idiv ecx ; -100/13	EDX	FF	FF	FF	F7
EAX: FF FF FF 9C		EAX	FF	FF	FF	F9
EDX: FF FF FF FF	idiv ecx ; -100/(-13)	EDX	FF	FF	FF	F7
EAX: FF FF FF 9C		EAX	00	00	00	07

Finally, here are two examples to help illustrate the difference between signed and unsigned division. Using signed division, −511 is divided by −32, giving a quotient of 15 and a remainder of −31. With the unsigned division, 65025 is divided by 255, giving a quotient of 255 and a remainder of 0.

Example

Before	Instruction Executed	After	
AX: FE 01	idiv bl ; -511/(-32)	AX	E1	0F
BL: E0			
AX: FE 01	div bl ; 65025/255	AX	00	FF
BL: FF			

With multiplication, the double-length destination in each single-operand format guarantees that the product will fit in the destination location—nothing can go wrong during a single-operand multiplication operation. However, there can be errors during division. One obvious cause is an attempt to divide by zero. A less obvious reason

Operand	Opcode	Bytes of Object Code
register 8	F6	2
register 16	F7	2
register 32	F7	2
memory byte	F6	2+
memory word	F7	2+
memory doubleword	F7	2+
64-bit mode		
register 64	F7	2
memory quadword	F7	2+

Figure 4.21 `div` and `idiv` instructions

is a quotient that is too large to fit in the single-length destination; if, say, 0002468A is divided by 0002; the quotient 12345 is too large to fit in the AX register. If an error occurs during the division operation, the 80x86 generates an exception. The routine, or interrupt handler, that services this exception will vary from system to system.

Figure 4.21 lists the allowable operand types for **div** and **idiv** instructions. These instructions have the same opcodes, with the *reg* field of the *ModR/M* byte distinguishing them as shown in Figure 4.9.

When arithmetic is being done with operands of a given length, the dividend must be converted to double length before a division operation is executed. For *unsigned* division, a doubleword-size dividend must be converted to quadword size with leading zero bits in the EDX register. This can be accomplished many ways, two of which are

```
mov    edx, 0
```

and

```
sub    edx, edx
```

Similar instructions can be used to put a zero in RDX, DX, or AH prior to unsigned division by a quadword, word, or byte, respectively.

The situation is more complicated for *signed* division. A positive dividend must be extended with leading 0 bits, but a negative dividend must be extended with leading 1 bits. The 80x86 has instructions specifically for this task. The **cbw**, **cwd**, **cdq**, and **cqo**

Instruction	Opcode	Bytes of Object Code
cbw	98	1
cwd	99	1
cdq	99	1
cqo	99	1

Figure 4.22 Instructions to prepare for signed division

instructions are the first ones we have seen that have no operand. The **cbw** instruction always has AL as its source and AX as its destination, **cwd** always has AX as its source and DX:AX as its destination, **cdq** always has EAX as its source and EDX:EAX as its destination, and **cqo** always has RAX as its source and RDX:RAX as its destination. The source register is not changed, but is extended as a signed number into AH, DX, EDX, or RDX. These instructions are summarized together in Figure 4.22.

The **cbw** (convert byte to word) instruction extends the 2's complement number in the AL register half to word length in AX. The **cwd** (convert word to double) instruction extends the word in AX to a doubleword in DX and AX. The **cdq** (convert double to quadword) instruction extends the doubleword in EAX to a quadword in EDX and EAX. The **cqo** instruction extends the quadword in RAX to a double quadword in RDX and RAX. Each instruction copies the sign bit of the original number to each bit of the high-order half of the result. None of these instructions affect flags. Some examples are:

Example

Before	Instruction Executed	After
EAX: FF FF FA 13	cdq	EDX	FF	FF	FF	FF
EDX: ?? ?? ?? ??		EAX	FF	FF	FF	13
AX: 07 0D	cwd	DX	00	00
DX: ?? ??		AX	07	0D

This section concludes with another simple program; this one to convert Celsius (centigrade) temperatures to Fahrenheit. Figure 4.23 gives the source code. The formula implemented is

$$F = (9/5) * C + 32$$

```
; program to convert Celsius temperature in memory at cTemp
; to Fahrenheit equivalent in memory at fTemp
; author:  R. Detmer
; date:  revised 6/2008

.586
.MODEL FLAT
.STACK  4096

.DATA
cTemp    DWORD   35     ; Celsius temperature
fTemp    DWORD   ?      ; Fahrenheit temperature

.CODE
main     PROC
         mov     eax, cTemp        ; start with Celsius temperature
         imul    eax,9             ; C*9
         add     eax,2             ; rounding factor for division
         mov     ebx,5             ; divisor
         cdq                       ; prepare for division
         idiv    ebx               ; C*9/5
         add     eax,32            ; C*9/5 + 32
         mov     fTemp, eax        ; save result

         mov     eax, 0       ; exit with return code 0
         ret
main     ENDP
END
```

Figure 4.23 Convert Celsius temperature to Fahrenheit

where F is the Fahrenheit temperature and C is the Celsius temperature. The program starts with a Celsius value of 35 stored in a doubleword in memory at *cTemp*, and ends with the corresponding Fahrenheit value stored in another doubleword at *fTemp*. Any value could be used, of course, instead of 35.

Since the arithmetic instructions covered so far perform only integer arithmetic, the program gives the integer to which the fractional answer would round. It is important to multiply 9 times *cTemp* before dividing by 5—the integer quotient 9/5 would be simply 1. Dividing *cTemp* by 5 before multiplying by 9 produces larger errors than if the multiplication is done first. (Why?) To get a rounded answer, half the divisor is added to the dividend before dividing. Since the divisor in this formula is 5, the number 2 is added for rounding. Notice that the **cdq** instruction is used to extend the partial result before division.

Figure 4.24 shows the debugger display at the end of the program. If you trace the arithmetic by hand, 35*9+2 is 317. Dividing 317 by 5 gives 63 with a remainder of 2 (still visible in EDX). Finally, adding 32 to 63 gives the 95 that shows as $5F_{16}$ in EAX and in the second doubleword of the memory display.

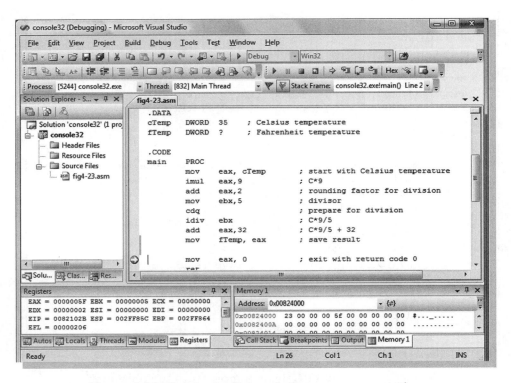

Figure 4.24 Celsius to Fahrenheit program execution

▬▬▬ **Exercises 4.4**

1. For each part of this problem, assume the "before" values when the given instruction is executed. Give the requested "after" values. Some of these instructions will cause division errors; identify such instructions.

Before	*Instruction*	*After*
*(a) EDX: 00 00 00 00		
EAX: 00 00 00 9A		
EBX: 00 00 00 0F	idiv ebx	EDX, EAX
(b) AX: FF 75		
byte at *count*: FC	idiv count	AX
(c) AX: FF 75		
byte at *count*: FC	div count	AX
*(d) DX: FF FF		
AX: FF 9A		
CX: 00 00	idiv cx	DX, AX
(e) EDX: FF FF FF FF		
EAX: FF FF FF 9A		
ECX: FF FF FF C7	idiv ecx	EDX, EAX
(f) DX: 00 00		
AX: 05 9A		
CX: FF C7	idiv cx	DX, AX
(g) DX: 00 00		
AX: 05 9A		
CX: 00 00	idiv cx	DX, AX
*(h) EDX: 00 00 00 00		
EAX: 00 00 01 5D		
EBX: 00 00 00 08	idiv ebx	EDX, EAX

*2. Give the opcode and the number of bytes of object code (including prefix bytes) for each instruction in Exercise 1.

3. This section mentioned two methods of zeroing EDX prior to unsigned division, using

```
mov   edx,0
```

or

```
sub   edx,edx
```

Which instruction requires fewer bytes of code?

Programming Exercises 4.4

1. The formula for converting a Fahrenheit to a Celsius temperature is

   $$C = (5/9) * (F - 32)$$

   Using the *windows32* or *windows64* framework, write a complete 80x86 assembly language program to prompt for a Fahrenheit temperature and calculate and display the corresponding Celsius temperature.

2. Using the *windows32* or *windows64* framework, write a complete 80x86 assembly language program that prompts for and inputs four grades with separate dialog boxes, and calculates the sum and the average (sum/4) of the grades. Display the sum and average on two lines of a message box, each line with an appropriate label.

3. Using the *windows32* or *windows64* framework, write a complete 80x86 assembly language program that prompts for and inputs four grades *Grade1*, *Grade2*, *Grade3*, and *Grade4*. Suppose that the last grade is a final exam grade that counts twice as much as the other three. Calculate the sum (adding the last grade twice) and the average (sum/5). Display the sum and average on two lines of a message box, each line with an appropriate label.

4. Using the *windows32* or *windows64* framework, write a complete 80x86 assembly language program that prompts for and inputs four grades *Grade1*, *Grade2*, *Grade3*, and *Grade4*, and four weights stored in doublewords *Weight1, Weight2, Weight3*, and *Weight4*. (This will take eight dialog boxes.) Each weighting factor indicates how many times the corresponding grade is to be counted in the sum. The weighted sum is

   WeightedSum = Grade1*Weight1+Grade2*Weight2+Grade3*Weight3+Grade4*Weight4

   and the sum of the weights is

   SumOfWeights = Weight1 + Weight2 + Weight3 + Weight4

   Calculate the weighted sum, the sum of the weights, and the weighted average (*WeightedSum/SumOfWeights*). Display the weighted sum and average on two lines of a message box, each line with an appropriate label.

4.5 Chapter Summary

The Intel 80x86 `mov` instruction is used to copy data from one location to another. All but a few combinations of source and destination locations are allowed. The `xchg` instruction swaps the data stored at two locations.

The 80x86 architecture has a full set of instructions for arithmetic with byte-length, word-length, doubleword-length, and quadword-length (in 64-bit mode) integers. The `add` and `sub` instructions perform addition and subtraction; `inc` and `dec` add and subtract 1, respectively. The `neg` instruction negates its operand; that is, takes the 2's complement of the operand.

There are two multiplication and two division mnemonics. The `imul` and `idiv` instructions assume that their operands are signed 2's complement numbers; `mul` and `div` assume that their operands are unsigned. Many multiplication instructions start with single-length operands and produce double-length products; other formats form a product the same length as the factors. Division instruction always start with a double-length dividend and single-length divisor; the operation results in a single-length quotient and a single-length remainder. The `cbw`, `cwd`, `cdq`, and `cqo` instructions aid in producing a double-length dividend before signed division. Flag settings indicate possible errors during multiplication; an error during division produces a hardware exception that invokes a procedure to handle the error.

Instructions that have operands in registers are generally faster than those that reference memory locations. Multiplication and division instructions are slower than addition and subtraction instructions.

CHAPTER 5

Branching and Looping

Computers derive much of their power from their ability to selectively execute code and from the speed at which they execute repetitive algorithms. Programs in high-level languages like Java or C++ use *if–then*, *if–then–else*, and *case* structures to selectively execute code, and loop structures such as *while* (pretest) loops, *until* (posttest) loops, and *for* (counter-controlled) loops to repetitively execute code. Some high-level languages have a *goto* statement for unconditional branching. Somewhat more primitive languages (like older versions of FORTRAN or BASIC) depend on fairly simple *if* statements and an abundance of *goto* statements for both selective execution and looping.

The 80x86 assembly language programmer's job is similar to the old FORTRAN or BASIC programmer's job. The 80x86 microprocessor can execute some instructions that are roughly comparable to *for* statements, but most branching and looping is done with 80x86 statements that are similar to, but even more primitive than, simple *if* and *goto* statements. The objective of this chapter is to describe the machine implementation of design/language structures such as *if–then*, *if–then–else*, *while*, *until*, and *for*. Loops are often used with arrays, and addressing modes useful for array access are also covered.

5.1   Unconditional Jumps

The 80x86 **jmp** ("jump") instruction corresponds to *goto* in a high-level language. As coded in assembly language, **jmp** usually has the form

        jmp   *statementLabel*

where *statementLabel* corresponds to the name field of some other assembly language statement. Recall that the name field is followed by a colon (:) when used to label an executable statement. The colon is not used in the **jmp** instruction itself. As an example, if there were alternative conditions under which a program should be terminated, its code might contain

        jmp   quit   ; exit from program
                  .
                  .
        quit: mov eax, 0   ; exit with return code 0
                ret

Figure 5.1 shows a complete example, a program that will loop indefinitely, calculating $1+2+ \ldots +n$ at the nth loop iteration. The program implements the following pseudocode design.

---

number := 0;
sum := 0;
forever loop
    add 1 to number;
    add number to sum;
end loop;

You must plan register and memory use to code a design like this. In this implementation, *number* is stored in EBX and *sum* is stored in EAX. No data is stored in memory.

Figure 5.2 shows the debugger window after the loop body has been executed one time. A breakpoint has been set at the **jmp** instruction, making it possible to examine the contents of *sum* (EAX) and *count* (EBX) before proceeding. Notice that both *sum* and count *are* 1 the first time the breakpoint is reached. Press F5 or click the Continue button ▶ to execute the **jmp** instruction and the loop body again. Figure 5.3 shows the debugger window after executing the loop body six times; *number* (EBX) contains 6 and *sum* (EAX) contains 15_{16} (21_{10}), the correct result for $1+2+3+4+5+6$. The program can be terminated by clicking the Stop button ■.

```
; program to find sum 1+2+...+n for n=1, 2, ...
; author:  R. Detmer
; revised:  6/2008

.586
.MODEL FLAT
.STACK  4096

.DATA

.CODE
main      PROC
          mov     ebx,0          ; number := 0
          mov     eax,0          ; sum := 0

forever: inc      ebx            ; add 1 to number
          add     eax, ebx       ; add number to sum
          jmp     forever        ; repeat

main      ENDP
END
```

Figure 5.1 Program with forever loop

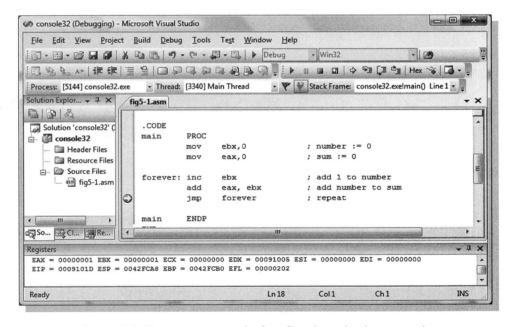

Figure 5.2 Program paused after first loop body execution

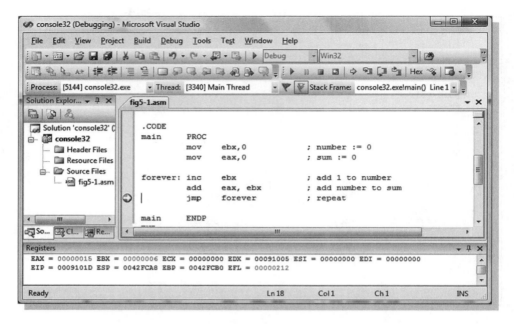

Figure 5.3 Program after six loop body iterations

The one `jmp` in the program in Figure 5.1 transfers control to a point that precedes the `jmp` statement itself. This is called a **backward reference**. The code

```
jmp     quit                    ; exit from program
        .
        .
quit:   mov eax, 0              ; exit with return code 0
```

illustrates a **forward reference**.

There are several 80x86 `jmp` instructions. All work by changing the value in the instruction pointer register EIP (RIP in 64-bit mode) so that the next instruction to be executed comes from a new address rather than from the address immediately following the current instruction. The most common jump instructions are **relative** jumps that change the instruction pointer by adding a positive or negative displacement for a forward or backward reference, respectively. There are also **indirect** jumps that get the new value for the instruction pointer from a register or from memory. We will not use indirect jumps in this book, but they are included in Figure 5.4 and discussed briefly. Not

Type	Opcode	Bytes of Object Code
relative near	E9	5
relative short	EB	2
register indirect	FF	2
memory indirect	FF	2+

Figure 5.4 jmp instructions

included are **far** jumps that change the code segment register as well as the instruction pointer; these are not used with flat memory model programming.

The object code for each relative jump instruction contains the displacement of the target instruction from the **jmp** itself. This displacement is added to the address of the next instruction to find the address of the target. The displacement is a signed number, positive for a forward reference and negative for a backward reference. For the relative **short** version of the instruction, only a single displacement byte is stored; this is sign-extended before the addition. The relative **near** format includes a 32-bit displacement. This is simply added to EIP in 32-bit mode, but is sign-extended before being added to RIP in 64-bit mode.

The 8-bit displacement in an relative short jump can serve for a target statement up to 128 bytes before or 127 bytes after the **jmp** instruction. This displacement is measured from the byte following the object code of the **jmp** itself since at the time an instruction is being executed, the instruction pointer logically contains the address of the next instruction to be executed. The 32-bit displacement in a relative near jump instruction can serve for a target statement up to 2,147,483,648 bytes before or 2,147,483,647 bytes after the **jmp** instruction.

There is no difference in the coding for a relative short jump and for a relative near jump. In order to generate more compact code the assembler uses a short jump if the target is within the smaller range. A near jump is automatically used if the target is more than 128 bytes away.

The indirect jump instructions use an address for the target rather than a displacement. However, this address is not encoded in the instruction itself. Instead, it is either in a register or in memory. Thus the format

```
jmp    edx
```

means to jump to the address stored in EDX. The memory indirect jump format can use any valid reference to memory. If *targetAddr* is declared as a **DWORD** in the data section, then

```
jmp     targetAddr
```

jumps to the address stored in that doubleword, not to that point in the data section. Using register indirect addressing, you could have

```
jmp     DWORD PTR [ebx]
```

that causes a jump to the address stored at the doubleword whose address is in EBX! Fortunately, these indirect forms are rarely needed.

Exercises 5.1

1. If the statement

   ```
   hardLoop:    jmp    hardLoop
   ```

   is executed, it continues to execute "forever." What is the object code for this statement? (If you can't figure it out, put the statement in a program, assemble the program, and look at the listing file.)

*2. Identify the type (i.e., relative near, relative short, register indirect, or memory indirect) of each jmp instruction in the following code fragment.

   ```
   .DATA
            ...
   addrStore DWORD   ?
            ...
   .CODE
            ...
   doAgain:
            ... (3 instructions)
            jmp  doAgain
            ... (200 instructions)
            jmp  doAgain
            ...
            jmp  addrStore
            ...
            jmp  eax
            ...
            jmp  DWORD PTR [edi]
   ```

Programming Exercise 5.1

1. Using the *console32* or *console64* framework, modify the program in Figure 5.1 so that after the nth iteration of the loop, EAX contains $1*2* \ldots *n$.

2. Using the *windows32* or *windows64* framework, write a program that will repeatedly prompt for a number using a dialog box. After each number is entered, display the sum and average of all numbers entered so far using separate message boxes for the sum and the average. (*Note:* You can terminate the program by clicking the stop button ■ when the dialog box is waiting for a number.)

5.2   Conditional Jumps, Compare Instructions, and *if* Structures

Conditional jump instructions make it possible to implement *if* structures, other selection structures, and loop structures in 80x86 machine language. There are many of these instructions. Each has the format

```
j--     targetStatement
```

where the last part of the mnemonic (shown here by dashes) identifies the condition under which the jump is to be executed. If the condition holds, then the jump takes place; otherwise, the next instruction (the one following the conditional jump) is executed.

With one exception (the **jcxz/jecxz** instruction, covered in Section 5.4), the "conditions" considered by the conditional jump instructions we consider are settings of various flags in the flag registers. For example, the instruction

```
jz      endWhile
```

means to jump to the statement with label *endWhile* if the zero flag ZF is set to 1; otherwise, fall through to the next statement. (The mnemonic **jz** stands for "jump if zero.")

Conditional jump instructions do not modify the flags; they only react to previously set flag values. Recall how the flags in the flag register get values in the first place. Some instructions (like **mov**) leave flags unchanged, some (like **add**) explicitly set some flags according to the value of a result, and still others (like **div**) unpredictably alter some flags, leaving them with unknown values.

Suppose, for example, that the value in the EAX register is added to a sum representing an account balance and three distinct treatments are needed, depending on whether the new balance is negative, zero, or positive. A pseudocode design for this could be

---

add value to balance;

if balance < 0
then
   . . . { design for negative balance }
elseif balance = 0
then
   . . . { design for zero balance }
else
   . . . { design for positive balance }
end if;

Assuming *balance* is stored in a doubleword in memory and *value* is stored in EAX, the following 80x86 code fragment implements this design.

```
                add    balance,eax  ; add value to balance
                jns    elseIfZero   ; jump if balance not
                                    ; negative
                ...                 ; code for negative balance
                jmp    endBalanceCheck
elseIfZero: jnz    elsePos      ; jump if balance not zero
                ...                 ; code for zero balance
                jmp    endBalanceCheck
elsePos:    ...                 ;code for positive balance

        endBalanceCheck:
```

Appropriate flags are set or cleared by the **add** instruction. No other instruction shown in the above code fragment changes the flags. The design checks first for (*balance* < 0). The code does this with the instruction

```
        jns    elseIfZero
```

which says to jump to *elseIfZero* if the sign flag is not set, that is, if (*balance* < 0) is *not* true. The code following this instruction corresponds to statements following the first *then* in the design, that is, what should be done if (*balance* < 0) *is* true. The statement

```
        jmp    endBalanceCheck
```

at the end of this block of statements is necessary so that the CPU skips the statements that correspond to the other cases. If the first conditional jump transfers control to *elseIfZero*, then the balance must be nonnegative (zero or positive). The design checks to see whether the balance is zero; the instruction

```
elseIfZero: jnz    elsePos
```

jumps to *elsePos* if the zero flag ZF=0. The last instruction that set flags is the **add** at the beginning, so the jump occurs if the balance was not zero. The code for the (*balance*=0) case follows this conditional jump and must again end with an unconditional jump to *endBalanceCheck*. Finally, the code that corresponds to the *else* in the design is at *elsePos*. Just as in a high-level language, a third check is not needed because the only remaining possibility is that *balance* is positive. This last block of code does not need a jump to *endBalanceCheck* since execution will fall through to this point.

The 80x86 code above directly corresponds to the order of statements in the design. When you code in assembly language, you should initially follow a careful design, and then, if there is a need to make the code really efficient, examine it to see whether there are places where you can improve it. This corresponds to what happens in many high-level language compilers. Most initially produce machine language that corresponds to the order of the high-level language statements being translated. Some compilers may then optimize the code, rearranging some statements for efficiency.

In the previous code, the label *endBalanceCheck* is on a line by itself. Technically this label references the address of whatever statement follows it, but it is far simpler to treat it as the part of the current design structure without worrying about what comes next. If what comes after this structure is changed, the code for this structure can remain the same. If the next statement requires another label, that is perfectly OK—multiple labels can reference the same instruction in memory. Labels are not part of object code, so extra labels do not add to the length of object code or to execution time.

When writing code to mirror a design, you may want to use labels like *if*, *then*, *else*, and *endif*. Unfortunately, **IF**, **ELSE**, and **ENDIF** are assembler directives so that they cannot be used as labels. In addition, **IF1**, **IF2**, and several other desirable labels are also reserved for use as directives. One solution is to use long, descriptive labels like *elseIfZero* in the above example. Since no reserved word contains an underscore, another solution is to use labels like *if_1* and *endif_2* that parallel keywords in the original design.

The terms **set a flag** and **reset a flag** are often used to mean "give the value 1" to a flag and "give the value 0" to a flag, respectively. (Sometimes the word **clear** is used instead of reset.) As you have seen, there are many instructions that set or reset flags. However, a `cmp` (compare) instruction's only job is to set or reset flags, and is probably the most common way to establish flag values.

Each **cmp** instruction compares two operands, and sets or resets AF, CF, OF, PF, SF, and ZF. The only job of a **cmp** instruction is to fix flag values; this is not just a side effect of some other operation. Each has the form

cmp   operand1, operand2

A **cmp** executes by calculating *operand1* minus *operand2*, exactly like a **sub** instruction; the value of the difference and what happens in performing the subtraction determines the flag settings. A **cmp** instruction is unlike **sub** in that the value at the *operand1* location is not changed. The flags that are of most interest in this book are CF, OF, SF, and ZF. The carry flag CF is set if there is a borrow for the subtraction and reset if no borrow is required. The overflow flag OF is set if there is an overflow and reset otherwise. The sign flag SF is set if the difference represents a negative 2's complement number (the leading bit is 1) and is reset if the number is zero or positive. Finally, the zero flag ZF is set if the difference is zero and is reset if it is nonzero.

Here are a few examples showing how the flags are set or reset when some representative byte-length numbers are compared. Recall that the subtraction operation is the same for signed and unsigned (2's complement) values. Just as a single-bit pattern can be interpreted as a signed number or a unsigned number, flag values have different interpretations after comparison of signed or unsigned values. The "interpretation" columns in the following table show the relationship of the operands under both signed and unsigned interpretations.

Example	Operand1	Operand2	Difference	CF	OF	SF	ZF	Signed	Unsigned
1	3B	3B	00	0	0	0	1	op1=op2	op1=op2
2	3B	15	26	0	0	0	0	op1>op2	op1>op2
3	15	3B	DA	1	0	1	0	op1<op2	op1<op2
4	F9	F6	03	0	0	0	0	op1>op2	op1>op2
5	F6	F9	FD	1	0	1	0	op1<op2	op1<op2
6	15	F6	1F	1	0	0	0	op1>op2	op1<op2
7	F6	15	E1	0	0	1	0	op1<op2	op1>op2
8	68	A5	C3	1	1	1	0	op1>op2	op1<op2
9	A5	68	3D	0	1	0	0	op1<op2	op1>op2

The column groups above are "Flags" (CF, OF, SF, ZF) and "Interpretation" (Signed, Unsigned).

What flag values characterize the relations equal, less than, and greater than? Equality is easy; the ZF flag is set if and only if *operand1* has the same value as *operand2* no matter whether the numbers are interpreted as signed or unsigned. This is illustrated by Example 1—less than and greater than take more analysis.

When you first think about less than, it seems as if the carry flag should be set for a borrow whenever *operand1* is less than *operand2*. This logic is correct if one interprets the operands as unsigned numbers. Examples 3, 5, 6, and 8 all have *operand1* < *operand2* as unsigned numbers, and these are exactly the examples where CF=1. Therefore, for unsigned numbers, CF=0 means *operand1* ≥ *operand2*. Strict greater-than inequality for unsigned numbers is characterized by CF=0 *and* ZF=0, that is *operand1* ≥ *operand2* and *operand1* ≠ *operand2*.

Examples 3, 5, 7, and 9 have *operand1* < *operand2* as signed numbers. What characterizes this situation is that SF≠OF. In the remaining examples, SF=OF and *operand1* ≥ *operand2* as signed numbers. Strict greater-than inequality for unsigned numbers is characterized by SF=OF *and* ZF=0, that is, *operand1* ≥ *operand2* and *operand1* ≠ *operand2*.

The **cmp** instructions are listed in Figure 5.5. Looking back at Figure 4.8, you see that the entries in the various columns are almost all the same as for **sub** instructions. There are alternative opcodes for some operand combinations—the ones listed are those chosen by the Visual Studio assembler.

A few reminders are in order about immediate operands. These can be coded in your choice of bases or as characters. Assuming that *wordOp* references a word in the data segment, each of the following is allowable.

```
cmp    eax, 356
cmp    wordOp, 0d3a6h
cmp    bh, '$'
```

Note that an immediate operand must be the second operand. The instruction

```
cmp    100, total     ; illegal
```

will not assemble since the first operand is immediate.

Finally, it is time to list the conditional jump instructions; they are shown in Figure 5.6. Many of these have alternative mnemonics that generate exactly the same machine code; these describe the same set of conditions a different way. Often one mnemonic is more natural than the other for implementation of a given design. The table is in three parts; the first two list instructions that are appropriate for use after comparison of signed and unsigned operands, respectively. The third part lists additional conditional jump instructions.

Operand 1	Operand 2	Opcode	Bytes of Object Code
register 8	immediate 8	80	3
register 16	immediate 8	83	3
register 32	immediate 8	83	3
register 16	immediate 16	81	4
register 32	immediate 32	81	6
AL	immediate 8	3C	2
AX	immediate 16	3D	3
EAX	immediate 32	3D	5
memory byte	immediate 8	80	3+
memory word	immediate 8	83	3+
memory doubleword	immediate 8	83	3+
memory word	immediate 16	81	4+
memory doubleword	immediate 32	81	6+
register 8	register 8	3A	2
register 16	register 16	3B	2
register 32	register 32	3B	2
register 8	memory byte	3A	2+
register 16	memory word	3B	2+
register 32	memory doubleword	3B	2+
memory byte	register 8	38	2+
memory word	register 16	39	2+
memory doubleword	register 32	39	2+
64-bit mode			
register 64	immediate 8	83	3
register 64	immediate 32	81	6
RAX	immediate 32	3D	5
memory quadword	immediate 8	83	3+
memory quadword	immediate 32	81	6+
register 64	register 64	3B	2
register 64	memory quadword	3B	2+
memory quadword	register 64	39	2+

Figure 5.5 cmp instructions

Appropriate for Use After Comparison of Signed Operands

Mnemonic	Description	Flags to Jump	Opcode Short	Opcode Near
jg jnle	jump if greater jump if not less or equal	SF=OF and ZF=0	7F	0F 8F
jge jnl	jump if greater or equal jump if not less	SF=OF	7D	0F 8D
jl jnge	jump if less jump if not greater or equal	SF≠OF	7C	0F 8C
jle jng	jump if less or equal jump if not greater	SF≠OF or ZF=1	7E	0F 8E

Appropriate for Use After Comparison of Unsigned Operands

Mnemonic	Description	Flags to Jump	Opcode Short	Opcode Near
ja jnbe	jump if above jump if not below or equal	CF=0 and ZF=0	77	0F 87
jae jnb	jump if above or equal jump if not below	CF=0	73	0F 83
jb jnae	jump if below jump if not above or equal	CF=1	72	0F 82
jbe jna	jump if below or equal jump if not above	CF=1 or ZF=1	76	0F 86

Other Conditional Jumps

Mnemonic	Description	Flags to Jump	Opcode Short	Opcode Near
je jz	jump if equal jump if zero	ZF=1	74	0F 84

Figure 5.6 Conditional jump instructions

Other Conditional Jumps

Mnemonic	Description	Flags to Jump	Opcode	
			Short	Near
jne jnz	jump if not equal jump if not zero	ZF=0	75	0F 85
js	jump if sign	SF=1	78	0F 88
jns	jump if not sign	SF=0	79	0F 89
jc	jump if carry	CF=1	72	0F 82
jnc	jump if not carry	CF=0	73	0F 83
jp jpe	jump if parity jump if parity even	PF=1	7A	0F 8A
jnp jpo	jump if not parity jump if parity odd	PF=0	7B	0F 8B
jo	jump if overflow	OF=1	70	0F 80
jno	jump if not overflow	OF=0	71	0F 81

Figure 5.6 Conditional jump instructions (continued)

Conditional jump mnemonics correspond to comparison of the first operand to the second operand in a preceding **cmp** instruction. For example, for the instruction jg, "jump if greater" means to jump if *operand1 > operand2*.

No conditional jump instruction changes any flag value. Each instruction has a short version and a near version. Just as with short unconditional jump instructions, a short conditional jump encodes a single-byte displacement and can transfer control 128 bytes before or 127 bytes after the address of the byte following the instruction itself. A short conditional jump requires 2 bytes of object code, one for the opcode and one for the displacement. A near conditional jump encodes a 32-bit displacement in addition to a 2-byte opcode, giving a total length of 6 bytes. It can transfer control up to 2,147,483,648 bytes backward or 2,147,483,647 forward.

One more pair of examples will illustrate the difference between the conditional jumps appropriate after comparison of signed and unsigned numbers. Suppose a value is stored in EAX and some action needs to be taken when that value is larger than 100. If the value is unsigned, one might code

```
cmp     eax, 100
ja      bigger
```

The jump would be chosen for any value bigger than 00000064_{16}, including values between 80000000_{16} and $FFFFFFFF_{16}$, that represent both large unsigned numbers and all negative 2's complement numbers. If the value in EAX is interpreted as signed, then the instructions

```
cmp     eax,100
jg      bigger
```

are appropriate. The jump will only be taken for values between 00000065 and 7FFFFFFF, not for those bit patterns that represent negative 2's complement numbers.

We now look at three examples showing implementation of *if* structures. The implementations are consistent with what a high-level language compiler would use. First consider the design

---

if value < 10
then
    add 1 to smallCount;
else
    add 1 to largeCount;
end if;

Suppose that *value* is stored in the EBX register and that *smallCount* and *largeCount* reference doublewords in memory. The following 80x86 code implements this design.

```
            cmp   ebx, 10        ; value < 10 ?
            jnl   elseLarge       ; skip if not
            inc   smallCount      ; add 1 to smallCount
            jmp   endValueCheck   ; exit
elseLarge:  inc   largeCount      ; add 1 to largeCount
endValueCheck:
```

Note that this code is completely self-contained; you do not need to know what comes before or after in the overall design to implement this portion. You must have a plan for making labels, though, to avoid duplicates and reserved words. A compiler often produces a label consisting of a letter followed by a sequence number, but most of the time we can do better as humans writing code.

Now consider the design

---

if (total ≥ 100) or (count = 10)
then
    add value to total;
end if;

Assume that *total* and *value* reference doublewords in memory, and that *count* is stored in the ECX register. Here is assembly language code to implement this design.

```
                cmp   total, 100      ; total >= 100 ?
                jge   addValue        ; do it if so
                cmp   ecx, 10         ; count = 10 ?
                jne   endAddCheck     ; skip if not
     addValue:  mov   ebx, value      ; copy value
                add   total, ebx      ; add value to total
     endAddCheck:
```

Notice that the design's *or* requires two **cmp** instructions. If either of the corresponding tests is passed, then the addition is performed. (Why was the addition done with two statements? Why not use **add total,value** ?) This code implements a shortcut *or*—if the first condition is true, then the second is not checked at all. The code implemented for some languages always checks both operands of an *or* operation, even if the first is true.

Finally consider the design

---

if (count > 0) and (ch = backspace)
then
    subtract 1 from count;
end if;

For this third example, assume that *count* is in the ECX register and *ch* is in the AL register. This design can be implemented as follows.

```
          cmp   ecx, 0          ; count > 0 ?
          jng   endCheckCh      ; done if not
          cmp   al, 08h         ; ch a backspace?
          jne   endCheckCh      ; done if not
          dec   count           ; subtract 1 from count
    endCheckCh:
```

This compound condition uses *and*, so both parts must be true in order to execute the action. This code implements a shortcut *and*—if the first condition is false, then the second is not checked at all.

In each of the previous implementation examples the order of the statements in the assembly language code follows the order of the design statements. It is important to adopt a consistent pattern of coding that accurately codes the design. Often to make the code flow the same as the design, you must use "negative" conditional jumps such as

```
    jng   endCheckCh      ; done if not
```

in the last example. It may be tempting to use the equivalent mnemonic `jle` instead of `jng`, but the original design contains (*count* > 0) and it is easy to make an error changing `jng` to the equivalent mnemonic `jle`. The mnemonic `jng` is closer to the original design than is `jle`. A common error is to use "less than" instead of "less than or equal to" as the opposite of "greater than."

Exercises 5.2

1. Assume for each part of this problem that the EAX register contains 00 00 00 4F and the doubleword referenced by *value* contains FF FF FF 38. Determine whether each of the conditional jump statements causes a jump to dest.

```
*(a) cmp   eax, value        (b) cmp   eax, value
     jl    dest                  jb    dest
 (c) cmp   eax, 04fh         (d) cmp   eax, 79
     je    dest                  jne   dest
*(e) cmp   value, 0          (f) cmp   value, -200
     jbe   dest                  jge   dest
 (g) add   eax, 200          (h) add   value, 200
     js    dest                  jz    dest
```

2. Each part of this problem gives a design with an *if* structure and some assumptions about how the variables are stored in an assembly language

program. Give a fragment of assembly language code that implements the design. The assembly language code should flow the same as the design.

*(a) design:

    if count = 0

    then

        count := value;

    end if;

Assumptions: *count* is in ECX; *value* references a doubleword in memory

(b) design:

    if count > value

    then

        count := 0;

    end if;

Assumptions: *count* is in ECX; *value* references a doubleword in memory

(c) design:

    if a + b = c

    then

        check := 'Y';

    else

        check := 'N';

    end if;

Assumptions: each of *a*, *b*, and *c* references a doubleword in memory; the character *check* is in the AL register

*(d) design:

    if (value ≤ -1000) or (value ≥ 1000)

    then

        value := 0;

    end if;

Assumption: *value* is in EDX

(e) design:

    if (ch $\geq$ 'a') and (ch $\leq$ 'z')

    then

        add 1 to lowerCount;

```
            else
                  if (ch ≥ 'A') and (ch ≤ 'Z')
                  then
                        add 1 to upperCount;
                  else
                        add 1 to otherCount;
                  end if;
            end if;
```

Assumptions: *ch* is in AL; each of *lowerCount*, *upperCount*, and *otherCount* references a doubleword in memory

5.3   Implementing Loop Structures

Most programs contain loops. Commonly used loop structures include *while*, *until*, and *for* loops. This section describes how to implement all three of these structures in 80x86 assembly language. The next section describes additional instructions that can be used to implement *for* loops.

A *while* loop can be indicated by the following pseudocode design.

```
while continuation condition loop
     . . . { loop body }
end while;
```

A while loop is a **pretest** loop—the continuation condition, a Boolean expression, is checked first; if it is *true*, then the body of the loop is executed. The continuation condition is then checked again. Whenever the value of the Boolean expression is *false*, execution continues with the statement following *end while*.

An 80x86 implementation of a *while* loop follows a pattern much like this one.

```
while:          .            ; code to check Boolean expression
                .
                .
body:           .            ; loop body
                .
                .
                jmp  while   ; go check condition again
endWhile:
```

It sometimes takes several statements to check the value of the Boolean expression. If it is determined that the value is *false*, then there will be a jump to *endWhile*. If it is determined that the continuation condition is true, then the code will either fall through to loop body or there will be a jump to its label. Notice that the loop body ends with a `jmp` to go check the condition again. Two common mistakes are to omit this jump or to jump to the body instead.

The label *while* in this model is not allowed in actual code since this is a reserved word for the assembler. In fact, the assembler has a `WHILE` directive that simplifies writing code for *while* loops. It is not used in this book as our main concern is understanding how structures are implemented at the machine language level.

For an example, suppose that the design

```
while (sum < 1000) loop
    . . . { loop body }
end while;
```

is to be coded in 80x86 assembly language. Assuming that *sum* references a doubleword in memory, one possible implementation is

```
whileSum:     cmp    sum, 1000      ; sum < 1000?
              jnl    endWhileSum    ; exit loop if not
               .                    ; loop body
               .
               .
              jmp    whileSum       ; check condition again
        endWhileSum:
```

The statement `jnl endWhileSum` directly implements the design. As discussed for *if* implementations, you should avoid the equivalent `jge` alternative both because `jnl` is closer to the design and because of the danger of choosing the wrong mnemonic when reversing the inequality.

For an example showing a complete loop body, suppose that the integer base 2 logarithm of a positive integer *number* needs to be determined. The integer base 2 logarithm of a number is the largest integer x such that $2^x \leq number$. The following design does the job.

```
x := 0;
twoToX := 1;
while twoToX ≤ number loop
    multiply twoToX by 2;
    add 1 to x;
end while;
subtract 1 from x;
```

Assuming that *number* references a doubleword in memory, the following 80x86 code implements the design, using the EAX register for *twoToX* and the ECX register for *x*.

```
            mov     ecx, 0       ; x := 0
            mov     eax, 1       ; twoToX := 1
whileLE:    cmp     eax, number  ; twoToX <= number?
            jnle    endWhileLE   ; exit if not
body:       add     eax, eax     ; multiply twoToX by 2
            inc     ecx          ; add 1 to x
            jmp     whileLE      ; go check condition again
endWhileLE:
            dec     ecx          ; subtract 1 from x
```

Figure 5.7 shows a sample run of this code. The value of *number* stored in memory is 750. A breakpoint has been set at the exit code. The program has executed from its beginning to the breakpoint. The ECX register contains 9, the correct value for $\log_2(750)$ since $2^9=512$, the largest power of 2 less than or equal to 750.

Often the continuation condition in a *while* is compound, having two parts connected by Boolean operators *and* or *or*. Both operands of an *and* must be true for a *true* conjunction. With an *or*, the only way the disjunction can be *false* is if both operands are *false*.

Changing a previous example to include a compound condition, suppose that the following design is to be coded.

```
while (sum < 1000) and (count ≤ 24) loop
    . . . { loop body }
end while;
```

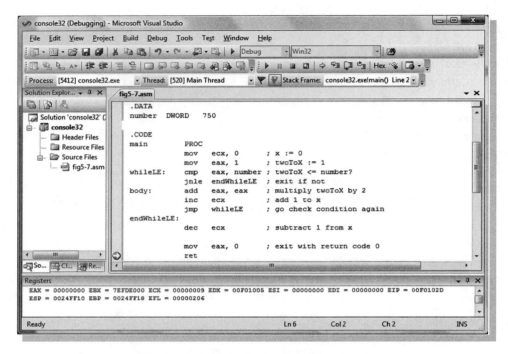

Figure 5.7 Calculating $\log_2(\text{number})$

Assuming that *sum* references a doubleword in memory and the value of *count* is in ECX, an implementation is

```
whileSum:   cmp    sum, 1000      ; sum < 1000?
            jnl    endWhileSum    ; exit if not
            cmp    ecx, 24        ; count <= 24?
            jnle   endWhileSum    ; exit if not
              .                   ; loop body
              .
              .
            jmp    whileSum       ; go check condition again
endWhileSum:
```

Modifying the example one more time, next is a design with an *or* instead of an *and*.

---
while (sum < 1000) or (flag = 1) loop
 . . . { loop body }
end while;

This time, assume that *sum* is in the EAX register, and that *flag* is a single byte in the BL register. Here is 80x86 code that implements the design.

```
whileSum:    cmp    eax, 1000      ; sum < 1000?
             jl     body           ; execute body if so
             cmp    bl,1           ; flag = 1?
             jne    endWhileSum    ; exit if not
body:        .                     ; loop body
             .
             .
             jmp    whileSum       ; go check condition again
endWhileSum:
```

Notice the difference in the previous two examples. For an *and* the loop is exited if either operand of the compound condition is *false*. For an *or* the loop body is executed if either operand of the compound condition is *true*.

The body of a *for* loop, a counter-controlled loop, is executed once for each value of a loop index (or counter) in a given range. In some high-level languages, the loop index can be some type other than integer; a design for assembly language implementation usually has an integer index. A *for* loop can be described by the following pseudocode.

---
for index := initialValue to finalValue loop
 . . . { loop body }
end for;

A *for* loop can easily be translated into a *while* structure.

---
index := initialValue;
while index ≤ finalValue loop
 . . . { loop body }
 add 1 to index;
end while;

Such a *while* is readily coded in 80x86 assembly language.

An *until* loop is a **posttest** loop—the condition is checked after the body of the loop is executed. In general, an *until* loop can be expressed as follows in pseudocode.

repeat
   . . . { loop body }
until *termination condition*;

The body of the loop is executed at least once; then the termination condition is checked. If it is *false*, then the body of the loop is executed again; if *true*, execution continues with the statement following the loop.

An 80x86 implementation of an *until* loop usually looks like the following code fragment.

```
until:      .            ; start of loop body
            .            .
            .            .
            .            ; code to check termination condition
endUntil:
```

If the code to check the termination condition determines that the value is *false*, then there will be a jump to *until*. If it is determined that the value is *true*, then the code will either fall through to *endUntil* or there will be a jump to that label.

Other loop structures can also be coded in assembly language. The *forever* loop is frequently useful. As it appears in pseudocode, it almost always has an *exit loop* statement to transfer control to the end of the loop; this is often conditional, that is, in an *if* statement.

This section ends with an example of a complete program. Suppose you really want to become a millionaire. You devise a scheme to go to work for a rich, but not very intelligent, employer. You negotiate a contract in which you agree to be paid 1 cent for the first day of work, 2 cents for the second day, 4 cents for the third day, 8 cents for the fourth day, and so on, with your wage doubling each day. What is the minimum number of days of work you should require in the contract to be sure that you earn a total of $1 million?

Obviously a loop is needed in the solution's design. A counter-controlled loop is not appropriate since we do not know how many times to iterate. Either a *while* loop or an *until* loop will work with a properly structured design. Here is a pseudocode design that uses a *while* loop.

---
nextDaysWage := 1;
totalEarnings := 0;
day := 0;
while totalEarnngs < 100000000 loop
    add nextDaysWage to totalEarnings;
    multiply nextDaysWage by 2;
    add 1 to day;
end loop;

Notice that the limit on total earnings is expressed in cents; $1 million has been converted to 100,000,000 cents. For an implementation, we choose to keep *totalEarnings* in EAX, *nextDaysWage* in EBX, and *day* in ECX. Figure 5.8 shows a screenshot with the debugger

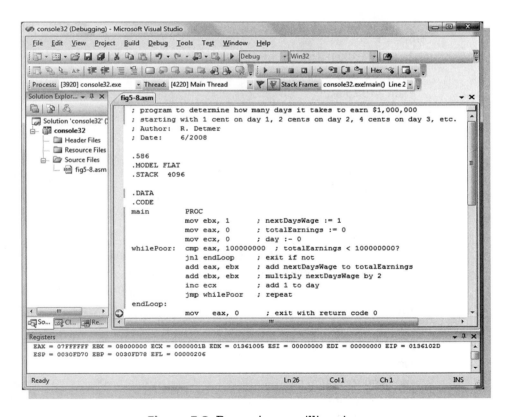

Figure 5.8 Becoming a millionaire

paused at the exit point of the program. How many days are needed to earn $1 million? What was your wage on the last day? What were your total earnings for these days?

Exercises 5.3

1. Each part of this problem contains a design with a *while* loop. Assume that *sum* references a doubleword in the data segment and that *count* is in the ECX register. Give a fragment of 80x86 code that implements the design.

   (a) sum := 0;
       count := 1;
       while (sum < 1000) loop
           add count to sum;
           add 1 to count;
       end while;

   *(b) sum := 0;
       count := 1;
       while (sum < 1000) and (count ≤ 50) loop
           add count to sum;
           add 1 to count;
       end while;

   (c) sum := 0;
       count := 100;
       while (sum < 1000) or (count ≥ 0) loop
           add count to sum;
           subtract 1 from count;
       end while;

2. Each part of this problem contains a design with an *until* loop. Assume that *sum* references a doubleword in the data segment and that *count* is in the ECX register. Give a fragment of 80x86 code that implements the design.

   (a) sum := 0;
       count := 1;
       repeat
           add count to sum;
           add 1 to count;
       until (sum > 5000);

  (b) sum := 0;
      count := 1;
      repeat
          add count to sum;
          add 1 to count;
      until (sum > 5000) or (count = 40) ;

 *(c) sum := 0;
      count := 1;
      repeat
          add count to sum;
          add 1 to count;
      until (sum $\geq$ 5000) and (count > 40);

3. Each part of this problem contains a design with a *for* loop. Assume that *sum* references a doubleword in the data segment and that *count* is in the ECX register. Give a fragment of 80x86 code that implements the design. (*Hint:* Change each *for* loop to the equivalent *while* structure.)

  (a) sum := 0;
      for count := 1 to 100 loop
          add count to sum;
      end for;

 *(b) sum := 0;
      for count := -10 to 50 loop
          add count to sum;
      end for;

  (c) sum := 1000;
      for count := 100 downto 50 loop
          subtract 2*count from sum;
      end for;

Programming Exercises 5.3

1. Modify the design for the program in Figure 5.8 to use an *until* loop instead of a *while* loop. Using the *console32* or *console64* framework, implement your modified design and run it under the debugger.

2. Keeping a *console32* program, modify the program in Figure 5.8 to look for the number of days it takes to earn $40 million. *Hint:* The program will fail if you simply change the immediate value in the cmp instruction. (Why?) An additional change to the program will make it work. What is the largest total earnings for which this design will work?

3. Using the *windows32* or *windows64* framework, design and implement a program that will use a dialog box to prompt for an integer n, compute the sum of the integers from 1 to n, and use a message box to display the sum.

4. Using the *console32* or *console64* framework, design and implement a program that will find the smallest integer n for which $1 + 2 + \ldots + n$ is at least 1000 and run it under the debugger.

5. Using the *windows32* or *windows64* framework, design and implement a program that will use a dialog box to prompt for an integer n, compute the sum $1^2 + 2^2 + 3^2 + \ldots + n^2$, and use a message box to display the sum.

6. The greatest common divisor of two positive integers is the largest integer that evenly divides both numbers. The following algorithm will find the greatest common divisor of *number1* and *number2*.

```
gcd := number1;
remainder := number2;
repeat
    dividend := gcd;
    gcd := remainder;
    remainder := dividend mod gcd;
until (remainder = 0);
```

Using the *windows32* or *windows64* framework, write a program that uses dialog boxes to prompt for and input values for *number1* and *number2*, implements the above design to find their greatest common divisor, and uses a message box to display the GCD.

5.4 *for* Loops in Assembly Language

Often the number of times the body of a loop must be executed is known in advance, either as a constant that can be coded when a program is written, or as the value of a variable that is assigned before the loop is executed. The *for* loop structure is ideal for coding such a loop.

The previous section showed how to translate a *for* loop into a *while* loop. This technique always works and is often the best way to code a *for* loop. However, the 80x86 microprocessor has instructions that make coding certain *for* loops very easy.

Consider the following two *for* loops, the first of which counts forward and the second of which counts backward.

```
for index := 1 to count loop
    . . . { loop body }
end for;
```

and

```
for index := count downto 1 loop
    . . . { loop body }
end for;
```

Each loop body executes *count* times. If the value of *index* is not needed within the body of the loop, then the loop that counts down is equivalent to the loop that counts up, although the design may not be as natural. Backward *for* loops are very easy to implement in 80x86 assembly language with the **loop** instruction.

The **loop** instruction has the format

```
loop    statementLabel
```

where *statementLabel* is the label of a statement that is a short displacement (128 bytes backward or 127 bytes forward) from the **loop** instruction. The loop instruction takes two bytes of object code, opcode E2 and the byte-size displacement.

The **loop** instruction causes the following actions to take place:

- The value in ECX is decremented.
- If the new value in ECX is zero, then execution continues with the statement following the loop instruction.

- If the new value in ECX is nonzero, then a jump to the instruction at *statementLabel* takes place.

Although the ECX register is a general register, it has a special place as a counter in the **loop** instruction and in several other 80x86 instructions. No other register can be substituted for ECX in these instructions. In practice this often means that when a loop is coded, ECX is not used for other purposes. In 64-bit mode, the action is exactly the same except that RCX is used instead of ECX.

The backward *for* loop structure

```
for count := 20 downto 1 loop
    . . . { loop body }
end for;
```

can be coded as follows in 80x86 assembly language using the **loop** instruction.

```
            mov    ecx, 20        ; number of iterations
forCount:    .                    ; loop body
             .
             .
            loop   forCount       ; repeat body 20 times
```

The counter in the ECX register will be 20 the first time the loop body is executed and will be decremented to 19 by the **loop** instruction. The value 19 is not zero, so control transfers to the start of the loop body at label *forCount*. The second time the loop body is executed, the ECX register will contain 19. The last time the loop body is executed, the value in ECX will be 1. ECX will be decremented to zero by the **loop** instruction, the jump to *forCount* will not be taken, and execution will continue with the instruction following the **loop** instruction.

The obvious label to mark the body of a *for* loop is *for*. Unfortunately this is a reserved word for the assembler. It is used for a directive that simplifies coding of *for* loops. Since our primary interest is in learning how the computer works at the machine level this directive is not used.

Now suppose that the doubleword in memory referenced by *number* contains the number of times a loop body is to be executed. The 80x86 code to implement a backward *for* loop could be

```
            mov    ecx, number     ; number of iterations
forIndex:   .                      ; loop body
            .
            .
            loop   forIndex        ; repeat body number times
```

This code gives surprising results if the value stored at *number* is zero. If it is zero, then the loop body is executed, the zero value is decremented to FFFFFFFF (borrowing to do the subtraction), the loop body is executed again, the value FFFFFFFF is decremented to FFFFFFFE, and so forth. The body of the loop is executed 4,294,967,296 times before the value in ECX gets back down to zero! To avoid this problem, one could code

```
            mov    ecx, number     ; number of iterations
            cmp    ecx, 0          ; number = 0 ?
            jz     endFor          ; skip loop if number = 0
forIndex:   .                      ; loop body
            .
            .
            loop   forIndex        ; repeat body number times
endFor:
```

If number is a signed value and might be negative, then

```
      jle   endFor        ; skip loop if number <= 0
```

is a more appropriate conditional jump.

There is another way to guard a *for* loop so that it is not executed when the value in ECX is zero. The 80x86 architecture has a **jecxz** conditional jump instruction that jumps to its destination if the value in the ECX register is zero. Using the **jecxz** instruction, the previous example can be coded as

```
            mov    ecx, number     ; number of iterations
            jecxz  endFor          ; skip loop if number = 0
forIndex:   .                      ; loop body
            .
            .
            loop   forIndex        ; repeat body number times
endFor:
```

The **jexcz** instruction is 2 bytes long, the opcode E3 plus a single-byte displacement. Like the other conditional jump instructions, **jecxz** affects no flag value. In 64-bit mode, there is also a **jrcxz** instruction that checks RCX. It has the same object code as **jecxz**.

The **jecxz** instruction can also be used to code a backward *for* loop when the loop body is longer than 127 bytes, too large for the **loop** instruction's single-byte displacement. For example, the structure

---

```
for counter := 50 downto 1 loop
    . . . { loop body }
end for;
```

---

could be coded as

```
                mov    ecx, 50        ; number of iterations
        forCounter:   .               ; loop body
                      .
                      .
                dec    ecx            ; decrement loop counter
                jecxz  endFor         ; exit if counter = 0
                jmp    forCounter     ; otherwise repeat body
        endFor:
```

However, since the **dec** instruction sets or resets the zero flag ZF, the conditional jump **jz endFor** can be used just as effectively.

It is often convenient to use a **loop** statement to implement a *for* loop, even when the loop index increases and must be used within the body of the loop. The **loop** statement uses ECX to control the number of iterations, while a separate counter serves as the loop index. For example, to implement the *for* loop

---

```
for index := 1 to 50 loop
    . . . { loop body using index }
end for;
```

---

the EBX register might be used to store *index* counting from 1 to 50, while the ECX register counts down from 50 to 1.

```
        mov    ebx, 1      ; index := 1
        mov    ecx, 50     ; number of iterations for loop
forNbr: .
        .                  ; use value in EBX for index
        .
        inc    ebx         ; add 1 to index
        loop   forNbr      ; repeat
```

Exercises 5.4

1. Each part of this problem has a *for* loop implemented with a `loop` statement. How many times is each loop body executed?

   (a)

   ```
           mov  ecx, 10
   forA:   .
           .                ; loop body
           .
           loop forA
   ```

   *(b)

   ```
           mov  ecx, 1
   forB:   .
           .                ; loop body
           .
           loop forB
   ```

   (c)

   ```
           mov  ecx, 0
   forC:   .
           .                ; loop body
           .
           loop forC
   ```

   *(d)

   ```
           mov  ecx, -1
   forD:   .
           .                ; loop body
           .
           loop forD
   ```

2. Each part of this problem contains a design with a *for* loop. Assume that *sum* references a doubleword in the data segment. Give a fragment of 80x86 code that implements the design. Use a `loop` statement appropriately in the code.

(a) sum := 0;
    for count := 50 downto 1 loop
        add count to sum;
    end for;

*(b) sum := 0;
    for count := 1 to 50 loop
        add count to sum;
    end for;

(c) sum := 0;
    for count := 1 to 50 loop
        add (2*count − 1) to sum;
    end for;

Programming Exercises 5.4

1. Using the *windows32* or *windows64* framework, design and implement a program that will use a dialog box to prompt for an integer n, compute the sum $1^2 + 2^2 + 3^2 + \ldots + n^2$, and use a message box to display the sum. Use a *for* loop in your design and implement it with a `loop` instruction.

2. The binomial coefficient $\binom{n}{k}$ is defined for integers $0 \leq k \leq n$ by $\binom{n}{k} = \dfrac{n!}{k!(n-k)!}$. Assuming that values for n and k are stored in doublewords in memory, design and implement a *windows32* or *windows64* program that will use dialog boxes to prompt for and input n and k, compute $\binom{n}{k}$ with the above formula, and use a message box to display the binomial coefficient. (*Hint:* Do not calculate $n!$ and $k!$ separately. Instead, calculate $\dfrac{n!}{k!}$ as $n*(n-1)*\ldots*(k+1)$.)

5.5 Arrays

Programs frequently use arrays to store collections of data values. Loops are commonly used to manipulate the data in arrays. Storage for an array can be reserved using the DUP directive in the data segment of a program. This section shows two ways to access one-dimensional arrays in 80x86 assembly language.

Suppose that you have a collection of *nbrElts* doubleword integers stored in memory at *nbrArray*, and that the value of *nbrElts* is also stored in a doubleword in memory. You want to process this array, first finding the average of the numbers and then adding 10 to each number that is smaller than the average. Here is a design to do this.

{ find sum and average }
sum := 0;
get address of first array element;
for count := nbrElts downto 1 loop
    add doubleword at address in array to sum;
    get address of next array element;
end for;
average := sum/nbrElts;

{ add 10 to each number less than average }
get address of first array element;
for count := nbrElts downto 1 loop
    if doubleword of array < average
    then
        add 10 to doubleword;
    end if;
    get address of next array element;
end for;

This design contains the curious statements "get address of first array element" and "get address of next array element." These reflect the particular assembly language implementation, one that works well if the task at hand involves moving sequentially through the elements stored in an array. The 80x86 feature that makes this possible is register indirect addressing, first discussed in Chapter 3. Our implementation code will use the EBX register to contain the address of the word currently being accessed; recall that [ebx] references the doubleword at the address in the EBX register rather than the doubleword in the register itself. In the 80x86 architecture any of the general registers EAX, EBX, ECX, and EDX or the index registers EDI and ESI are appropriate for use as a "pointer." However, the

ECX register is often reserved for use as a loop counter. Similarly, the ESI and EDI registers are often reserved for use with strings that are usually arrays of characters. String operations will be covered in Chapter 8. The program listing appears in Figure 5.9.

For our *console32* implementation, we allow space for 100 doublewords in *nbrArray*, but only use the first 5 to test. The sum is calculated in EAX and, after division

```
; given an array of doubleword integers, (1) find their average
; and (2) add 10 to each number smaller than average
; author:  R. Detmer
; revised:  6/2008

.586
.MODEL FLAT
.STACK   4096

.DATA
nbrArray     DWORD     25, 47, 15, 50, 32, 95 DUP (?)
nbrElts      DWORD     5
.CODE
main         PROC
; find sum and average
             mov     eax,0            ; sum := 0
             lea     ebx,nbrArray     ; get address of nbrArray
             mov     ecx,nbrElts      ; count := nbrElts
             jecxz   quit             ; quit if no numbers
forCount1:   add     eax,[ebx]        ; add number to sum
             add     ebx,4            ; get address of next array elt
             loop    forCount1        ; repeat nbrElts times

             cdq                      ; extend sum to quadword
             idiv    nbrElts          ; calculate average

; add 10 to each array element below average
             lea     ebx,nbrArray     ; get address of nbrArray
             mov     ecx,nbrElts      ; count := nbrElts
forCount2:   cmp     [ebx],eax        ; number < average ?
             jnl     endIfSmall       ; continue if not less
             add     DWORD PTR [ebx], 10   ; add 10 to number
endIfSmall:
             add     ebx,4            ; get address of next array elt
             loop    forCount2        ; repeat

quit:        mov     eax, 0      ; exit with return code 0
             ret
main         ENDP
END
```

Figure 5.9 Process array

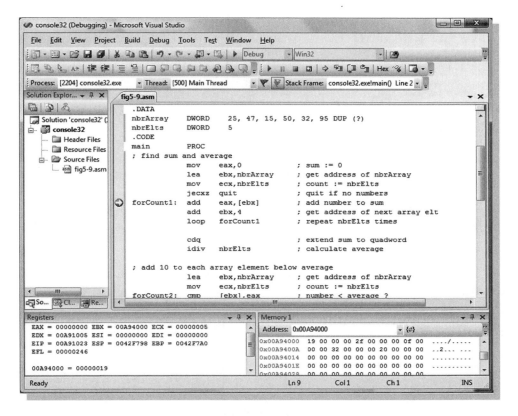

Figure 5.10 Setting up an array process loop

by *nbrElts*, the average is in the same register. Figure 5.10 shows the program executing under the debugger, stopped at a breakpoint right before the first loop starts iterating. Notice that ECX contains the number of elements and EBX contains 00A94000, the same address that the memory display shows for the address of *nbrArray* (&nbrarray). The **lea** instruction has placed this address into EBX.

The mnemonic **lea** stands for "load effective address." The **lea** instruction has the format

```
lea     destination, source
```

The destination is usually a 32-bit general register; the source is any reference to memory. The address of the source is loaded into the register. (Contrast this with **mov** *destination, source* where the *value* at the source address is copied to the destination.) The **lea** instruction has opcode 8D.

Notice that you get the address of the next doubleword in the array by adding 4 to the current address in EBX since each doubleword is 4 bytes long. Step through a couple of

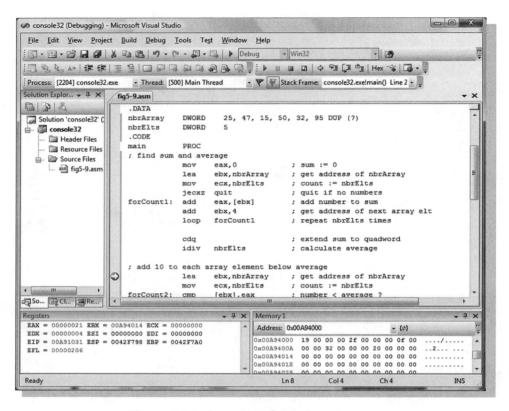

Figure 5.11 Average of numbers in array

iterations of the loop to watch EBX change as the next array elements are added to *sum*. Then clear the first breakpoint and set a breakpoint at the second **lea** instruction and let the first loop complete. Figure 5.11 shows the debugger display. ECX has decremented to zero. EAX contains 21_{16} and this is correct because the average of these five numbers is 33.8.

Finally, set another breakpoint at the end of the program and click the Continue button. Figure 5.12 shows the final display. Notice that in memory 19_{16} has been changed to 23_{16}, $0f_{16}$ has been changed to 19_{16}, and 20_{16} has been changed to $2a_{16}$, that is, each number less than 21_{16} has had 10 added to it.

Figure 5.13 shows the same program rewritten for a 64-bit environment. It still processes an array of doublewords, but other details are changed. In particular, RBX is used to point to each array element. Also, RCX is used as the counter register by the loop instruction in 64-bit mode, but we cannot simply copy the value of *nbrElts* to RCX since the sizes don't match. To solve this problem, all 64 bits of RCX are cleared before copying the value of *nbrElts* to the low-order 32 bits. The only other changes to the program are eliminating the directives that the 64-bit assembler does not use.

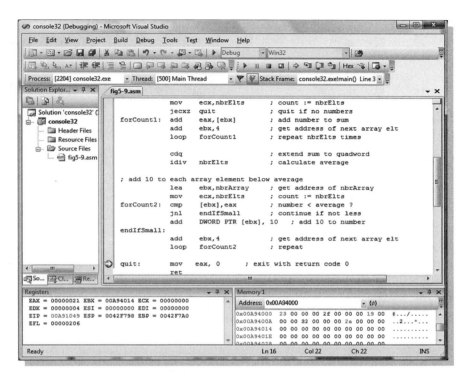

Figure 5.12 Small numbers in array changed

```
; given an array of doubleword integers, (1) find their average
; and (2) add 10 to each number smaller than average
; author:  R. Detmer
; revised:  6/2008

.DATA
nbrArray    DWORD    25, 47, 15, 50, 32, 95 DUP (?)
nbrElts     DWORD    5
.CODE
main        PROC
; find sum and average
            mov     eax,0           ; sum := 0
            lea     rbx,nbrArray    ; get address of nbrArray
            mov     rcx, 0          ; clear all of RCX
            mov     ecx,nbrElts     ; count := nbrElts
            jrcxz   quit            ; quit if no numbers
forCount1:  add     eax,[rbx]       ; add number to sum
            add     rbx,4           ; get address of next array elt
            loop    forCount1       ; repeat nbrElts times
```
                                                              (continued)

Figure 5.13 Process array (64-bit version)

```
                cdq                     ; extend sum to quadword
                idiv    nbrElts         ; calculate average

; add 10 to each array element below average
                lea     rbx,nbrArray    ; get address of nbrArray
                mov     rcx, 0          ; clear all of RCX
                mov     ecx,nbrElts     ; count := nbrElts
forCount2:      cmp     [rbx],eax       ; number < average ?
                jnl     endIfSmall      ; continue if not less
                add     DWORD PTR [rbx], 10    ; add 10 to number
endIfSmall:
                add     rbx,4           ; get address of next array elt
                loop    forCount2       ; repeat

quit:           mov     rax, 0       ; exit with return code 0
                ret
main            ENDP
END
```

Figure 5.13 Process array (64-bit version) (continued)

If you were planning to code this program in a high-level language like Java or C++, the first loop design might look like

---

```
for index := 0 to nbrElts-1 loop
    add nbrArray[index] to sum;
end for;
```

Figure 5.14 gives a *console32* program that comes close to directly implementing this design. Only the body of *main* is shown since the rest is identical to the first version of the program in Figure 5.9. What is new is that ECX performs exactly the function of *index* in the above design—it counts from 0 up to *nbrElts*−1. Instead of using register indirect addressing to reference the array element, we use **indexed addressing**. The address format **nbrArray[4*ecx]** is assembled into an address with a displacement that is the address of *nbrArray*, ECX as an index register, and 4 as a **scaling factor** for the index. When executed, the operand used is at the address that is at the sum of the displace-

```
; find sum and average
            mov     eax,0               ; sum := 0
            mov     ecx,0               ; index := 0
for1:       cmp     ecx,nbrElts         ; index < nbrElts
            jnl     endFor1             ; exit if not
            add     eax,nbrArray[4*ecx]  ; add number to sum
            inc     ecx                 ; increment index
            jmp     for1                ; repeat
endFor1:
            cdq                         ; extend sum to quadword
            idiv    nbrElts             ; calculate average

; add 10 to each array element below average
            mov     ecx,0               ; index := 0
for2:       cmp     ecx,nbrElts         ; index < nbrElts
            jnl     endFor2             ; exit if not
            cmp     nbrArray[4*ecx],eax  ; number < average ?
            jnl     endIfSmall          ; continue if not less
            add     DWORD PTR nbrArray[4*ecx], 10    ; add 10 to number
endIfSmall:
            inc     ecx                 ; increment index
            jmp     for2                ; repeat
endFor2:
quit:       mov     eax, 0       ; exit with return code 0
            ret
```

Figure 5.14 Process array using indexed addressing

ment and four times the contents of the index register. In other words, the first operand is at *nbrArray*+0, the second at *nbrArray*+4, and so on. The advantage of using indexed addressing is that array elements do not have to be accessed in sequential order.

The 80x86 architecture has additional addressing modes. The most complicated is **based and indexed**. One format in assembly language looks like `100[ebx+8*ecx]`. In this example the address of the operand is calculated as the contents of EBX plus eight times the contents of ECX plus 100. Notice that the function of the displacement 100 in this example is exactly the same as the function of the starting address *nbrArray* in the previous example. The only allowable scaling factor values are 2, 4, and 8.

Recall that object code often contains a *ModR/M* byte. If the *R/M* field has value 100 and the *Mod* field has value 00, 01, or 10, then an additional *SIB* **byte** follows the *ModR/M* byte to encode information about the scale factor, the index register, and the base register. The scale field is 2 bits long and has values 00 for no scaling, 01 for scale factor 2, 10 for 4, and 11 for 8. The remaining two fields are each 3 bits long and designate index and base registers using the encodings shown in Figure 4.3. In 64-bit mode, *REX* prefixes extend this encoding.

Exercises 5.5

1. Modify the program in Figure 5.9, replacing the second loop by one that changes each number larger than average to zero.
2. Modify the program in Figure 5.9, replacing the second loop by one that changes each number within 5 of the average to the average. Include values equal to *average*−5 or to *average*+5.
3. Assemble each instruction in a *console32* program, examine the listing file, and explain how each field of the *ModR/M* byte and each field in the *SIB* byte relates to the corresponding part of the assembly language source code.

   *(a) add   1000[ebx+4*esi], edx
   (b) mov   DWORD PTR 1000[ecx+8*edi], 5000

Programming Exercises 5.5

1. The following design will input numbers into an array or doublewords, using the sentinel value −9999 to terminate input.

   nbrElts := 0;
   get address of array;
   prompt for and input number;
   while number ≠ −9999 loop
        add 1 to nbrElts;
        store number at address;
        add 4 to address;
        prompt for and input number;
   end while;

   Implement this design in a *windows32* or *windows64* program that uses a dialog box to prompt for and input each number. Assume that no more than 100 numbers will be entered. Use a single message box to report the sum of the numbers, how many numbers were entered (not counting the sentinel value), the average of the numbers, and the count of array entries that are greater than or equal to the average value.

2. Using the *windows32* or *windows64* framework, write a program that uses a dialog box to input a string of characters into *charStr*, recalling that the *input* macro terminates a string with a null byte (00). Process this string as an array of characters, replacing each uppercase letter in *charStr* by its lowercase equivalent, leaving every other character unchanged. Use a message box to display the modified string.

3. There are many ways to determine prime numbers. Here is a design for one way to find the first 100 primes. Implement this design in 80x86 assembly language. Using the *console32* or *console64* framework, write a program that stores the primes in an array of doublewords *primeArray*, and examine the contents of *primeArray* using the debugger.

```
prime[1] := 2; { first prime number }
prime[2] := 3; { second prime number }
primeCount := 2;
candidate := 5; { first candidate for a new prime }
while primeCount < 100 loop
    index := 1;
    while (index ≤ primeCount)
            and (prime[index] does not evenly divide candidate) loop
        add 1 to index;
    end while;
    if (index > primeCount)
    then {no existing prime evenly divides the candidate, so it is a new prime}
        add 1 to primeCount;
        prime[primeCount] := candidate;
    end if;
    add 2 to candidate;
end while;
```

4. It is often necessary to search an array for a given value. Using the *windows32* or *windows64* framework, write a program that inputs a

collection of integers into an array of doublewords and then sequentially searches for values stored in the array. Implement the following design.

```
nbrElts := 0;
get address of array;
prompt for and input number;
while (number > 0) loop
    add 1 to nbrElts;
    store number at address in array;
    get address of next array element;
    prompt for and input number;
end while;
repeat
    prompt for and input keyValue;
    get address array;
    count := 1;
    forever loop
        if count > nbrElts
        then
            display keyValue, "not in array";
            exit loop;
        end if;
        if keyValue = current element of array
        then
            display keyValue, "is element", count;
            exit loop;
        end if;
        add 1 to count;
        get address of next array element;
    end loop;
    prompt for and input response;
until (response = 'N') or (response = 'n')
```

5. Suppose that *nbrArray* is a 1-based array of doubleword integers (that is, the first index is 1, not 0). The first *nbrElts* values in *nbrArray* can be sorted into increasing order using the **selection sort** algorithm.

```
for position := 2 to nbrElts-1 loop
    smallSpot := position;
    smallValue := nbrArray [position];
    for i := position+1 to nbrElts loop
        if nbrArray [i] < smallValue
        then
            smallSpot := i;
            smallValue := nbrArray [i];
        end if;
    end for;
    nbrArray [smallSpot] := nbrArray [position];
    nbrArray [position] := smallValue;
end for;
```

Implement this algorithm in a *console32* or *console64* program, testing with an array of 20 doubleword integers. Use scaled and indexed addressing appropriately to address array elements, noting that the algorithm as written starts with index 1, not index 0. Execute your program under the debugger.

5.6 Chapter Summary

This chapter introduced 80x86 instructions that can be used to implement many high-level design or language features including *if* statements, various loops structures, and arrays.

The `jmp` instruction unconditionally transfers control to a destination statement. It has several versions, including one that jumps to a short destination 128 bytes before or 127 bytes after the `jmp`, and one that jumps to a near destination a 32-bit displacement away. The `jmp` instruction is used in implementing various loop structures, typically transferring control back to the beginning of the loop, and in the *if–then–else* structure at the end of the "then code" to transfer control to *endif* so that the *else* code is not also executed. A `jmp` statement corresponds directly to the *goto* statement that is available in most high-level languages.

Conditional jump instructions examine the settings of one or more flags in the flag register and jump to a destination statement or fall through to the next instruction depending on the flag values. Conditional jump instructions have short and near displacement versions. There is a large collection of conditional jump instructions. They are used in *if* statements and loops, often in combination with compare instructions, to check Boolean conditions.

The cmp (compare) instructions have the sole purpose of setting or resetting flags in the flags register. Each compares two operands and assigns flag values. The comparison is done by subtracting the second operand from the first. The difference is not retained as it is with a sub instruction. Compare instructions often precede conditional jump instructions.

Loop structures like *while*, *until*, and *for* loops can be implemented using compare, jump, and conditional jump instructions. The loop instruction provides another way to implement many *for* loops. To use the loop instruction, a counter is placed in the ECX register prior to the start of the loop. The loop instruction itself is at the bottom of the loop body; it decrements the value in ECX and transfers control to a destination (normally the first statement of the body) if the new value in ECX is not zero. This results in the body of the loop being executed the number of times originally placed in the ECX register. The conditional jump jecxz instruction can be used to guard against executing such a loop when the initial counter value is zero.

Storage for an array can be reserved using the DUP directive in the data segment of a program. The elements of an array can be sequentially accessed by putting the address of the first element of the array in a register, and adding the size of an array element repeatedly to get to the next element. The current element is referenced using register indirect addressing. The lea (load effective address) instruction is commonly used to load the initial address of the array. More complicated addressing modes can be used for nonsequential access of array elements.

CHAPTER **6**

Procedures

The 80x86 architecture enables implementation of procedures that are similar to those in a high-level language. In fact, 80x86 procedures can be called from high-level language programs or can call high-level language procedures. There are three main concepts involved: (1) how to transfer control from a calling program to a procedure and back, (2) how to pass parameter values to a procedure and results back from the procedure, and (3) how to write procedure code that is independent of the calling program. In addition, sometimes a procedure must allocate local variable space. The hardware stack is used to accomplish each of these jobs. This chapter begins with a discussion of the 80x86 stack. Sections 6.1 to 6.3 cover operations in 32-bit mode only, while Section 6.4 describes differences for 64-bit mode. The final section discusses macros, sometimes used to substitute for procedure calls, and used by the *io.h* file in *windows32* and *windows64* projects to call procedures.

6.1   The 80x86 Stack

Programs in this book have allocated stacks with the code

```
.STACK   4096
```

This **.STACK** directive tells the assembler to reserve 4096 bytes of uninitialized storage. The operating system initializes the stack pointer register ESP to the address of the first byte above the 4096 bytes in the stack. A larger or smaller stack could be allocated, depending on the anticipated usage in the program.

The stack is most often used by pushing doublewords on it, or by popping them off it. This is done automatically as part of the execution of **call** and **return** instructions (see Section 6.2). It is also done manually with **push** and **pop** instructions. This section covers the mechanics of **push** and **pop** instructions, describing how they use the stack.

Source code for a push instruction has the syntax

```
push source
```

The source operand can be a register 16, a register 32, a segment register, a word in memory, a doubleword in memory, an immediate byte, an immediate word, or an immediate doubleword. The only byte-size operand is immediate, and is sign-extended to a word or doubleword to get the value actually pushed on the stack. Figure 6.1 lists some allowable

Operand	Opcode	Bytes of Object Code
EAX or AX	50	1
ECX or CX	51	1
EDX or DX	52	1
EBX or BX	53	1
ESP or SP	54	1
EBP or BP	55	1
ESI or SI	56	1
EDI or DI	57	1
memory word	FF	2+
memory doubleword	FF	2+
immediate byte	6A	2
immediate word	68	3
immediate doubleword	68	5

Figure 6.1 push instructions

operand types, omitting segment registers that we will not use. The usual mnemonic for a push instruction is just **push**. However, if there is ambiguity about the size of the operand (as there would be with a small immediate value) then you can use **pushw** or **pushd** mnemonics to specify word-size or doubleword-size operands, respectively. The **WORD PTR** and **DWORD PTR** operators are used with memory operands when needed.

When a **push** instruction is executed for a doubleword-size operand, the stack pointer ESP is decremented by 4. Recall that initially ESP contains the address of the byte just above the allocated space. Subtracting 4 makes ESP point to the top doubleword in the stack. The operand is then stored at the address in ESP, that is, at the high-memory end of the stack space. Execution is similar for a word-size operand, except that ESP is decremented by 2 before the operand is stored.

Example

We now show an example of execution of two **push** instructions. It assumes that ESP initially contains 00600200. The first **push** decrements ESP to 006001FC and then stores the contents of EAX at that address. Notice that the low-order and high-order bytes are reversed in memory. The second **push** decrements ESP to 006001F8 and stores FFFFFF10 (-240_{10}) at that address.

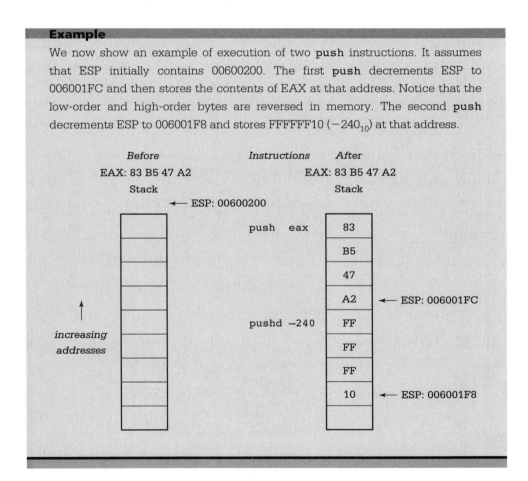

You can use the debugger to watch these instructions actually execute. After you assemble a program starting with

```
mov    eax, 83b547a2h
push eax
pushd -240
```

the assembly listing displays

```
00000000 B8 83B547A2 mov   eax, 83b547a2h
00000005 50          push eax
00000006 68 FFFFFF10 pushd -240
```

This is expected from the opcodes listed in Figure 4.1 for **mov** and Figure 6.1 for **push**. Figure 6.2 shows the WinDbg display after the EAX register has been initialized with 83B547A2. We just want to see the top few bytes of the stack, so we note that ESP contains 002BFC98. (It might have another value at another time or on another computer.) To display the top 16 bytes, we open a memory view starting at address 0x0044FD88. These bytes are shown on the top two lines of the memory window. Notice that the stack contains "junk" values; zeros in this case.

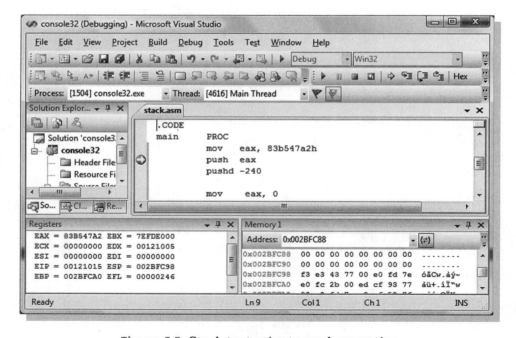

Figure 6.2 Stack test prior to push operation

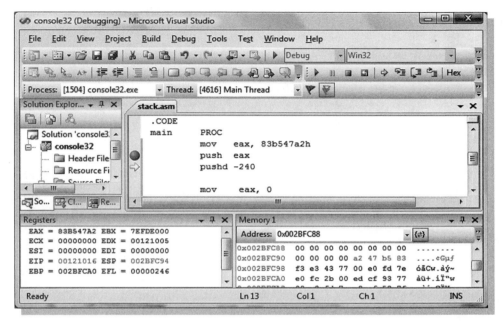

Figure 6.3 EAX has been pushed onto the stack

Now execute the **push** instruction. The resulting display is shown in Figure 6.3. Notice that ESP now contains 0044FD94, that is, it has been decremented by 4. The last 4 bytes on the second memory line (in red) show the doubleword stored at the new stack pointer address. The bytes from EAX have been stored backward in memory. Finally, execute the **pushd** instruction. The resulting display is shown in Figure 6.4. ESP now contains 0044FD90, again decremented by 4. The first 4 bytes of the second memory line show the value of −240, again with the bytes of FFFFFF10 stored in reverse order.

If additional operands were pushed onto the stack, ESP would be decremented further and the new values stored. No **push** instruction affects any flag bit.

Notice that a stack "grows downward," contrary to the image that you may have of a typical software stack.[1] Also notice that the only value on the stack that is readily available is the last one pushed; it is at the address in ESP. Furthermore, ESP changes frequently as you push values and as procedure calls are made. In the next section you will learn a way to establish a fixed reference point in the middle of the stack

---

[1]Of course, if you draw the picture so that lower memory addresses are at the top, then it "grows upward." The author's preference is to draw the pictures so that when ESI is decremented, its "pointer" moves down.

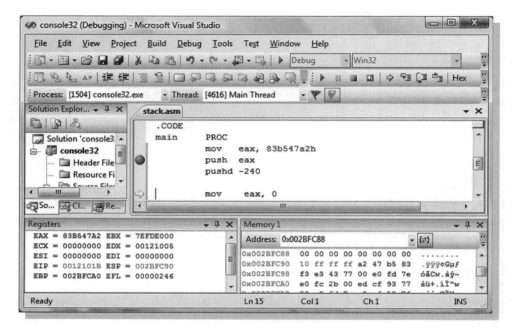

Figure 6.4 −240 has been pushed onto the stack

using the EBP register, so that values near that point can be accessed without having to pop off all the intermediate values.

Pop instructions do the opposite job of push instructions. Each pop instruction has the format

pop *destination*

where *destination* can reference a word or doubleword in memory, any register 16, any register 32, or any segment register except CS. (The **push** instruction does not exclude CS.) The **pop** instruction gets a doubleword-size value from the stack by copying the doubleword at the address in ESP to the destination, then incrementing ESP by 4. The operation for a word-size value is similar, except that ESP is incremented by 2. Figure 6.5 gives information about **pop** instructions for different destination operands. Segment registers are again omitted. Pop instructions do not affect flags.

Example

Here is an example to show how pop instructions work. The doubleword at the address in ESP is copied to ECX before ESP is incremented by 4. The values popped from the stack are physically still there even though they logically have been removed. Note again that the bytes of a doubleword are stored backward in memory in the 80x86 architecture.

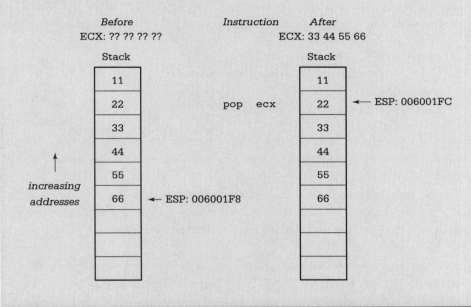

Figure 6.5 pop instructions

Operand	Opcode	Bytes of Object Code
EAX or AX	58	1
ECX or CX	59	1
EDX or DX	5A	1
EBX or BX	5B	1
ESP or SP	5C	1
EBP or BP	5D	1
ESI or SI	5E	1
EDI or DI	5F	1
memory word	8F	2+
memory doubleword	8F	2+

We have noted previously that registers are a scarce resource when programming. One use of push and pop instructions is to temporarily save the contents of a register on the stack. Suppose, for example, that you are using EDX to store some program variable, but need to do a division that requires you to extend a dividend into EDX:EAX prior to the operation. One way to avoid losing the value in EDX is to push it on the stack.

```
push edx    ; save variable
cdq         ; extend dividend to quadword
idiv divisor ; divide
pop  edx    ; restore variable
```

This example assumes that you don't need the remainder the division operation puts in EDX. If you do need the remainder, it could be copied somewhere else before popping the saved value back to EDX.

As the above example shows, push and pop instructions are often used in pairs. When we examine how the stack is used to pass parameters to procedures, you will see a way to logically discard values from the stack without popping them to a destination location.

In a 32-bit environment the stack is created on a doubleword boundary, that is, the address in ESP will be a multiple of 4. It is important to keep the stack top on a doubleword boundary for certain system calls. Therefore, with few exceptions, you should always push doubleword values on the stack, even though the 80x86 architecture allows words to be used.

In addition to the ordinary push and pop instructions, there are special mnemonics to push and pop flag registers. These are **pushf** (**pushfd** for the extended flag register) and **popf** (**popfd** for the extended flag register). These are summarized in Figure 6.6. They are sometimes used in procedure code. Obviously, **popf** and **popfd** instructions change flag values; these are the only push or pop instructions that change flags.

Instruction	Opcode	Bytes of Object Code
pushf/pushfd	9C	1
popf/popfd	9D	1

Figure 6.6 pushf and popf instructions

The 80x86 architecture has **pushad** and **popad** instructions that push or pop all general-purpose registers with a single instruction. These are rarely useful and do not work in 64-bit mode, so they are not used in this book.

Exercises 6.1

1. For each instruction, give the opcode and the number of bytes of object code including prefix bytes. Assume that *double* references a double-word in memory.

   (a) push ax   (b) pushd 10

   *(c) push ebp   (d) pop ebx

   (e) pop double   (f) pop dx

   (g) pushfd

2. For each part of this problem, assume the "before" values when the given instructions are executed. Give the requested "after" values. Trace execution of the instructions by drawing pictures of the stack

Before	Instructions	After
*(a) ESP: 06 00 10 00	push ecx	ESP, ECX
ECX: 01 A2 5B 74	pushd 10	
(b) ESP: 02 00 0B 7C	pushd 20	ESP, EBX
EBX: 12 34 56 78	push ebx	
(c) ESP: 00 10 F8 3A	push eax	ESP, EAX, EBX, ECX
EAX: 12 34 56 78	pushd 30	
	pop ebx	
	pop ecx	

3. Many microprocessors do not have an instruction equivalent to xchg. With such systems, a sequence of instructions like the following can be used to exchange the contents of two registers:

   ```
   push eax
   push ebx
   pop  eax
   pop  ebx
   ```

   Explain why this sequence works to exchange the contents of the EAX and EBX registers. Compare the number of bytes of code required to execute this sequence with those required for the instruction xchg eax,ebx.

4. Another alternative to the xchg instruction is to use

```
push  eax
mov   eax, ebx
pop   ebx
```

Explain why this sequence works to exchange the contents of the EAX and EBX registers. Compare the number of bytes of code required to execute this sequence with those required for the instruction xchg eax,ebx.

6.2   32-Bit Procedures with Value Parameters

The word **procedure** is used in high-level languages to describe a subprogram that is almost a self-contained unit. The main program or another subprogram can call a procedure by including a statement that consists of the procedure name followed by a parenthesized list of arguments to be associated with the procedure's formal parameters.

Many high-level languages distinguish between a procedure that performs an action and a function that returns a value. A **function** is similar to a procedure except that it is called by using its name and argument list in an expression. It returns a value associated with its name; this value is then used in the expression. All subprograms in C/C++ are technically functions in this sense, but these languages allow for functions that return no value.

In assembly language and in some high-level languages the term *procedure* is used to describe both types of subprograms: those that return values and those that do not. The word *procedure* is used in both senses in this book.

Procedures are valuable in assembly language for the same reasons as in high-level languages—they help divide programs into manageable tasks and they isolate code that can be used multiple times within a single program, or that can be saved and reused in other programs. Sometimes assembly language can be used to write more efficient code than is produced by a high-level language compiler and this code can be put in a procedure called by a high-level program that does tasks that don't need to be as efficient.

Recall the major main concepts listed in the introduction to this chapter: (1) how to transfer control from a calling program to a procedure and back, (2) how to pass parameter values to a procedure and results back from the procedure, and (3) how to write procedure code that is independent of the calling program. These can be handled in many ways in assembly language, and this section describes one particular protocol, called **cdecl** in Microsoft documentation. It is the default convention used in C programs in the Visual Studio environment. Figure 6.7 gives a complete *windows32* program that is used to illustrate aspects of this protocol.

```
; Input x and y, call procedure to evaluate 3*x+7*y, display result
; Author: R. Detmer
; Date:  6/2008
.586
.MODEL FLAT
INCLUDE io.h
.STACK 4096

.DATA
number1 DWORD   ?
number2 DWORD   ?
prompt1 BYTE   "Enter first number x", 0
prompt2 BYTE   "Enter second number y", 0
string BYTE   20 DUP (?)
resultLbl BYTE "3*x+7*y", 0
result BYTE   11 DUP (?), 0

.CODE
_MainProc PROC
    input   prompt1, string, 20    ; read ASCII characters
    atod    string       ; convert to integer
    mov     number1, eax  ; store in memory

    input  prompt2, string, 20 ; repeat for second number
    atod    string
    mov     number2, eax

    push    number2      ; 2nd parameter
    push    number1      ; 1st parameter
    call    fctn1        ; fctn1(number1, number2)
    add     esp, 8       ; remove parameters from stack

    dtoa    result, eax    ; convert to ASCII characters
    output resultLbl, result ; output label and result

    mov     eax, 0 ; exit with return code 0
    ret
_MainProc ENDP
```

(continued)

Figure 6.7 Procedure example

```
; int fctn1(int x, int y)
; returns 3*x+4*y
fctn1   PROC
    push    ebp        ; save base pointer
    mov     ebp, esp   ; establish stack frame
    push    ebx        ; save EBX

    mov     eax, [ebp+8]    ; x
    imul    eax, 3          ; 3*x
    mov     ebx, [ebp+12]   ; y
    imul    ebx, 7          ; 7*y
    add     eax, ebx        ; 3*x + 7*y

    pop     ebx        ; restore EBX
    pop     ebp        ; restore EBP
    ret                ; return
fctn1   ENDP

END
```

Figure 6.7 Procedure example *(continued)*

The code for a procedure always follows a `.CODE` directive. The body of a procedure is bracketed by **PROC** and **ENDP** directives. Each of these directives has a label that gives the name of the procedure. With *windows32* programs *_MainProc* is a procedure. Additional assembly language procedures can go in the same code segment before or after *_MainProc*. They can even be in separate files; information for how to do this is in the next section.

Let's first look at how to transfer control from *_MainProc* to the procedure *fctn1*. This is done by the instruction

```
call fctn1
```

In general, a `call` instruction saves the address of the next instruction (the one immediately following the call), then transfers control to the procedure code. It does this by pushing EIP onto the stack and then changing EIP to contain the address of the first instruction of the procedure.

Transferring control back from a procedure is accomplished by reversing the above steps. A `ret` (return) instruction pops the stack into EIP, so that the next instruction to be executed is the one at the address that was pushed on the stack by the call. There is almost always at least one **ret** instruction in a procedure and there can be more than one. If there is only one **ret**, it is ordinarily the last instruction in the procedure since subsequent instructions would be unreachable without "spaghetti code." Although a **call** instruction must identify its destination, the **ret** does not—control will transfer to the instruction following the most recent call. The address of that instruction is stored on the 80x86 stack.

The syntax of the 80x86 call statement is

call *destination*

Figure 6.8 lists some of the 80x86 **call** instructions. No **call** instruction modifies any flag. All of the procedure calls used in this book will be the first type, near relative. For a near relative call, the 5 bytes of the instruction consist of the E8 opcode plus the displacement from the next instruction to the first instruction of the procedure. The transfer of control when a procedure is called is similar to the transfer of a relative jump, except that the old contents of EIP are pushed.

Near indirect calls encode a register 32 or a reference to a doubleword in memory. When the call is executed, the contents of that register or doubleword are used as the address of the procedure. This makes it possible for a call instruction to go to different procedures different times.

All far calls must provide both new CS contents and new EIP contents. With far direct calls, both of these are coded in the instruction, and these 6 bytes plus the 1 for the opcode make the 7 seen in Figure 6.8. With far indirect calls, these are located at a 6-byte block in memory, and the address of that block is coded in the instruction. The extra byte is a *ModR/M* byte. Far calls were very important when the segmented memory model was used.

Operand	Opcode	Bytes of Object Code
near relative	E8	5
near indirect using register	FF	2
near indirect using memory	FF	2+
far direct	9A	7
far indirect	FF	6+

Figure 6.8 call instructions

The return instruction **ret** is used to transfer control from a procedure body back to the calling point. Its basic operation is simple; it simply pops the address previously stored on the stack and loads it into the instruction pointer EIP. Since the stack contains the address of the instruction following the call, execution will continue at that point. A near return just has to restore EIP. A far return instruction reverses the steps of a far call, restoring both EIP and CS; both of these values are popped from the stack. No **ret** instruction changes any flag.

There are two formats for the **ret** instruction. The more common form has no operand, and is simply coded

```
ret
```

The other version has a single operand, and is coded

```
ret   count
```

The operand *count* is added to the contents of ESP after completion of the other steps of the return process (popping EIP and, for a far procedure, CS). This can be useful if other values (parameters in particular) have been saved on the stack just for the procedure call; this is not used with the *cdecl* protocol, however. Figure 6.9 lists the various formats of **ret** instructions.

Using a high-level language, a procedure definition often includes **parameters** (sometimes called *formal parameters*) that are associated with **arguments** (also called *actual parameters*) when the procedure is called. For the procedure's pass-by-value (in) parameters, values of the arguments (which may be expressions) are copied to the parameters when the procedure is called, and these values are then referenced in the procedure using their local names (the identifiers used to define the parameters). Reference (pass-by-location or in-out) parameters associate a parameter identifier with an argument that is a single variable, and can be used to pass a value either to the proce-

Type	Operand	Opcode	Bytes of Object Code
near	none	C3	1
near	immediate	C2	3
far	none	CB	1
far	immediate	CA	3

Figure 6.9 ret instructions

dure from the caller or from the procedure back to the caller. Reference parameters are covered in the next section.

Our example code in Figure 6.7 has two arguments (*number1* and *number2*) in *_MainProc* that are passed by value to two parameters (*x* and *y*) in *fctn1*. We now look at how to pass parameter values to a procedure and results back from the procedure. The second part of this is simple—if the procedure returns a single doubleword value, then it puts that value in EAX to be used by the calling program. Notice that this is exactly what *fctn1* does in the program in Figure 6.7; after some preliminaries (explained next), it computes the desired value in EAX where it is available back in *_MainProc*. With the *cdecl* protocol, only the EAX register may be used for this purpose.

Doubleword parameters are passed to the procedure by pushing them on the stack. In the *cdecl* protocol, the parameters are pushed on the stack in the opposite order in which they appear in the parameter list—the last parameter value is pushed first and the first parameter value is pushed last. The code that calls *fctn1* in *_MainProc* is

```
push   number2    ; 2nd parameter
push   number1    ; 1st parameter
call   fctn1      ; fctn1(number1, number2)
add    esp, 8     ; remove parameters from stack
```

The first two statements obviously push the argument values on the stack prior to the procedure call. The purpose of the last statement is to remove the values from the stack following return from the procedure. If the stack is not cleaned up and a program repeatedly calls a procedure, eventually the stack will fill up causing a run-time error with modern operating systems. Arguments could be removed using the alternative form of the **ret** statement that specifies an operand, but the *cdecl* protocol specifically leaves the stack cleanup task to the calling program. The arguments could be removed by popping the values off the stack, but it is more efficient to simply add the number of bytes of parameters to ESP, moving the stack pointer above the values.

Now, we look at how a procedure retrieves parameter values from the stack. Upon entry to the procedure, the stack looks like the left illustration in Figure 6.10. The two arguments—now the parameter values—have been pushed on the stack by the calling program and the return address has been pushed on the stack by the **call** instruction. The first instructions executed by the procedure are

```
push   ebp        ; save base pointer
mov    ebp, esp   ; establish stack frame
push   ebx        ; save EBX
```

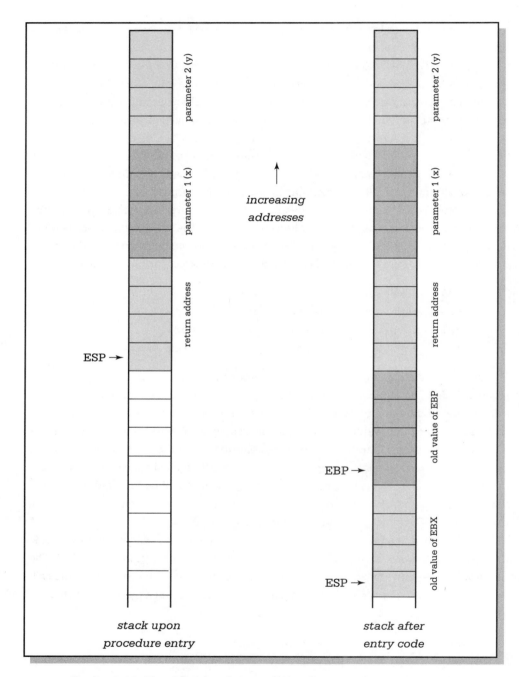

Figure 6.10 Establishing base pointer in procedure entry code

This is known as **entry code**. The first two instructions will always be the pair shown. They preserve EBP so that it can be restored before returning, and set EBP to point at a fixed place in the stack that can be used to locate parameters. The third instruction is needed in this procedure so that EBX can be used for computations within the procedure and then restored before return; this makes its use in the procedure transparent to the calling program. After these three instructions are executed, the stack looks like the right illustration in Figure 6.10.

There are 8 bytes stored between the address stored in EBP and the first parameter (x) value. Parameter 1 can be referenced using based addressing by [ebp+8]. The second parameter (y) value is 4 bytes higher on the stack; its reference is [ebp+12]. The code

```
mov    eax, [ebp+8]    ; x
imul   eax, 3          ; 3*x
mov    ebx, [ebp+12]   ; y
imul   ebx, 7          ; 7*y
add    eax, ebx        ; 3*x + 7*y
```

copies the value of the first parameter from the stack into EAX and the value of the second parameter from the stack into EBX in order to compute the desired promised result.

You may wonder why EBP is used at all. Why not just use ESP as a base register? The principal reason is that ESP is likely to change, but the instruction **mov ebp,esp** loads EBP with a fixed reference point in the stack. This fixed reference point will not change as other instructions in the procedure are executed, even if the stack is used for other purposes, for example, to push additional registers or to call other procedures.

We now come to the third major concept, how to write procedure code that is independent of and preserves the environment for the calling program. You have already seen most of the code for this. Basically, the entry code pushes each register that will be used by the procedure, and the **exit code** pops them in the opposite order. Obviously, you must not save and restore EAX when a value is being returned in EAX. The exit code for our example consists of

```
pop    ebx           ; restore EBX
pop    ebp           ; restore EBP
ret                  ; return
```

EBP is always restored last since it is always saved first. This example only used EBX for computations, but it is not unusual to save and restore several registers. Figure 6.11 summarizes the *cdecl* protocol.

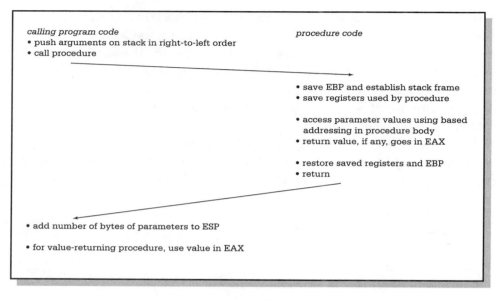

calling program code
- push arguments on stack in right-to-left order
- call procedure

procedure code
- save EBP and establish stack frame
- save registers used by procedure

- access parameter values using based
  addressing in procedure body
- return value, if any, goes in EAX

- restore saved registers and EBP
- return

- add number of bytes of parameters to ESP

- for value-returning procedure, use value in EAX

Figure 6.11 *cdecl* protocol

Exercises 6.2

*1. Suppose that the procedure *exercise1* is called by the instruction

```
call exercise1
```

If this call statement is at address 00402000 and ESP contains 00406000 before the call, what return address will be on the stack when the first instruction of procedure *exercise1* is executed? What will be the value in ESP?

2. Suppose that a procedure begins with this entry code

```
push ebp      ; save EBP
mov  ebp,esp  ; new base pointer
push ecx      ; save registers
push esi
...
```

Assume that this procedure has three doubleword parameters whose formal order is first *x*, then *y*, and last *z*. Draw a picture of the stack following execution of the above code. Include parameters, return address, and show the bytes to which EBP and ESP point. Give the based address with which each parameter can be referenced.

Programming Exercises 6.2

For each of these exercises follow the *cdecl* protocol for the specified procedure and write a short *console32* or *windows32* test-driver program to test the procedure.

1. Write a procedure *discr* that could be described in C/C++ by

   ```
   int discr(int a, int b, int c)
   ; return the discriminant b*b-4*a*c
   ```

   that is, its name is *discr*, it has three integer parameters, and it is a value-returning procedure.

2. Write a value-returning procedure *min2* to find the smaller of two doubleword integer parameters.

3. Write a value-returning procedure *max3* to find the largest of three doubleword integer parameters.

4. Programming Exercise 5.3.6 has an algorithm for finding the greatest common divisor of two positive integers. Write a procedure *gcd* to implement this algorithm. It might be described in C/C++ by int gcd(int number1, int number2), that is, its name is *gcd*, it has two integer parameters, and it is a value-returning procedure.

6.3   Additional 32-Bit Procedure Options

The previous section's main example showed how to pass arguments to parameters by value. With a reference parameter, the address of the argument instead of its value is passed to the procedure. Reference parameters are used for several purposes, two of which are to send a large argument (for example, an array or a structure) to a procedure, or to send results back to the calling program as argument values. This section begins with an example that illustrates both of these uses of reference parameters.

Consider the procedure for which C++ function prototype could be written

```
void minMax(int arr[], int count, int& min, int& max);
// Set min to smallest value in arr[0],..., arr[count-1]
// Set max to largest value in arr[0],..., arr[count-1]
```

In C++, the notation int arr[ ] indicates that the address of the integer array *arr* will be passed, and int& instead of int says that the addresses of integer variables *min* and *max* will be passed. Figure 6.12 shows an implementation of this procedure in a

```
; procedure minMax to find smallest and largest elements in an
; array and test driver for minMax
; author: R. Detmer
; date: 6/2008

.586
.MODEL FLAT
.STACK 4096

.DATA
minimum    DWORD   ?
maximum    DWORD   ?
nbrArray   DWORD   25, 47, 95, 50, 16, 95 DUP (?)

.CODE
main  PROC
     lea  eax, maximum ; 4th parameter
     push eax
     lea  eax, minimum ; 3rd parameter
     push eax
     pushd 5        ; 2nd parameter (number of elements)
     lea  eax, nbrArray ; 1st parameter
     push eax
     call minMax    ; minMax(nbrArray, 5, minimum, maximum)
     add  esp, 16   ; remove parameters from stack

quit:  mov  eax, 0    ; exit with return code 0
     ret
main   ENDP

; void minMax(int arr[], int count, int& min, int& max);
; Set min to smallest value in arr[0],..., arr[count-1]
; Set max to largest value in arr[0],..., arr[count-1]
minMax PROC
     push ebp       ; save base pointer
     mov  ebp,esp   ; establish stack frame
     push eax       ; save registers
     push ebx
     push ecx
     push edx
     push esi
```

(continued)

Figure 6.12 Procedure using address parameters

```
       mov   esi,[ebp+8]  ; get address of array arr
       mov   ecx,[ebp+12] ; get value of count
       mov   ebx, [ebp+16] ; get address of min
       mov   edx, [ebp+20] ; get address of max

       mov   DWORD PTR [ebx], 7fffffffh ; largest possible integer
       mov   DWORD PTR [edx], 80000000h ; smallest possible integer
       jecxz exitCode   ; exit if there are no elements

forLoop:
       mov   eax, [esi]  ; a[i]
       cmp   eax, [ebx]  ; a[i] < min?
       jnl   endIfSmaller ; skip if not
       mov   [ebx], eax  ; min := a[i]
endIfSmaller:
       cmp   eax, [edx]  ; a[i] > max?
       jng   endIfLarger  ; skip if not
       mov   [edx], eax  ; max := a[i]
endIfLarger:
       add   esi, 4     ; point at next array element
       loop  forLoop    ; repeat for each element of array

exitCode:
       pop   esi     ; restore registers
       pop   edx
       pop   ecx
       pop   ebx
       pop   eax
       pop   ebp
       ret           ; return
minMax ENDP
END
```

Figure 6.12 Procedure using address parameters *(continued)*

console32 program. It also includes a simple test driver that establishes locations for an array and the smallest and largest numbers to be stored, and calls *minMax*, pushing the four parameters, three of which are addresses. Note that there are 16 bytes of parameters to remove after the call.

The *minMax* procedure follows a straightforward design that is in the comments of the procedure. Notice that several registers are used and their contents are saved in the entry code and restored in the exit code. The reader should draw the stack picture to see where the parameters are placed on the stack. Immediately after the entry code, the various parameters are copied into registers. The *minMax* procedure uses indirect addressing extensively, based addressing to retrieve the parameters, and register indirect addressing to access the array sequentially. Register indirect addressing is also used as EBX and EDX point at *min* and *max*, in this case the doublewords allocated for *minimum* and *maximum*, respectively, in the test driver. As an alternative to starting *min* at the largest possible integer and *max* at the smallest possible integer, each could have been initialized to the first array element's value. This takes slightly more code. Figure 6.13 shows a debugger window with the program paused following the call; the memory window has been set to start at the address of *minimum*.

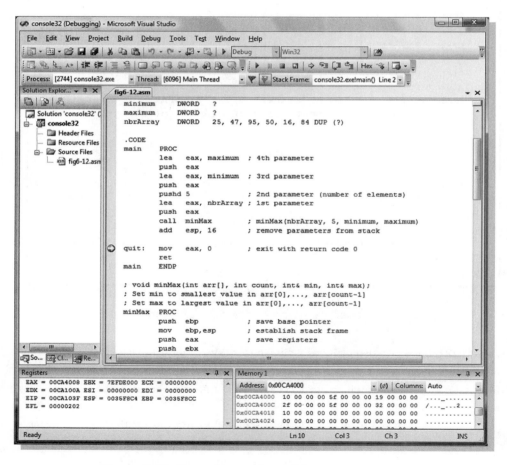

Figure 6.13 Procedure using address parameters

- save EBP and establish stack frame
- **subtract number of bytes of local space from ESP**
- save registers used by procedure

- access parameter values using based addressing in procedure body
- return value, if any, goes in EAX

- restore saved registers
- **copy EBP to ESP**
- restore EBP
- return

Figure 6.14 Procedure code with local variable space

Procedure *minMax* required the use of several registers in its implementation. Using registers is almost always preferable to using memory but there simply aren't enough of them to implement complex algorithms. Some procedures need to have local variables in memory. The standard way to do this is to allocate space for them on the stack. Figure 6.14 outlines procedure code to do this. It is a minor modification of the right side of Figure 6.11 with the new steps shown in bold.

Here is a simplified, not-to-scale picture of the stack with local storage reserved.

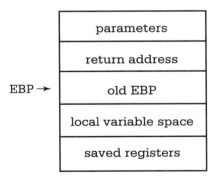

Just as doubleword parameters above the reference point can be referenced by [ebp+8], [ebp+12], and so on. The first doubleword in the local variable space below the reference point can be accessed by [ebp-4], the next below by [ebp-8], and so on. C and C++ compilers normally allocate all local variables on the stack. There are several difficulties with doing this in assembly language, not the least of which is remembering where a particular local variable is stored in the stack.

The two new steps are obviously implemented by **sub   esp,n** and **mov esp,ebp**, where *n* is the number of bytes of local storage you want to reserve. You may be wondering why the "deallocation" step isn't **add   esp,n**. The answer is that it could be, but the **mov** instruction is both simpler and safer. It is safer because it will still restore the correct value to ESP even if the saved registers were not properly popped off the stack.

A **recursive** procedure or function is one that calls itself, either directly or indirectly. The best algorithms for manipulating many data structures are recursive. It is frequently very difficult to code certain algorithms in a programming language that does not support recursion.

It is almost as easy to code a recursive procedure in 80x86 assembly language as it is to code a non-recursive procedure. If parameters are passed on the stack and local variables are stored on the stack, then each call of the procedure gets new storage allocated for its parameters and local variables. There is no danger of the arguments passed to one call of a procedure being confused with those for another call because each call has its own stack frame. If registers are properly saved and restored, then the same registers can be used by each call of the procedure.

This section gives one example of a recursive procedure in 80x86 assembly language. It solves the Towers of Hanoi puzzle, pictured in Figure 6.15 with four disks. The object of the puzzle is to move all disks from source spindle A to destination spindle B, one at a time, never placing a larger disk on top of a smaller disk. Disks can be moved to spindle C, a spare spindle. For instance, if there are only two disks, the small disk can be

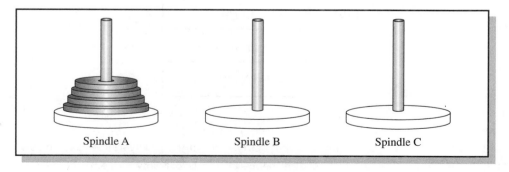

Figure 6.15 Towers of Hanoi puzzle

moved from spindle A to C, the large one can be moved from A to B, and finally the small one can be moved from C to B.

In general, the Towers of Hanoi puzzle is solved by looking at two cases. If there is only one disk, then the single disk is simply moved from the source spindle to the destination. If the number of disks *nbrDisks* is greater than one, then the top (*nbrDisks*-1) disks are moved to the spare spindle, the largest one is moved to the destination, and finally the (*nbrDisks*-1) smaller disks are moved from the spare spindle to the destination. Each time (*nbrDisks*-1) disks are moved, exactly the same procedure is followed, except that different spindles have the roles of source, destination, and spare. Figure 6.16 expresses the algorithm in pseudocode.

Figure 6.17 lists 80x86 code that implements the design as a *windows32* program. The code is a fairly straightforward translation of the pseudocode design, with each recursive procedure call in *move* implemented just like the call in the main program. Note that although the spindles are designated by single characters, these characters are passed in doublewords to ensure that the stack stays on a doubleword boundary. A high-level language compiler would probably calculate *nbrDisks-1* twice—once for each recursive call where it is used—but we can be a little more efficient and calculate it

```
procedure move(nbrDisks, source, destination, spare);
begin
    if NbrDisks = 1
    then
        display "Move disk from ", source, " to ", destination
    else
        move(nbrDisks-1, source, spare, destination);
        move(1, source, destination, spare);
        move(nbrDisks-1, spare, destination, source);
    end if;
end procedure move;

begin {main program}
    prompt for and input number;
    move(number, 'A', 'B', 'C');
end;
```

Figure 6.16 Pseudocode for Towers of Hanoi Solution

```
; program to print instructions for "Towers of Hanoi" puzzle
; author: R. Detmer
; revised: 6/2008
.586
.MODEL FLAT
INCLUDE io.h
.STACK 4096

.DATA
prompt BYTE   "How many disks?",0
number BYTE   16 DUP (?)
outLbl BYTE   "Move disk", 0
outMsg BYTE   "from spindle "
source BYTE   ?, 0ah, 0dh
    BYTE   'to spindle '
dest   BYTE   ?, 0

.CODE
_MainProc PROC
    mov   al,'C'     ; argument 4: 'C'
    push  eax
    mov   al,'B'     ; argument 3: 'B'
    push  eax
    mov   al,'A'     ; argument 2: 'A'
    push  eax
    input prompt, number,16   ; read ASCII characters
    atod  number      ; convert to integer
    push  eax        ; argument 1: number
    call  move       ; Move(number,Source,Dest,Spare)
    add   esp,16     ; remove parameters from stack

    mov   eax, 0 ; exit with return code 0
    ret
_MainProc ENDP

move   PROC NEAR32
; procedure move(nbrDisks : integer; { number of disks to move }
;        source, dest, spare : character { spindles to use } )
; all parameters are passed in doublewords on the stack

    push  ebp         ; save base pointer
    mov   ebp,esp     ; establish stack frame
```

(continued)

Figure 6.17 Towers of Hanoi solution

```
    push  eax       ; save registers
    push  ebx

    cmp  DWORD PTR [ebp+8],1 ; nbrDisks = 1?
    jne  elseMore    ; skip if more than 1
    mov  ebx,[ebp+12]  ; source
    mov  source,bl    ; copy character to output
    mov  ebx,[ebp+16]  ; destination
    mov  dest,bl     ; copy character to output
    output outLbl, outMsg ; display move instruction
    jmp  endIfOne    ; return
elseMore:
    mov  eax,[ebp+8]   ; get nbrDisks
    dec  eax        ; nbrDisks - 1
    push  DWORD PTR [ebp+16] ; par 4: old destination is new spare
    push  DWORD PTR [ebp+20] ; par 3: old spare is new destination
    push  DWORD PTR [ebp+12] ; par 2: source does not change
    push  eax       ; par 1: nbrDisks-1
    call  move       ; move(nbrDisks-1,source,spare,destination)
    add  esp,16      ; remove parameters from stack

    push  DWORD PTR [ebp+20] ; par 4: spare unchanged
    push  DWORD PTR [ebp+16] ; par 3: destination unchanged
    push  DWORD PTR [ebp+12] ; par 2: source does not change
    pushd 1         ; par 1: 1
    call  move       ; move(1,source,destination,spare)
    add  esp,16      ; remove parameters from stack

    push  DWORD PTR [ebp+12] ; par 4: original source is spare
    push  DWORD PTR [ebp+16] ; par 3: original destination
    push  DWORD PTR [ebp+20] ; par 2: source is original spare
    push  eax       ; parameter 1: nbrDisks-1
    call  move       ; move(nbrDisks-1,spare,destination,source)
    add  esp,16      ; remove parameters from stack
endIfOne:
    pop  ebx       ; restore registers
    pop  eax
    pop  ebp        ; restore base pointer
    ret          ; return
move  ENDP
END
```

Figure 6.17 Towers of Hanoi solution *(continued)*

just one time. This value is computed in EAX and will be there after the intervening code because subsequent calls save and restore EAX. The last thing to note is that variables in the data section are used by procedure *move*. In general, use of global variables is discouraged, but here it is simpler and more efficient than allocating local variables on the stack. They are only being used for display of a single instruction and do not need to be preserved between calls. Figure 6.18 shows a sample run of this program.

One of the reasons for using procedures is so that code that performs a useful task can be reused in other programs. Although you can always just copy and paste code from one program to another, it is often more convenient to package a procedure in a separate file, and then simply include the file in another project. We now return to the first example of this section and show how it can be split into separate files. The test-driver code is shown in Figure 6.19 and the procedure code is in Figure 6.20. There is lit-

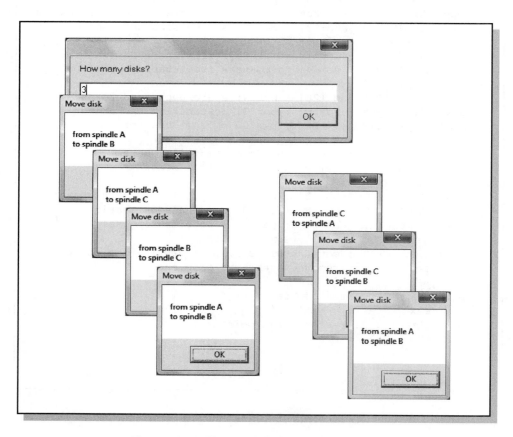

Figure 6.18 Towers of Hanoi sample run

```
; and test driver for minMax
; author: R. Detmer
; date: 6/2008

.586
.MODEL FLAT
.STACK 4096

.DATA
minimum    DWORD   ?
maximum    DWORD   ?
nbrArray   DWORD   25, 47, 95, 50, 16, 84 DUP (?)

EXTERN minMax:PROC

.CODE
main  PROC
    lea   eax, maximum ; 4th parameter
    push eax
    lea   eax, minimum ; 3rd parameter
    push eax
    pushd 5         ; 2nd parameter (number of elements)
    lea   eax, nbrArray ; 1st parameter
    push eax
    call minMax     ; minMax(nbrArray, 5, minimum, maximum)
    add   esp, 16    ; remove parameters from stack

quit:  mov   eax, 0    ; exit with return code 0
    ret
main  ENDP
END
```

Figure 6.19 Test driver for *minMax* in separate file

tle new here except that the test-driver file needs an **EXTERN** directive to identify *minMax* as a procedure. The procedure file must repeat directives that are also used in the test-driver file: **.586**, **.MODEL FLAT**, **.CODE** and **END**. It is not necessary to have another **.STACK** directive, and in a *windows32* program **INCLUDE io.h** is only needed if the procedure is using the macros defined in *io.h*.

How can you call a high-level language procedure from assembly language or an assembly language procedure from a high-level language? The answer is by carefully following the calling protocol used by the compiler for the high-level language. The

```
; procedure minMax to find smallest and largest elements in an array
; author: R. Detmer   date: 6/2008
.586
.MODEL FLAT
.CODE
; void minMax(int arr[], int count, int& min, int& max);
; Set min to smallest value in arr[0],..., arr[count-1]
; Set max to largest value in arr[0],..., arr[count-1]
minMax PROC
    push ebp       ; save base pointer
    mov  ebp,esp   ; establish stack frame
    push eax       ; save registers
    push ebx
    push ecx
    push edx
    push esi

    mov  esi,[ebp+8]  ; get address of array arr
    mov  ecx,[ebp+12] ; get value of count
    mov  ebx, [ebp+16] ; get address of min
    mov  edx, [ebp+20] ; get address of max

    mov  DWORD PTR [ebx], 7fffffffh ; largest possible integer
    mov  DWORD PTR [edx], 80000000h ; smallest possible integer
    jecxz exitCode    ; exit if there are no elements

forLoop:
    mov  eax, [esi]  ; a[i]
    cmp  eax, [ebx]  ; a[i] < min?
    jnl  endIfSmaller ; skip if not
    mov  [ebx], eax  ; min := a[i]
endIfSmaller:
    cmp  eax, [edx]  ; a[i] > max?
    jng  endIfLarger ; skip if not
    mov  [edx], eax  ; max := a[i]
endIfLarger:
    add  esi, 4    ; point at next array element
    loop forLoop     ; repeat for each element of array

exitCode:
    pop  esi      ; restore registers
    pop  edx
    pop  ecx
    pop  ebx
    pop  eax
    pop  ebp
    ret           ; return
minMax ENDP
END
```

Figure 6.20 *minMax* in separate file

Visual Studio C compiler uses the *cdecl* protocol. The *windows32* projects that you have been using for programs with input and output already do this. For example, the file *framework.c* contains the code

```
int MainProc(void);
// prototype for user's main program

int WINAPI WinMain(HINSTANCE hInstance, HINSTANCE
hPrevInstance,
  LPSTR lpCmdLine, int nCmdShow)
{
  _hInstance = hInstance;
  return MainProc();
}
```

Execution begins with *WinMain* that basically just calls your assembly language procedure *MainProc*. However, recall that the name of your procedure is not *MainProc*, but *_MainProc*. The code generated by the C compiler follows the *cdecl* **text decoration** convention of appending a leading underscore. In general, to call an assembly language procedure from a Visual Studio C program, prototype the function to describe it, name the assembly language procedure with the same name prefixed with an underscore, and follow the *cdecl* protocols in the assembly language code.

A *windows32* project also calls C functions in *framework.c* from expansions of the *output* and *input* macros. For example, the definition code for the *output* macro contains

```
lea   eax,outStr      ; string address
push  eax             ; string parameter on stack
lea   eax,outLbl      ; label address
push  eax             ; string parameter on stack
call  _showOutput     ; showOutput(outLbl, outStr)
add   esp, 8          ; remove parameters
```

This is clearly a call to procedure *_showOutput*, which is *showOutput* in *framework.c*. The assembly language code must add the underscore to the name because the assembler does not decorate the name, but the C compiler will. In general, text decoration is only a concern when you are mixing high-level and assembly language procedures, not when you are entirely writing in assembly language where no text decoration is generated or in C where the compiler takes care of text decoration automatically.

The Visual Studio programming environment uses several other procedure protocols, one of which is **stdcall**. The *stdcall* protocol is similar to *cdecl*, the biggest differences being that the procedure rather than the caller must remove parameters from the stack (which makes the **ret** instruction with an operand very handy!) and the text decoration convention is much more complex, involving not only a leading underscore but a trailing at sign (@) followed by a decimal number that is the number of bytes of parameters. The **fastcall** protocol gives yet another set of conventions. With *fastcall*, parameters are passed in registers. The important point here is that when you are mixing assembly language and a high-level language, you must know what protocol the high-level language compiler is using and follow it carefully.

Exercises 6.3

*1. Give entry code and exit code for a procedure that reserves 8 bytes of storage on the stack for local variables. Assuming that this space is used for two doublewords, give the based address with which each local variable can be referenced.

2. Figure 6.11 gave the steps for calling code and procedure code using the *cdecl* protocol. Write down the corresponding lists for the *stdcall* protocol.

Programming Exercises 6.3

For each of these exercises follow the *cdecl* protocol for the specified procedure and write a short *console32* or *windows32* test-driver program to test the assembly language procedure.

1. Suppose that a procedure is described in C/C++ by void toUpper(char str[]), that is, its name is *toUpper*, and it has a single parameter that is the address of an array of characters. Assuming that the character string is null-terminated, implement *toUpper* so that it changes each lowercase letter in the string to its uppercase equivalent, leaving all other characters unchanged.

2. Suppose that a procedure is described in C/C++ by int upperCount(char str[]), that is, its name is *upperCount*, it has a single parameter that is the address of an array of characters, and it returns an integer. Assuming that the character string is null-terminated, implement *upperCount* so that it returns a count of how many uppercase letters appear in the string.

3. Programing Exercise 5.5.5 gave the selection sort algorithm. Implement this algorithm in a procedure whose C/C++ description could be

```
void selectionSort(int nbrArray[], int nbrElts)
; sort nbrArray[0] .. nbrArray[nbrElts-1]
; into increasing order using selection sort
```

The first parameter will be the address of the array.

4. Write a procedure *avg* to find the average of a collection of doubleword integers in an array. Procedure *avg* will have three parameters in the following order:

   (1) The address of the array.

   (2) The number of integers in the array (passed as a doubleword).

   (3) The address of a doubleword at which to store the result.

5. Write a value-returning procedure *search* to search an array of doublewords for a specified doubleword value. Procedure *search* will have three parameters:

   (1) The value for which to search (a doubleword integer).

   (2) The address of the array.

   (3) The number n of doublewords in the array (passed as a doubleword).

   Return the position $(1,2,...,n)$ at which the value is found, or return 0 if the value does not appear in the array.

6. The factorial function is defined for a nonnegative integer argument n by

$$factorial(n) = \begin{cases} 1 \text{ if } n = 0 \\ n \times factorial(n-1) \text{ if } n > 0 \end{cases}$$

   Write a value-returning procedure named *factorial* that implements this recursive definition.

7. The greatest common divisor (GCD) of two positive integers m and n can be calculated recursively by the function described below in pseudocode.

```
function gcd(m, n : integer) : integer;
if n = 0
then
    return m;
else
    remainder := m mod n;
    return gcd(n, remainder);
end if;
```

Write a value-returning procedure named *gcd* that implements this recursive definition.

6.4 64-Bit Procedures

This section describes the differences in the 32-bit procedure protocol and the 64-bit procedure protocol. First we look at the additional **push** and **pop** instructions available in 64-bit mode. These are shown in Figures 6.21 and 6.22. The entries in these tables are very similar to those for 32-bit mode instructions (see Figures 6.1 and 6.5 in this chapter's first section). There are entries for all 16 64-bit general registers. The REX prefix 41 is used for R8–R15.

One important difference in 32- and 64-bit modes is that you cannot use 32-bit register or memory operands with 64-bit **push** and **pop** instructions. The available immediate operands sizes for **push** remain byte, word, and doubleword—quadword is not added. Also, the **pushad** and **popad** instructions in 32-bit mode do not exist in 64-bit mode, nor are there instructions to push and pop all 16 64-bit registers.

Operand	Opcode	Bytes of Object Code
64-bit mode		
RAX or R8	50	1
RCX or R9	51	1
RDX or R10	52	1
RBX or R11	53	1
RSP or R12	54	1
RBP or R13	55	1
RSI or R14	56	1
RDI or R15	57	1
memory word	FF	2+
memory quadword	FF	2+
immediate byte	6A	2
immediate word	68	3
immediate doubleword	68	5

Figure 6.21 64-bit mode push instructions

Operand	Opcode	Bytes of Object Code
64-bit mode		
RAX or R8	58	1
RCX or R9	59	1
RDX or R10	5A	1
RBX or R11	5B	1
RSP or R12	5C	1
RBP or R13	5D	1
RSI or R14	5E	1
RDI or R15	5F	1
memory word	8F	2+
memory quadword	8F	2+

Figure 6.22 64-bit mode pop instructions

Just as it is important to keep the stack on a doubleword boundary in a 32-bit environment, it is important to keep it on a quadword boundary in a 64-bit environment. Therefore, you almost always push and pop quadwords.

The 64-bit versions of instructions **call** and **ret** are very similar to the 32-bit versions. The tables for **call** and **ret** instructions are not repeated since they are exactly the same tables as in 32-bit instructions mode shown in Figures 6.8 and 6.9. A **push** instruction pushes a 64-bit return address onto the stack before loading RIP with the procedure's address, and a **pop** instruction pops the 64-bit return address from the stack into RIP.

Where the 64-bit protocol is most different is in parameter conventions. With the 32-bit architecture, registers are often a scarce resource. The 64-bit architecture doubles the number of available registers, making it more practical to pass arguments in registers and the 64-bit protocol takes advantage of this. Arguments that can be passed as quadwords (including bytes, words, and doublewords) are extended to quadword length, if necessary. The first four arguments are always passed in the registers shown in Figure 6.23. Additional arguments, if any, are passed on the stack.

In a 64-bit environment, a calling procedure must reserve space on the stack for arguments. Normally, the procedure does this in entry code. The *windows64* programs in this book start with

```
sub     rsp, 120   ; reserve stack space for MainProc
```

Argument	Register
1	RCX
2	RDX
3	R8
4	R9

Figure 6.23 64-bit registers used to pass arguments

that generates enough space for 15 quadwords. The bottom part of the reserved space is reserved for arguments. If there is a fifth argument, then it is copied to [RSP+32], a sixth to [RSP+40], and so on. After the return address (8 bytes) is pushed on the stack, the called procedure will then find these values at [RSP+40], [RSP+48], and so on. Why start 32 bytes from the bottom? This is to leave space in the stack for the first four parameters, even though they are in the registers. The called procedure can use this space to copy any of the first four argument values.

Registers can be pushed by entry code and popped by exit code similar to the way they are done in the 32-bit environment. However, this is usually done before the local stack space is reserved. Once the local stack space is established, there should be no change to RSP before a subsequent procedure is called. This makes it possible to use RSP and based addressing to locate parameters and local variables. However, you can use RBP as a frame pointer if needed.

RAX is used to return a single quadword value. Microsoft documentation labels registers RAX, RCX, RDX, and R8–R11 as **volatile**, meaning that the called procedure is free to change them. Similarly, RBX, RDI, RSI, RBP, RSP, and R12–R15 are called **nonvolatile**, meaning that a called procedure has the responsibility of preserving them. In practice, sometimes it is safest to preserve any register that you don't want destroyed by a called procedure. For example, in *windows64* projects, the *atod* macro includes the code

```
mov     [rsp+32], rcx   ; save register used to pass parameters
mov     [rsp+40], rbx   ; save registers destroyed by atodproc
mov     [rsp+48], rdx
lea     rcx,source      ; source address to rcx
call    atodproc        ; call atodproc(source)
```

```
mov     rcx, [rsp+32]   ; restore register used to pass parameters
mov     rbx, [rsp+40]   ; restore registers destroyed by atodproc
mov     rdx, [rsp+48]
```

Notice that the registers are saved in the stack area above the area reserved for copying the first four parameters. This code preserves RBX even though it should be nonvolatile.

Figure 6.24 shows the listing of a *console64* version of the program whose *console32* version appeared in Figure 6.12. It is noticeably simpler than the 32-bit version.

```
; procedure minMax to find smallest and largest elements in an
; array and test driver for minMax    —    64-bit version
; author: R. Detmer
; date: 7/2008

.DATA
minimum    QWORD   ?
maximum    QWORD   ?
nbrArray   QWORD   25, 47, 95, 50, 16, 95 DUP (?)

.CODE
main       PROC
           sub  rsp, 32        ; local stack space
           lea  rcx, nbrArray  ; 1st parameter
           mov  rdx, 5         ; 2nd parameter (number of elements)
           lea  r8, minimum    ; 3rd parameter
           lea  r9, maximum    ; 4th parameter
           call minMax     ; minMax(nbrArray, 5, minimum, maximum)

quit:      add  rsp, 32    ; clean up stack
           mov  rax, 0     ; exit with return code 0
           ret
main       ENDP

; void minMax(int arr[], int count, int& min, int& max);
; Set min to smallest value in arr[0],..., arr[count-1]
; Set max to largest value in arr[0],..., arr[count-1]
minMax PROC
    push rax        ; save registers
    push rsi
```

(continued)

Figure 6.24 Procedure using address parameters

```
        mov  rsi,rcx  ; get address of array arr (1st parameter)
        mov  rcx,rdx  ; get value of count (2nd parameter)

        mov  rax, 7fffffffffffffffh ; largest possible integer
        mov  QWORD PTR [r8], rax
        mov  rax, 8000000000000000h ; smallest possible integer
        mov  QWORD PTR [r9], rax
        jrcxz exitCode    ; exit if there are no elements

forLoop:
    mov  rax, [rsi]   ; a[i]
    cmp  rax, [r8]    ; a[i] < min?
    jnl  endIfSmaller ; skip if not
    mov  [r8], rax    ; min := a[i]
endIfSmaller:
    cmp  rax, [r9]    ; a[i] > max?
    jng  endIfLarger  ; skip if not
    mov  [r9], rax    ; max := a[i]
endIfLarger:
    add  rsi, 8       ; point at next array element
    loop forLoop      ; repeat for each element of array

exitCode:
    pop  rsi     ; restore registers
    pop  rax
    ret          ; return
minMax ENDP
END
```

Figure 6.24 Procedure using address parameters

The four arguments are simply placed in registers and then used in the procedure. The procedure *minMax* itself does not call additional procedures, so does not need to establish local stack space. One difference is that the 32-bit *minMax* simply places the largest and smallest possible values in the caller's data at the addresses passed in the third and fourth parameters, respectively, but since there is no immediate quadword to memory **mov** in the 64-bit architecture the immediate values are first placed in RAX and then copied to their destinations.

We conclude this section with an example of an assembly language procedure called from a C main program. The C test driver is shown in Figure 6.25 and the assem-

```
/* C test driver for assembly language procedure add5 */
/* author: R. Detmer */
/* date: 7/2008 */

int add5(int x1, int x2, int x3, int x4, int x5);
/* returns sum of arguments */

#include <stdio.h>

int main()
{
    int a=5;
    int b=7;
    int c=9;

    int sum;

    sum = add5(a, 6, b, 8, c);
    printf("The sum is %d\n", sum);
    return 0;
}
```

Figure 6.25 C test driver for 64-bit procedure

bly language procedure is shown in Figure 6.26. These are separate source files in a *console64* project. One of the satisfying things about this program is that if you launch it with control-F5, you can actually see the output in the console window!

You may wonder why *add5* uses EAX instead of RAX to accumulate the sum. With the Visual Studio 2008 C compiler, an `int` is a 32-bit integer. The C compiler passes the five arguments in quadwords, but the high-order half of each quadword is undefined, so *add5* just adds the low-order doublewords that contain the integers. This C compiler uses `long long` to designate a quadword integer; `long int` is still 32 bits.

Another point of this example is to show how a fifth argument is handled in a procedure—in this case it is located at [RSP+40] since no registers needed to be saved in *add5*. Finally, note that the C compiler did not use text decoration so that the called procedure could be named simply *add5*.

```
; procedure add5 to add five parameters
; 64-bit version
; author: R. Detmer
; date: 7/2008

.CODE

; void add5(int x1, int x2, int x3, int x4, int x5);
; returns sum of arguments
add5    PROC
        mov  eax, ecx     ; x1
        add  eax, edx     ; x2
        add  eax, r8d     ; x3
        add  eax, r9d     ; x4
        add  eax, DWORD PTR [rsp+40]    ; x5
        ret               ; return
add5    ENDP
END
```

Figure 6.26 64-bit procedure to add five integers

Exercises 6.4

1. Suppose that the entry code for a 64-bit procedure saves no register and reserves no local stack space. How do you find each of the following quadword parameter values in the body of the procedure?

   (a) parameter 1   *(b) parameter 3

   (c) parameter 5   *(d) parameter 7

2. Suppose that the entry code for a 64-bit procedure is

   ```
   push   rsi
   push   r12
   ```

   How do you find each of the following quadword parameter values in the body of the procedure?

   (a) parameter 1   *(b) parameter 3

   (c) parameter 5   *(d) parameter 7

3. Suppose that the entry code for a 64-bit procedure is

   ```
   push   rsi
   push   r12
   sub    rsp, 48
   ```

How do you find each of the following quadword parameter values in the body of the procedure?

(a) parameter 1   *(b) parameter 3

(c) parameter 5   *(d) parameter 7

Programming Exercises 6.4

For each of these exercises follow the 64-bit protocol for the specified procedure and write a short *console64* or *windows64* test-driver program to test the procedure.

1. Write a value-returning procedure *min2* to find the smaller of two quadword integer parameters.

2. Write a value-returning procedure *max6* to find the largest of six quadword integer parameters.

3. Suppose that a value-returning procedure is described in C/C++ by int alphaCount(char str[]), that is, its name is *alphaCount*, it has a single parameter that is the address of an array of characters, and it returns a doubleword integer. Assuming that the character string is null-terminated, implement *alphaCount* so that it returns a count of how many letters (lowercase or uppercase) appear in the string.

4. Programing Exercise 5.5.5 gave the selection sort algorithm. Implement this algorithm in a procedure whose C/C++ description could be

```
void selectionSort(long long nbrArray[], int nbrElts)
; sort nbrArray[0] .. nbrArray[nbrElts-1]
; into increasing order using selection sort
```

The first parameter will be the address of the array. Notice that the array is an array of quadwords and the count of how many elements is a doubleword.

5. Write a procedure *avg* to find the average of a collection of quadword integers in an array. Procedure *avg* will have three parameters in the following order:

(1) The address of the array.

(2) The number of integers in the array (passed as a doubleword).

(3) The address of a doubleword at which to store the result.

6. The factorial function is defined for a nonnegative integer argument n by

$$factorial(n) = \begin{cases} 1 \text{ if } n = 0 \\ n \times factorial(n-1) \text{ if } n > 0 \end{cases}$$

Write a value-returning procedure named *factorial* that implements this recursive definition. Pass the argument as a doubleword integer, but return a quadword result.

6.5   Macro Definition and Expansion

A macro was defined in Chapter 3 as a statement that is shorthand for a sequence of other statements. The assembler expands a macro to the statements it represents, and then assembles these new statements. The *windows32* and *windows64* programs in previous chapters have made extensive use of macros defined in the file *io.h*. This section explains how to write macro definitions and tells how the assembler uses these definitions to expand macros into other statements.

A macro definition resembles a procedure definition in a high-level language. The first line gives the name of the macro being defined and a list of parameters; the main part of the definition consists of a collection of model statements that describe the action of the macro in terms of the parameters. A macro is called much like a high-level language procedure, too—the name of the macro is followed by a list of arguments.

These similarities are superficial. A procedure call in a high-level language is compiled into a sequence of instructions to push parameters on the stack followed by a **call** instruction, whereas a macro call actually expands into statements given in the macro, with the arguments substituted for the parameters used in the macro definition. Code in a macro is repeated every time a macro is called, but there is just one copy of the code for a procedure. Macros often execute more rapidly than procedure calls since there is no overhead for passing parameters or for **call** and **ret** instructions, but this is usually at the cost of more bytes of object code.

Every macro definition is bracketed by **MACRO** and **ENDM** directives. The format of a macro definition is

```
name   MACRO   list of parameters
       assembly language statements
       ENDM
```

The parameters in the **MACRO** directive are ordinary symbols, separated by commas. The assembly language statements may use the parameters as well as registers, immediate operands, or symbols defined outside the macro. The statements may even include macro calls.

```
add2    MACRO nbr1, nbr2
; put sum of two doubleword parameters in EAX
        mov   eax, nbr1
        add   eax, nbr2
        ENDM
```

Figure 6.27 Macro to add two integers

A macro definition can appear anywhere in an assembly language source code file as long as the definition comes before the first statement that calls the macro. It is good programming practice to place macro definitions near the beginning of a source file or in a separate file that is included with the **INCLUDE** directive.

This section gives several examples of macro definitions and macro calls. Figure 6.27 lists the definition of a macro *add2* that finds the sum of two parameters, putting the result in the EAX register. The parameters used to define the macro are *nbr1* and *nbr2*. These labels are local to the definition. The same names could be used for other purposes in the program, although some human confusion might result.

The statements to which **add2** expands depends on the arguments used in a call. For example, the macro call

```
add2 value, 30   ; value + 30
```

expands to

```
; put sum of two doubleword parameters in EAX
mov   eax, value
add   eax, 30
```

The statement

```
add2 value1, value2   ; value1 + value2
```

expands to

```
; put sum of two doubleword parameters in EAX
mov   eax, value1
add   eax, value2
```

The macro call

```
add2 eax, ebx    ; sum of two values
```

expands to

```
; put sum of two doubleword parameters in EAX
mov   eax, eax
add   eax, ebx
```

Note that the instruction **mov eax, eax** is legal, even if it accomplishes nothing.

However, the macro call

```
add2 ebx, eax    ; sum of two values
```

expands to

```
; put sum of two doubleword parameters in EAX
mov   eax, ebx
add   eax, eax
```

that will double the value in EBX, not add the values in EBX and EAX.

In each of these examples the first argument is substituted for the first parameter *nbr1* and the second argument is substituted for the second parameter *nbr2*. Each macro results in **mov** and **add** instructions, but because the types of arguments differ, the object code will vary.

If one of the arguments is missing, the macro will still be expanded. For instance, the macro

```
add2 value
```

expands to

```
; put sum of two doubleword parameters in EAX
mov eax, value
add   eax,
```

The argument *value* replaces *nbr1* and an empty string replaces *nbr2*. The assembler will report an error, but it will be for the illegal **add** instruction that results from the macro expansion, not directly because of the missing argument.

Similarly, the macro call

```
add2   , value
```

expands to

```
; put sum of two doubleword parameters in EAX
mov   eax,
add   eax, value
```

The comma in the macro call separates the first missing argument from the second argument, *value*. An empty argument replaces the parameter *nbr1*. The assembler will again report an error, this time for the illegal **mov** instruction.

Note again that the definition and expansion for the *add2* macro contain no **ret** instruction. Although macros look much like procedures, they generate in-line code when the macro call is expanded at assembly time.

Figure 6.28 shows the definition of a macro *swap* that will exchange the contents of two doublewords in memory. It is very similar to the 80x86 **xchg** instruction that will not work with two memory operands.

As with the *add2* macro, the code generated by calling the *swap* macro depends on the arguments used. For example, the call

```
swap [ebx], [ebx+4]  ; swap adjacent words in array
```

expands to

```
; exchange two doublewords in memory
    push  eax
    mov   eax, [ebx]
    xchg  eax, [ebx+4]
    mov   [ebx], eax
    pop   eax
```

It might not be obvious to the user that the *swap* macro uses the EAX register, so the **push** and **pop** instructions in the macro protect the user from unexpectedly losing the contents of this register.

```
swap    MACRO dword1, dword2
; exchange two doublewords in memory
    push  eax
    mov   eax, dword1
    xchg  eax, dword2
    mov   dword1, eax
    pop   eax
    ENDM
```

Figure 6.28 Macro to swap two memory words

```
min2    MACRO first, second
; put smaller of two doublewords in the EAX register
     LOCAL endIfMin
     mov   eax, first
     cmp   eax, second
     jle   endIfMin
     mov   eax, second
endIfMin:
     ENDM
```

Figure 6.29 Macro to find smaller of two memory words

Figure 6.29 gives a definition of a macro *min2* that finds the minimum of two doubleword signed integers, putting the smaller in the EAX register. The code for this macro must implement a design with an *if* statement, and such a design usually has at least one assembly language statement with a label. If an ordinary label were used, then it would appear every time a *min2* macro call was expanded and the assembler would produce error messages because of duplicate labels. The solution is to use a **LOCAL** directive to define a symbol *endIfMin* that is local to the *min2* macro.

The **LOCAL** directive is used only within a macro definition and goes at the beginning of the definition. It lists one or more symbols, separated by commas, that are used within the macro definition. Each time the macro is expanded and one of these symbols is needed, it is replaced by a symbol starting with two question marks and ending with four hexadecimal digits (??0000, ??0001, etc.). The same *??dddd* symbol replaces the local symbol each instance the local symbol is used in one particular expansion of a macro call. The same symbols may be listed in **LOCAL** directives in different macro definitions or may be used as regular symbols in code outside of macro definitions.

The macro call

```
min2  [ebx], ecx  ; find smaller of two values
```

might expand to the code

```
; put smaller of two doublewords in the EAX register
     mov   eax, [ebx]
     cmp   eax, ecx
     jle   ??000C
     mov   eax, ecx
??000C:
```

Here, *endIfMin* has been replaced the two instances it appears within the macro definition by *??000C* in the expansion. Another expansion of the same macro in a single file would have a different number after the question marks.

The assembler has several directives that control how macros and other statements are shown in listing files. The most useful are

- `.LIST` that causes statements to be included in the listing file,
- `.NOLIST` that completely suppresses the listing of all statements, and
- `.NOLISTMACRO` that selectively suppresses macro expansions while allowing the programmer's original statements to be listed.

The file *io.h* ends starts with a `.NOLIST` directive so that macro definitions do not clutter the listing of a program that includes it. Similarly *io.h* ends with `.NOLISTMACRO` and `.LIST` directives so that macro expansion listings do not obscure the programmer's code, but original statements are listed.

We conclude this section by looking at two of the macro definitions in *io.h*. Figure 6.30 shows the *atod* and *dtoa* macro definitions. Like the other macro definitions in

```
atod       MACRO   source          ; convert ASCII string to integer in EAX
           lea     eax,source      ; source address to AX
           push    eax             ; source parameter on stack
           call    atodproc        ; call atodproc(source)
           add     esp, 4          ; remove parameter
           ENDM

dtoa       MACRO   dest,source     ; convert double to ASCII string
           push    ebx             ; save EBX
           lea     ebx, dest       ; destination address
           push    ebx             ; destination parameter
           mov     ebx, [esp+4]    ; in case source was EBX
           mov     ebx, source     ; source value
           push    ebx             ; source parameter
           call    dtoaproc        ; call dtoaproc(source,dest)
           add     esp, 8          ; remove parameters
           pop     ebx             ; restore EBX
           ENDM
```

Figure 6.30 *atod* and *dtoa* macro definitions

io.h, these simply expand to procedure calls, and the real work is done by the procedures. The expansion of *atod* is simpler, both because it has only one parameter, and because *atodproc* returns the needed value in EAX. This means that EAX can also be used temporarily to push the necessary parameter onto the stack.

The situation is more complicated with *dtoa*. There is no safe choice of a register to use to push parameter values onto the stack. You can save and restore any register—here EBX is used—but if that register contains the source value, then its contents will be destroyed when the destination parameter is handled. To ensure that the expansion works even when the original source argument is EBX, the instruction **mov ebx,[esp+4]** restores the original value of EBX after handling the destination parameter and before handling the source parameter. This could have been accomplished by a pair of **pop** and **push** instructions.

Exercises 6.5

1. Using the macro definition for *add2* given in Figure 6.27, show the sequence of statements to which each of the following macro calls expands.

    *(a) add2 25, ebx

    (b) add2 ecx, edx

    (c) add2   ; no argument

2. Using the macro definition for *swap* given in Figure 6.28, show the sequence of statements to which each of the following macro calls expands.

    *(a) swap value1, value2

    (b) swap temp, [ebx]

    (c) swap value

3. Using the macro definition for *min2* given in Figure 6.29, show the sequence of statements to which each of the following macro calls expands.

    *(a) min2 value1, value2

      (Assume the local symbol counter is at 000A.)

    (b) min2 ecx, value

      (Assume the local symbol counter is at 0019.)

━━━ **Programming Exercises 6.5**

Assemble each macro definition below in a short *console32* or *console64* test-driver program.

1. Write a definition of a macro *add3* that has three doubleword integer parameters and puts the sum of the three numbers in the EAX register.

2. Write a definition of a macro *max2* that has two doubleword integer parameters and puts the maximum of the two numbers in the EAX register.

3. Write a definition of a macro *min3* that has three doubleword integer parameters and puts the minimum of the three numbers in the EAX register.

4. Write a definition of a macro *toUpper* with one parameter; the address of a byte in memory. The code generated by the macro will examine the byte, and if it is the ASCII code for a lowercase letter, replace it by the ASCII code for the corresponding uppercase letter.

6.6 Chapter Summary

This chapter has discussed protocols for implementing procedures in the 80x86 architecture. There are three main concepts involved: (1) how to transfer control from a calling program to a procedure and back, (2) how to pass parameter values to a procedure and results back from the procedure, and (3) how to write procedure code that is independent of the calling program. The stack serves several important purposes in procedure implementation. When a procedure is called the address of the next instruction is stored on the stack before control transfers to the first instruction of the procedure. A return instruction retrieves this address from the stack in order to transfer control back to the correct point in the calling program. Argument values (or their addresses) can be pushed onto the stack to pass them to a procedure; when this is done, the base pointer EBP and based addressing provide a convenient mechanism for accessing the values in the procedure. The stack can be used to provide space for a procedure's local variables. The stack is also used to "preserve the environment"—for example, register contents can be pushed onto the stack when a procedure begins and popped off before returning to the calling program so that the calling program does not need to worry about what registers might be altered by the procedure.

In the 32-bit environment there are several protocols used for procedures. This chapter emphasized the *cdecl* protocol that is also used by the Visual Studio C compiler. Following this protocol makes it possible to have a C function call an assembly language procedure, or an assembly language procedure call a C function.

There is just one standard procedure protocol in the 64-bit environment. It uses registers rather than the stack to pass the first four argument values.

A macro is a statement that is shorthand for a sequence of other statements. The assembler expands a macro to the statements it represents, and then assembles these new statements.

CHAPTER 7

Bit Manipulation

A computer contains many integrated circuits that enable it to perform its functions. Each chip incorporates from a few to many thousand **logic gates**, each an elementary circuit that performs Boolean **and, or, exclusive or**, or **not** operations on bits that are represented by electronic states. The CPU is usually the most complex integrated circuit in a PC.

Previous chapters have examined the 80x86 microprocessors' instructions for moving data, performing arithmetic operations, branching, and utilizing subroutines. The 80x86 and other CPUs can also execute instructions that perform Boolean operations on multiple pairs of bits at one time. This chapter defines the Boolean operations and describes the 80x86 instructions that implement them. It also covers instructions that cause bit patterns to shift or rotate in a byte, word, or doubleword. Although bit manipulation instructions are very primitive, they are widely used in assembly language programming, often because they provide the sort of control that is rarely available in a high-level language.

7.1   Logical Operations

Many high-level languages allow variables of Boolean type, that is, variables that are capable of storing *true* or *false* values. Virtually all high-level languages allow expressions with Boolean values to be used in conditional (*if*) statements. In assembly language the Boolean value *true* is identified with the bit value 1 and the Boolean value *false* is identified with the bit value 0. Figure 7.1 gives the definitions of the Boolean operations using bit values as the operands. The *or* operation is sometimes called "inclusive or" to distinguish it from "exclusive or" (*xor*). The only difference between *or* and *xor* is for two 1 bits; 1 *or* 1 is 1, but 1 *xor* 1 is 0, that is, exclusive or corresponds to one operand or the other *true*, but not both.

bit1	*bit2*	*bit1* **and** *bit2*	(a) **and** operation
0	0	0	
0	1	0	
1	0	0	
1	1	1	

bit1	*bit2*	*bit1* **or** *bit2*	(b) **or** operation
0	0	0	
0	1	1	
1	0	1	
1	1	1	

bit1	*bit2*	*bit1* **xor** *bit2*	(c) **xor** operation
0	0	0	
0	1	1	
1	0	1	
1	1	0	

bit	**not** *bit*	(d) **not** operation
0	1	
1	0	

Figure 7.1 Definitions of logical operations

The 80x86 has **and**, **or**, **xor** and **not** instructions that implement the logical operations. The formats of these instructions are

```
and    destination, source
or     destination, source
xor    destination, source
not    destination
```

The first three instructions act on pairs of bytes, words, doublewords, or quadwords performing the logical operations on the bits in corresponding positions from the two operands. For example, when the instruction **and ebx,ecx** is executed, bit 0 from the EBX register is "anded" with bit 0 from the ECX register, bit 1 from EBX is "anded" with bit 1 from ECX, and so forth to bit 31 from EBX and bit 31 from ECX. The results of these 32 *and* operations are put in the corresponding positions in the destination EBX.

The **not** instruction has only a single operand. It changes each 0 bit in that operand to 1 and each 1 bit to 0. For example, if the AL register contains 10110110 and the instruction **not al** is executed, then the result in AL will be 01001001. This is sometimes called "taking the 1's complement" of the operand.

The **not** instruction does not affect any flag. However, each of the other three Boolean instructions affects CF, OF, PF, SF, and ZF. The carry flag CF and overflow flag OF flags are both reset to 0. The sign flag SF and the zero flag ZF are set or reset according to the value of the result of the operation. For instance, if the result is a pattern of all 0 bits, then ZF will be set to 1; if any bit of the result is not 0, then ZF will be reset to 0. The parity flag, which we have not used, is set or reset corresponding to the parity of just the low-order byte of the result.

The **and**, **or** and **xor** instructions all accept the same types of operands and require the same number of bytes of object code. They are summarized together in Figure 7.2. Information about the **not** instruction is given in Figure 7.3.

It is interesting to note that Figure 7.2 is almost identical to Figure 4.8 that showed **add** and **sub** instructions. Also, Figure 7.3 is almost identical to Figure 4.11 that showed **neg** instructions. In both cases, the available operand formats are identical and even many of the opcodes are the same. Recall that when the opcodes are the same, the *ModR/M* byte of the instruction distinguishes between **add**, **sub**, **and**, **or**, and **xor** instructions; Figure 4.9 showed the *reg* field for these instructions.

Following are some examples showing how the logical instructions work. Many hex calculators perform the logical operations directly. To compute the results by hand, you expand each hex value to binary, do the logical operations on corresponding pairs of

Destination Operand	Source Operand	Opcode			Bytes of Object Code
		and	or	xor	
register 8	immediate 8	80	80	80	3
register 16	immediate 8	83	83	83	3
register 32	immediate 8	83	83	83	3
register 16	immediate 16	81	81	81	4
register 32	immediate 32	81	81	81	6
AL	immediate 8	24	0C	34	2
AX	immediate 16	25	0D	35	3
EAX	immediate 32	25	0D	35	5
memory byte	immediate 8	80	80	80	3+
memory word	immediate 8	83	83	83	3+
memory doubleword	immediate 8	83	83	83	3+
memory word	immediate 16	81	81	81	4+
memory doubleword	immediate 32	81	81	81	6+
register 8	register 8	22	0A	32	2
register 16	register 16	23	0B	33	2
register 32	register 32	23	0B	33	2
register 8	memory byte	22	0A	32	2+
register 16	memory word	23	0B	33	2+
register 32	memory doubleword	23	0B	33	2+
memory byte	register 8	20	08	30	2+
memory word	register 16	21	09	31	2+
memory doubleword	register 32	21	09	31	2+
64-bit mode					
register 64	immediate 8	83	83	83	3
register 64	immediate 32	81	81	81	6
RAX	immediate 32	25	0D	35	5
memory quadword	immediate 8	83	83	83	3+
memory quadword	immediate 32	81	81	81	6+
register 64	register 64	23	0B	33	2
register 64	memory quadword	23	0B	33	2+
memory quadword	register 64	21	09	31	2+

Figure 7.2 and, or and xor instructions

Destination Operand	Opcode	Bytes of Object Code
register 8	F6	2
register 16	F7	2
register 32	F7	2
memory byte	F6	2+
memory word	F7	2+
memory doubleword	F7	2+
64-bit mode		
register 64	F7	2
memory quadword	F7	2+

Figure 7.3 not instruction

bits and convert the result back to hex. These expansions are shown in the examples. We have chosen word-size operands to keep the examples smaller.

Example

Before	Instruction	Bitwise Operation	After
AX: E2 75	and ax,cx	1110 0010 0111 0101 1010 1001 1101 0111 1010 0000 0101 0101	AX A0 55 SF 1 ZF 0
DX: E2 75	or dx,value	1110 0010 0111 0101 1010 1001 1101 0111 1110 1011 1111 0111	DX EB F7 SF 1 ZF 0
BX: E2 75	xor bx,0a9d7h	1110 0010 0111 0101 1010 1001 1101 0111 0100 1011 1010 0010	BX 4B A2 SF 0 ZF 0
AX: E2 75	not ax	1110 0010 0111 0101 0001 1101 1000 1010	AX 1D 8A

Each of the logical instructions has a variety of uses. One application of the **and** instruction is to clear selected bits in a destination. Note that if any bit value is "anded" with 1, the result is the original bit. On the other hand, if any bit value is "anded" with 0, the result is 0. Because of this, selected bits in a destination can be cleared by "anding" the destination with a bit pattern that has 1s in positions that are not to be changed and 0s in positions that are to be cleared.

For example, to clear all but the last 4 bits in the EAX register, the following instruction can be used.

```
and   eax, 0000000fh   ; clear high-order 28 bits of EAX
```

If EAX originally contained 4C881D7B, this *and* operation would yield 0000000B:

```
0100 1100 1000 1000 0001 1101 0111 1011 4C881D7B
0000 0000 0000 0000 0000 0000 0000 1111 0000000F
0000 0000 0000 0000 0000 0000 0000 1011 0000000B
```

Only one of the leading zeros is needed in 0000000fh, but coding seven zeros helps clarify the purpose of this operand. The trailing hex digit f corresponds to 1111 in binary, providing the four 1s that will leave the last 4 bits in EAX unchanged.

A value that is used with a logical instruction to alter bit values is often called a mask. The assembler accepts numeric values in decimal, hexadecimal, binary, and octal formats. Hex and binary are preferred for constants used as masks since the bit pattern is obvious for binary values or easy to figure out for hex values.

As illustrated above, the **and** instruction is useful when selected bits of an operand need to be cleared. The **or** instruction is useful when selected bits of an operand need to be set to 1 without changing other bits. Observe that if the value 1 is combined with either a 0 or 1 using the *or* operation, then the result is 1. However, if the value 0 is used as one operand, then the result of an *or* operation is the other operand.

The *exclusive or* instruction will complement selected bits of a byte or word without changing other bits. This works since 0 *xor* 1 is 1 and 1 *xor* 1 is 0, that is, combining any bit with 1 using an *xor* operation results in the opposite of the bit value.

A second use of logical instructions is to implement high-level language Boolean operations. One byte in memory could be used to store eight Boolean values. If such a byte is at *flags*, then the statement

```
and   flags, 11011101b   ; flag5 := false;  flag1 := false
```

assigns value *false* to bits 1 and 5, leaving the other values unchanged. (Recall that bits are numbered from right to left, starting with zero for the rightmost bit.)

If the byte in memory at *flags* is being used to store eight Boolean values, then an *or* instruction can assign *true* values to any selected bits. For instance, the instruction

```
or    flags, 00001100b    ; flag3 := true;  flag2 := true
```

assigns *true* values to bits 2 and 3 without changing the other bits.

If the byte in memory at *flags* is being used to store eight Boolean values, then an *xor* instruction can negate selected values. For instance, the design statement

flag6 := NOT flag6;

can be implemented as

```
xor   flags, 01000000b    ; flag6 := not flag6
```

A third application of logical instructions is to perform certain arithmetic operations. Suppose that the value in the EAX register is interpreted as an unsigned integer. The expression (*value* mod 32) could be computed using the following sequence of instructions.

```
mov   edx,0       ; extend value to quadword
mov   ebx,32      ; divisor
div   ebx         ; divide value by 32
```

Following these instructions, the remainder (value mod 32) will be in the EDX register. The following alternative sequence leaves the same result in the EDX register without, however, putting the quotient in EAX.

```
mov   edx,eax       ; copy value to DX
and   edx,0000001fh ; compute value mod 32
```

This choice is more efficient than the first one. It works because the value in EDX is a binary number; as a sum it is

$$bit31*2^{31} + bit30*2^{30} + \dots + bit2*2^2 + bit1*2 + bit0$$

Since each of these terms from bit31*2^{31} down to bit5*2^5 is divisible by 32 (2^5), the remainder upon division by 32 is the bit pattern represented by the trailing 5 bits, those left after masking by 0000001F. Similar instructions will work whenever the second operand of the *mod* operation is a power of 2.

A fourth use of logical instructions is to manipulate ASCII codes. Recall that the ASCII codes for digits are 30_{16} for 0, 31_{16} for 1, and so forth, to 39_{16} for 9. Suppose that the AL register contains the ASCII code for a digit, and that the corresponding integer value is needed in EAX. If the value in the high-order 24 bits in EAX is known to be zero, then the instruction

```
sub    eax, 00000030h        ; convert ASCII code to integer
```

will do the job. If the high-order bits in EAX are unknown, then the instruction

```
and    eax, 0000000fh        ; convert ASCII code to integer
```

is a much safer choice. It ensures that all but the last 4 bits of EAX are cleared. For example, if the EAX register contains 5C3DF036, junk in the high-order bits and the ASCII code for the character 6 in AL, then **and** **eax,0000000fh** produces the integer 00000006 in EAX.

The **or** instruction can be used to convert an integer value between 0 and 9 in a register to the corresponding ASCII character code. For example, if the integer is in BL, then the following instruction changes the contents of BL to the ASCII code.

```
or    bl,30h        ; convert digit to ASCII code
```

If BL contains 04, then the **or** instruction will yield 34:

```
0000 0100    04
0011 0000    30
0011 0100    34
```

With the 80x86 processors, the instruction **add** **bl,30h** does the same job using the same number of object code bytes. However, the *or* operation is more efficient than addition with some CPUs.

An **xor** instruction can be used to change the case of the ASCII code for a letter. Suppose that the CL register contains the ASCII code for some uppercase or lowercase letter. The ASCII code for an uppercase letter and the ASCII code for the corresponding lowercase letter differ only in the value of bit 5. For example, the code for the uppercase letter S is 53_{16} (01010011_2) and the code for lowercase s is 73_{16} (01110011_2). The instruction

```
xor   cl, 00100000b      ; change case of letter in CL
```

"flips" the value of bit 5 in the CL register, changing the value to the ASCII code for the other case letter. Similarly, if CL contains the ASCII code of a letter of unknown case, then **or cl, 00100000b** will force it to be lowercase, and **and cl, 11011111b** will force it to be uppercase.

The 80x86 instruction set includes **test** instructions that function the same as **and** instructions except that destination operands are not changed. This means that the only job of a **test** instruction is to set flags. (Remember that a **cmp** instruction is essentially a **sub** instruction that sets flags but does not change the destination operand.) One application of a **test** instruction is to examine a particular bit of a byte or word. The following instruction tests bit 13 of the EDX register.

```
test   edx, 00002000h   ; check bit 13
```

Note that 00002000 in hex is the same as 0000 0000 0000 0000 0010 0000 0000 0000 in binary, with bit 13 equal to 1. Often this **test** instruction would be followed by a **jz** or **jnz** instruction, and the effect would be to jump to the destination if bit 13 were 0 or 1, respectively.

The **test** instruction can also be used to get information about a value in a register. For example,

```
test   ecx, ecx    ; set flags for value in ECX
```

"ands" the value in the ECX register with itself, resulting in the original value. ("Anding" any bit with itself gives the common value.) The flags are set according to the value in ECX. The instruction

```
and   ecx, ecx      ; set flags for value in ECX
```

will accomplish the same goal and is equally efficient. However, using **test** makes it clear that the only purpose of the instruction is testing.

The various forms of the **test** instruction are listed in Figure 7.4. They are almost the same as for **and**, **or** and **xor** instructions. Notice that the figure does not show a source operand in memory. However, the assembler lets you code a register destination with a memory source and transposes the operands to have the memory operand first, one of the allowable formats.

Destination Operand	Source Operand	Opcode	Bytes of Object Code
register 8	immediate 8	F6	3
register 16	immediate 16	F7	4
register 32	immediate 32	F7	6
AL	immediate 8	A8	2
AX	immediate 16	A9	3
EAX	immediate 32	A9	5
memory byte	immediate 8	F6	3+
memory word	immediate 16	F7	4+
memory doubleword	immediate 32	F7	6+
register 8	register 8	84	2
register 16	register 16	85	2
register 32	register 32	85	2
memory byte	register 8	84	2+
memory word	register 16	85	2+
memory doubleword	register 32	85	2+
64-bit mode			
register 64	immediate 32	F7	6
RAX	immediate 32	A9	5
memory quadword	immediate 32	F7	6+
register 64	register 64	85	2
memory quadword	register 64	85	2+

Figure 7.4 test instructions

Exercises 7.1

1. For each part of this problem, assume the "before" values when the given instruction is executed. Give the requested "after" values. (The operands are word size to reduce the number of pairs of bits to combine.)

	Before	Instruction	After
*(a)	BX: FA 75		
	CX: 31 02	and bx,cx	BX, SF, ZF
*(b)	BX: FA 75		
	CX: 31 02	or bx,cx	BX, SF, ZF

*(c) BX: FA 75

     CX: 31 02   `xor`   `bx,cx`   BX, SF, ZF

*(d) BX: FA 75   `not`   `bx`   BX

 (e) AX: FA 75   `and`   `ax,000fh`   AX, SF, ZF

 (f) AX: FA 75   `or`   `ax,0fff0h`   AX, SF, ZF

 (g) AX: FA 75   `xor`   `ax,0ffffh`   AX, SF, ZF

 (h) AX: FA 75   `test` `ax,0004h`   AX, SF, ZF

2. Recall the two methods given in this section for computing (*value* mod 32) when *value* is an unsigned integer in the EAX register:

```
mov   edx,0        ; extend value to quadword
mov   ebx,32       ; divisor
div   ebx          ; divide value by 32
```

and

```
mov   edx,eax       ; copy value to DX
and   edx,0000001fh ; compute value mod 32
```

Find the total number of bytes of object code necessary for each of these methods.

*3. Suppose that *value* is an unsigned integer in the EAX register. Give appropriate instructions to compute (*value* mod 8) putting the result in the EBX register and leaving EAX unchanged.

4. Suppose that each bit of the doubleword at *flags* represents a Boolean value, with bit 0 for *flag0*, and so forth, up to bit 31 for *flag31*. For each of the following design statements, give a single 80x86 instruction to implement the statement.

   (a) flag2 := true;

 *(b) flag5 := false; flag16 := false; flag19 := false;

   (c) flag12 := NOT flag12

5. (a) Suppose that the AL register contains the ASCII code for an uppercase letter. Give a logical instruction (other than xor) that will change its contents to the code for the corresponding lowercase letter.

  *(b) Suppose that the AL register contains the ASCII code for a lowercase letter. Give a logical instruction (other than xor) that will change its contents to the code for the corresponding uppercase letter.

▦ Programming Exercises 7.1

1. The Pascal programming language includes the predefined function *odd* that has a single doubleword integer parameter and returns *true* for an odd integer and *false* for an even integer. Following the *cdecl* protocol, write a procedure that implements this function in assembly language, returning −1 in EAX for *true* and 0 in EAX for *false*. Use an appropriate logical instruction to generate the return value. Test your procedure by assembling it with a main program that calls it.

2. In two-dimensional graphics programming a rectangular region of the plane is mapped to the display; points outside this region are **clipped**. The region, bounded by four lines $x = x_{min}$, $x = x_{max}$, $y = y_{min}$, and $y = y_{max}$, can be pictured

0110	0100	0101	
			$y = y_{max}$
0010	0000	0001	
			$y = y_{min}$
1010	1000	1001	
$x = x_{min}$	$x = x_{max}$		

An **outcode** (or region code) is associated with each point (x, y) of the plane. This 4-bit code is assigned according to the following rules:

- bit 0 (rightmost) is 1 if the point is to the right of the region, that is $x > x_{max}$; it is 0 otherwise.
- bit 1 is 1 if the point is left of the region $(x < x_{min})$.
- bit 2 is 1 if the point is above the region $(y > y_{max})$.
- bit 3 is 1 if the point is below the region $(y < y_{min})$.

The diagram above shows the outcodes for each of the nine regions of the plane.

(a) Suppose that the outcode for point (x_1, y_1) is in the low-order 4 bits of AL, that the outcode for point (x_2, y_2) is in the low-order 4 bits of BL, and that other bits of these registers are reset to 0. Give a single 80x86 statement that will set ZF to 1 if the two points are both inside the rectangular region and to 0 otherwise. The value in AL or BL may be changed.

(b) Suppose that the outcode for point (x_1, y_1) is in the low-order 4 bits of AL, that the outcode for point (x_2, y_2) is in the low-order 4 bits of BL, and that other bits of these registers are reset to 0. Give a single 80x86 statement that will set ZF to 0 if the two points are both on the same side of the rectangular region. ("Both on the same side" means both right of $x = x_{max}$, both left of $x = x_{min}$, both above $y = y_{max}$, or both below $y = y_{min}$.) The value in AL or BL may be changed.

(c) Write a procedure *setcode* that returns the outcode for a point (x, y). Specifically, *setcode* has six doubleword integer parameters: x, y, x_{min}, x_{max}, y_{min}, and y_{max} in this order. Return the outcode in the low-order 4 bits of the AL register, assigning 0 to each of the higher-order bits in EAX. Follow the *cdecl* protocol. Test your procedure by assembling it with a main program that calls it.

7.2 Shift and Rotate Instructions

The logical instructions introduced in the previous section enable the assembly language programmer to set or clear bits in a word or byte stored in a register or memory. Shift and rotate instructions enable the programmer to change the position of bits within a doubleword, word, or byte. This section describes the shift and rotate instructions and gives examples of some ways that they are used.

Shift instructions slide the bits in a location given by the destination operand to the left or to the right. The direction of the shift can be determined from the last character of the mnemonic—**sal** and **shl** are left shifts; **sar** and **shr** are right shifts. Shifts are also categorized as logical or arithmetic—**shl** and **shr** are logical shifts; **sal** and **sar** are arithmetic shifts. The difference between logical and arithmetic shifts is explained below. The table in Figure 7.5 summarizes the mnemonics.

The source code format of any shift instruction is

```
s--    destination, count
```

There are three versions of the *count* operand. This operand can be the number 1, another number serving as a byte-size immediate operand, or the register specification CL. The original 8086/8088 CPU had only the first and third of these options.

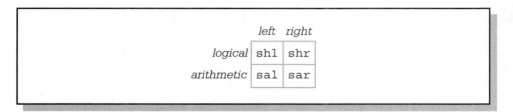

Figure 7.5 Shift instructions

An instruction having the format

s-- *destination,* 1

causes a shift of exactly one position within the destination location. With the format

s-- *destination, immediate8*

an immediate operand of 0 to 255 can be coded. However, most of the 80x86 family mask this operand by 00011111_2, that is, they reduce it mod 32 before performing the shift. (This is 00111111_2 for mod 64 in 64-bit mode.) This makes sense because you cannot do over 32 meaningful shift operations to an operand no longer than a doubleword. In the final format,

s-- *destination,* cl

the unsigned count operand is in the CL register. Again, most 80x86 CPUs reduce the count mod 32 or mod 64 before beginning the shifts.

Arithmetic and logical left shifts are identical; the mnemonics **sal** and **shl** are synonyms that generate the same object code. When a left shift is executed, the bits in the destination slide to the left and 0 bits fill in on the right. The bits that fall off the left are lost except for the very last one shifted off; it is saved in the carry flag CF. The sign flag SF, zero flag ZF, and parity flag PF are assigned values corresponding to the final value in the destination location. The overflow flag OF is undefined for a multiple-bit shift; for a single-bit shift (*count*=1) it is reset to 0 if the sign bit of the result is the same as the sign bit of the original operand value, and set to 1 if they are different.

Arithmetic and logical right shifts are not the same. With both, the bits in the destination slide to the right and the bits that fall off the right are lost except for the very last one shifted off that is saved in CF. For a logical right shift (**shr**) 0 bits fill in on the left. However, with an arithmetic right shift (**sar**) copies of the original sign bit are used to fill in on the left. Therefore, for an arithmetic right shift, if the original operand represents a negative 2's complement number, then the new operand will have leading 1 bits for each position shifted and will also be negative. As with left shifts, the values of SF, ZF, and PF depend on the result of the operation. The overflow flag OF is undefined for a multiple-bit shift. For a single-bit logical right shift **shr**, OF is set to the sign bit of the original operand. Notice that this is equivalent to saying that it is reset to 0 if the sign bit in the result is the same as the sign bit in the original operand value, and set to 1 if they are different, so OF with a logical right shift gives an indication of sign change. With a single-bit arithmetic right shift **sar** OF is always cleared—the sign bits of the original and new value are always the same.

Some hex calculators can directly do shift operations. For hand evaluation, you write the operand in binary, shift filling in with 0's or 1's as appropriate, regroup the bits, and then translate the new bit pattern back to hex. Things are a little simpler for a multiple-bit shift that shifts four positions or some multiple of four positions; in this case each group of 4 bits corresponds to one hex digit, so one can think of shifting hex digits instead of bits. Here are a few examples that illustrate execution of shift instructions; each example begins with a word containing the hex value A9 D7 (1010 1001 1101 0111 in binary). The bit(s) shifted off are separated by a vertical line in the original value. An arrow shows the direction bits are shifted. The added bit(s) are in bold in the new value.

Example

Before	Instruction	Operation in Binary	After
CX: A9 D7	sal cx,1	1|010 1001 1101 0111 0101 0011 1010 1110	CX 53 | AE SF 0 ZF 0 CF 1 OF 1
AX: A9 D7	shr ax,1	1010 1001 1101 011|1 **0**101 0100 1110 1011	AX 54 | EB SF 0 ZF 0 CF 1 OF 1
BX: A9 D7	sar bx,1	1010 1001 1101 011|1 **1**101 0100 1110 1011	BX D4 | EB SF 1 ZF 0 CF 1 OF 0

| word at | sal ace,4 | 1010 |1001 1101 0111 | ace | 9D | 70 |
| ace: A9 D7 | | 1011 1101 0111 **0000** | | | |

SF 1 ZF 0
CF 0 OF ?

| DX: A9 D7 | shr dx,4 | 1010 1001 1101|0111 | DX | 0A | 9D |
| | | **0000** 1010 1001 1101 | | | |

SF 0 ZF 0
CF 0 OF ?

| AX: A9 D7 | sar ax,cl | 1010 1001 1101|0111 | AX | FA | 9D |
| CL: 04 | | **1111** 1010 1001 1101 | | | |

SF 1 ZF 0
CF 0 OF ?

Figure 7.6 gives the opcode and number of bytes required using various operand types in shift instructions. All four types of shifts discussed so far, as well as the rotate instructions discussed next, share opcodes. The size of the destination and the type of the count operand are implied by the opcode. As with some other instructions, the *reg* field of the *ModR/M* byte of the object code is used to choose among the different types of shifts and rotates, as well as between register and memory destinations. (See Figure 4.9.)

The shift instructions are quite primitive, but they have many applications. One of these is to do certain multiplication and division operations. In fact, for processors without multiplication instructions, shift instructions are a crucial part of routines to perform multiplication. Even with the 80x86 architecture, some products may be computed more rapidly with shift operations than with multiplication instructions.

In a multiplication operation where the multiplier is 2, a single-bit left shift of the multiplicand results in the product in the original location. The product will be correct unless the overflow flag OF is set. It is easy to see why this works for unsigned numbers; shifting each bit to the left one position makes it the coefficient of the next higher power of 2 in the binary representation of the number. A single-bit left shift also correctly doubles a signed operand. In fact, one can use multiplication by 2 on a hex calculator to find the result of a single-bit left shift.

Destination Operand	Count Operand	Opcode	Bytes of Object Code
register 8	1	D0	2
register 16/32	1	D1	2
memory byte	1	D0	2+
memory word/doubleword	1	D1	2+
register 8	immediate 8	C0	3
register 16/32	immediate 8	C1	3
memory byte	immediate 8	C0	3+
memory word/doubleword	immediate 8	C1	3+
register 8	CL	D2	2
register 16/32	CL	D3	2
memory byte	CL	D2	2+
memory word/doubleword	CL	D3	2+
64-bit mode			
register 64	1	D1	2+
memory quadword	1	D1	2+
register 64	immediate 8	C1	3
memory quadword	immediate 8	C1	3
register 64	CL	D3	2
memory quadword	CL	D3	2

Figure 7.6 Shift and rotate instructions

A single-bit right shift can be used to efficiently divide an unsigned operand by 2. Suppose, for example, that the EBX register contains an unsigned operand. Then the logical right shift `shr ebx,1` shifts each bit in EBX to the position corresponding to the next lower power of 2, resulting in half the original value. The original units bit is copied into the carry flag CF, and is the remainder for the division.

If EBX contains a signed operand, then the arithmetic right shift `sar ebx,1` does almost the same job as an `idiv` instruction with a divisor of 2. The difference is that if the dividend is an odd, negative number, then the quotient is rounded down; that is, it is one smaller than it would be using an `idiv` instruction. For a concrete example, suppose that the EDX register contains FFFFFFFF and the EAX register contains FFFFFFF7, so that EDX:EAX has the quadword 2's complement representation for −9. Assume also that ECX contains 00000002. Then `idiv ecx` gives a result of FFFFFFFC in EAX and FFFFFFFF in EDX, that is, a quotient of −4 and a remainder of −1. However, if FFFFFFF7 is in EBX, then `sar ebx,1` gives a result of FFFFFFFB in EBX and 1 in CF, a quotient of −5 and a remainder of +1. Both quotient–remainder pairs satisfy the equation

$$\text{dividend} = \text{quotient*divisor} + \text{remainder}$$

but with the −5 and +1 combination, the sign of the remainder differs from the sign of the dividend, contrary to the rule followed by `idiv`.

Instead of multiplying an operand by 2, it can be doubled by either adding it to itself or by using a left shift. A shift is sometimes slightly more efficient than addition and either is generally more efficient than multiplication. To divide an operand by 2, a right shift is the only alternative to division, and is typically much faster; however, as we have seen, the right shift is not quite the same as division by 2 for a negative dividend. To multiply or divide an operand by 4, 8, or some other small power of 2, either repeated single-bit shifts or one multiple-bit shift can be used.

Shifts can be used in combination with other logical instructions to combine distinct groups of bits into a byte, word, or doubleword, or to separate the bits in a byte, word, or doubleword into different groups. Figure 7.7 shows a procedure *hexToAscii* that will convert a doubleword operand to a sequence of 8 bytes in memory; each byte containing the ASCII code for the corresponding hex digit in the operand. For example, if the operand is B70589A4, then the procedure will generate 42 37 30 35 38 39 41 34. A test driver that hard-codes this particular source operand is shown with the procedure. The screenshot in Figure 7.8 shows the test program about to exit. You can see the result highlighted in memory.

To do its job, *hexToAscii* must extract eight groups of 4 bits each from the operand. Each group of 4 bits represents a decimal value from 0 to 15, and each group must be converted to the corresponding ASCII character. This character is a digit 0 through 9 for integer value 0 (0000_2) through 9 (1001_2) or a letter A through F for integer value 10 (1010_2) through 15 (1111_2).

The eight characters are stored right to left in contiguous bytes of memory as they are generated. The operand is initially copied into EAX and then is repeatedly

```
; hex to ASCII procedure and test driver
; author:  R. Detmer
; revised:  7/2008

.586
.MODEL FLAT
.STACK  4096

; test driver for hexToAscii procedure
.DATA
source      DWORD    0b70589a4h
dest        BYTE     8 DUP (?)
.CODE
main        PROC
            lea      eax, dest    ; destination address
            push     eax          ; second operand
            push     source       ; source (1st operand)
            call     hexToAscii   ; hexToAscii(source, dest)
            add      esp, 8       ; discard parameters
quit:       mov      eax, 0       ; exit with return code 0
            ret
main        ENDP

hexToAscii  PROC
; Convert doubleword to string of eight ASCII codes
; Parameters:
; (1) doubleword containing source value
; (2) doubleword containing destination address of 8 byte long area
            push     ebp                ; establish stack frame
            mov      ebp, esp
            push     eax                ; save registers
            push     ebx
            push     ecx
            push     edx
            mov      eax, [ebp+8]       ; source value to EAX
            mov      edx, [ebp+12]      ; destination address to EDX
            mov      ecx, 8             ; loop count
forIndex:   mov      ebx, eax           ; copy value
            and      ebx, 0000000fh     ; mask off all but last 4 bits
ifDigit:    cmp      bl, 9              ; digit <= 9?
            jnle     elseHex            ; skip if not
```

(continues)

Figure 7.7 Procedure to convert a doubleword to hex

```
                or      bl, 30h          ; convert digit to ASCII
                jmp     endIfDigit       ; exit if
elseHex:        add     bl, 'A'-10       ; convert letter to ASCII
endIfDigit:
                mov     [edx+ecx-1], bl  ; store in memory
                shr     eax, 4           ; shift next digit to right
                loop    forIndex         ; iterate loop

                pop     edx              ; restore registers
                pop     ecx
                pop     ebx
                pop     eax
                pop     ebp              ; restore base pointer
                ret                      ; return
hexToAscii      ENDP
END
```

Figure 7.7 Procedure to convert a doubleword to hex *(continued)*

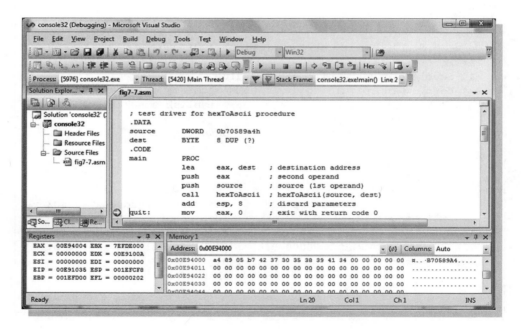

Figure 7.8 Result of calling *hexToAscii*

shifted right to get the next 4 bits at the right-hand end. The design for the middle of the program is

```
for index := 8 downto 1 loop
    copy value to EBX;
    mask off all but last 4 bits in EBX;
    if value in BL ≤ 9
    then
        convert value in BL to a character 0 through 9;
    else
        convert value in BL to a letter A through F;
    end if;
    store BL in memory at address destination+index-1;
    shift value right 4 bits to position next group of 4 bits;
end for;
```

In the code, the instruction

```
and   ebx, 0000000fh   ; mask off all but last 4 bits
```

masks off all but the last 4 bits in EDX. The *if* is implemented by

```
ifDigit:    cmp     bl, 9           ; digit <= 9?
            jnle    elseHex         ; skip if not
            or      bl, 30h         ; convert digit to ASCII
            jmp     endIfDigit      ; exit if
elseHex:    add     bl, 'A'-10      ; convert letter to ASCII
endIfDigit:
```

A value from 0 to 9 is converted to the ASCII code for a digit using the **or** instruction; **add edx,30h** would work just as well here. To convert numbers 0A to 0F to the corresponding ASCII codes 41 to 46 for letters A to F, the value 'A'−10 is added to the number. This actually adds the decimal number 55, but the code used is clearer than **add bl,55**. After the ASCII code is stored, the **shr** instruction shifts the value in EAX right 4 bits, discarding the hex digit that was just converted to a character.

In addition to the shift instructions discussed in this book, there are "double-shift" instructions that use a register as a source of fill bits for a register or memory destination, instead of using just 0's or 1's to fill. These instructions have mnemonics **shrd** and **shld**, and syntax

```
sh-d   destination, source register, count
```

We don't need these instructions in this book.

Rotate instructions are similar to shift instructions. With shift instructions the bits that are shifted off one end are discarded while vacated space at the other end is filled by 0's (or 1's for a right arithmetic shift of a negative number). With rotate instructions the bits that are shifted off one end of the destination are used to fill in the vacated space at the other end.

Rotate instruction formats are the same as single-shift instruction formats. A single-bit rotate instruction has the format

```
r--    destination, 1
```

and there are two multiple-bit versions

```
r--    destination, immediate8
r--    destination, cl
```

The instructions **rol** (rotate left) and **ror** (rotate right) can be used for byte, word, doubleword, or quadword operands in a register or in memory. As each bit "falls off" one end, it is copied to the other end of the destination. In addition, the last bit copied to the other end is also copied to the carry flag CF. The overflow flag OF is the only other flag affected by rotate instructions. It is undefined for multi-bit rotates, and familiarity with its definition for single-bit rotate instructions is not needed in this book.

As an example, suppose that the DX register contains D25E and the instruction

```
rol   dx, 1
```

is executed. In binary, the operation looks like

```
1  1  0  1    0  0  1  0    0  1  0  1    1  1  1  0
```

resulting in 1010 0100 1011 1101 or A4BD. The carry flag CF is set to 1 since a 1 bit rotated from the left end to the right.

Opcodes and number of bytes for rotate instructions are identical to those for shift instructions. They were shown in Figure 7.6.

The rotate instruction

```
ror     eax, 4          ; shift next digit to right
```

could be used instead of the shift instruction in procedure *hexToAscii* (see Figure 6.7). Since eight 4-bit rotations result in all bits being rotated back to their original positions this leaves the value in EAX unchanged at the end. There is no advantage in this particular program, but there could be in similar applications.

There is an additional pair of rotate instructions, **rcl** (rotate through carry left) and **rcr** (rotate through carry right). Each of these instructions treats the carry flag CF as if it were part of the destination. This means that **rcl eax,1** shifts bits 0 through 30 of EAX left one position, copies the old value of bit 31 into CF and copies the old value of CF into bit 0 of EAX. The rotate through carry instructions obviously alter CF; they also affect OF, but no other flag. The opcodes for rotate through carry instructions are the same as the corresponding shift instructions, and were shown in Figure 7.6.

Exercises 7.2

1. For each part of this problem, assume the "before" values when the given instruction is executed. Give the requested "after" values.

	Before	*Instruction*		*After*
*(a)	AX: A8 B5	shl	ax, 1	AX, CF, OF
(b)	AX: A8 B5	shr	ax, 1	AX, CF, OF
*(c)	AX: A8 B5	sar	ax, 1	AX, CF, OF
*(d)	AX: A8 B5	rol	ax, 1	AX, CF
(e)	AX: A8 B5	ror	ax, 1	AX, CF
(f)	AX: A8 B5			
	CL: 04	sal	ax, cl	AX, CF
(g)	AX: A8 B5	shr	ax, 4	AX, CF
(h)	AX: A8 B5			
	CL: 04	sar	ax, cl	AX, CF
(i)	AX: A8 B5			
	CL: 04	rol	ax, cl	AX, CF
(j)	AX: A8 B5	ror	ax, 4	AX, CF
*(k)	AX: A8 B5	rcl	ax, 1	AX, CF
	CF: 1			
(l)	AX: A8 B5	rcr	ax, 1	AX, CF
	CF: 0			

2. Compare the total number of bytes of object code for each of these alternative ways of dividing the unsigned integer in the EAX register by 32:

```
*(a) mov   edx,0     ; extend value to doubleword
     mov   ebx,32    ; divisor
     div   ebx       ; value div 32
 (b) shr   eax,1     ; divide by 2
     shr   eax,1     ; divide by 2
     shr   eax,1     ; divide by 2
     shr   eax,1     ; divide by 2
     shr   eax,1     ; divide by 2
 (c) shr   eax,5     ; divide by 32
```

3. Compare the total number of bytes of object code for each of these alternative ways of multiplying the value in the EAX register by 32:

```
 (a) mov   ebx,32    ; multiplier
     mul   ebx       ; value * 32
*(b) imul  eax,32    ; value * 32
 (c) shl   eax,1     ; multiply by 2
     shl   eax,1     ; multiply by 2
     shl   eax,1     ; multiply by 2
     shl   eax,1     ; multiply by 2
     shl   eax,1     ; multiply by 2
 (d) shl   eax,5     ; multiply by 32
```

4. Suppose that each of *value1*, *value2*, and *value3* references a byte in memory and that an unsigned integer is stored in each byte. Assume that the first value is no larger than 31 so that it has at most 5 significant bits and at least 3 leading 0 bits. Similarly assume that the second value is no larger than 15 (4 significant bits) and the third value is no larger than 127 (7 bits).

   (a) Give code to pack all three of these numbers into a 16-bit word in the AX register, copying the low-order 5 bits from *value1* to bits 11–15 of AX, the low-order 4 bits from *value2* to bits 7–10 of AX, and the low-order 7 bits from *value3* into bits 0–6 of AX.

   *(b) Give code to unpack the 16-bit number in the AX register into 5-bit, 4-bit, and 7-bit numbers, padding each value with zeros on the left to make 8 bits, and storing the resulting bytes at *value1*, *value2*, and *value3*, respectively.

*5. The instructions

```
mov   ebx, eax   ; value
shl   eax, 1     ; 2*value
add   eax, ebx   ; 3*value
```

multiplies the value in EAX by 3. Write similar code sequences that use shift and addition instructions to efficiently multiply by 5, 7, 9, and 10.

Programming Exercises 7.2

1. Write a procedure *binaryToAscii* that converts a doubleword integer to a string of exactly 32 0 or 1 characters representing its value as an unsigned binary number. Follow *cdecl* protocols. The procedure will have two parameters:

   (1) The doubleword value.

   (2) The address of the 32-byte-long destination string.

   Use a rotate instruction to extract the bits one at a time, left to right; recalling that jc or jnc instructions look at the carry bit. Write a short test driver to test your procedure.

2. A byte can be represented using three octal digits. Bits 7 and 6 determine the left octal digit (which is never larger than 4); bits 5, 4, and 3 the middle digit; and bits 2, 1, and 0 the right digit. For instance, 11010110_2 is 11 010 110$_2$ or 326_8. The value of a word is represented in *split octal* by applying the 2–3–3 system to the high-order and low-order bytes separately. Write a procedure *splitOctal* that converts a word to a string of exactly seven characters representing the value of the number in split octal; two groups of three digits separated by a space. Follow *cdecl* protocols. The procedure will have two parameters:

   (1) The word value (passed as the low-order word of a doubleword).

   (2) The address of the 7-byte-long destination string.

   Write a short test driver to test your procedure.

7.3 Converting an ASCII String to a 2's Complement Integer

The *atod* macro has been used to scan an area of memory containing an ASCII representation of an integer, producing the corresponding doubleword-length 2's complement integer in the EAX register. This section describes the *windows32* version of *atod* and the procedure it calls as examples of this sort of operation. Code is similar for the *windows64* components.

The *atod* macro expands into the following sequence of instructions.

```
lea     eax,source          ; source address to EAX
push    eax                 ; source parameter on stack
call    atodproc            ; call atodproc(source)
add     esp, 4              ; remove parameter
```

These instructions simply call procedure *atodproc* passing a single argument, the address of the string of ASCII characters to be scanned. The EAX register is not saved by the macro code since the result is to be returned in EAX. The actual source identifier is used in the expanded macro, not the name *source*.

The actual ASCII to 2's complement integer conversion is done by the procedure *atodproc* whose source code is in the file *io.asm* in the *windows32* package. This source code is shown in Figure 7.9. The procedure begins with standard entry code and ends with standard exit code. The first job of *atodproc* is to skip leading spaces, if any.

```
; atodproc(source)
; Procedure to scan data segment starting at source address, interpreting
; ASCII characters as an doubleword-size integer value returned in EAX.

; Leading blanks are skipped.  A leading - or + sign is acceptable.
; Digit(s) must immediately follow the sign (if any).
; Memory scan is terminated by any non-digit.

; No error checking is done. If the number is outside the range for a
; signed word, then the return value is undefined.

atodproc    PROC
            push    ebp                 ; save base pointer
            mov     ebp, esp            ; establish stack frame
            sub     esp, 4              ; local space for sign
            push    ebx                 ; Save registers
            push    edx
            push    esi
            pushfd                      ; save flags

            mov     esi,[ebp+8]         ; get parameter (source addr)
```

(continues)

Figure 7.9 ASCII to doubleword integer conversion

```
WhileBlankD:cmp     BYTE PTR [esi],' '  ; space?
        jne     EndWhileBlankD      ; exit if not
        inc     esi                 ; increment character pointer
        jmp     WhileBlankD         ; and try again
EndWhileBlankD:

        mov     eax,1               ; default sign multiplier
IfPlusD:    cmp     BYTE PTR [esi],'+'  ; leading + ?
        je      SkipSignD           ; if so, skip over
IfMinusD:   cmp     BYTE PTR [esi],'-'  ; leading - ?
        jne     EndIfSignD          ; if not, save default +
        mov     eax,-1              ; -1 for minus sign
SkipSignD:  inc     esi             ; move past sign
EndIfSignD:

        mov     [ebp-4],eax         ; save sign multiplier
        mov     eax,0               ; number being accumulated

WhileDigitD:cmp     BYTE PTR [esi],'0'  ; compare next character to '0'
        jl      EndWhileDigitD      ; not a digit if smaller than '0'
        cmp     BYTE PTR [esi],'9'  ; compare to '9'
        jg      EndWhileDigitD      ; not a digit if bigger than '9'
        imul    eax,10              ; multiply old number by 10
        mov     bl,[esi]            ; ASCII character to BL
        and     ebx,0000000Fh       ; convert to single-digit integer
        add     eax,ebx             ; add to sum
        inc     esi                 ; increment character pointer
        jmp     WhileDigitD         ; go try next character
EndWhileDigitD:

; if value is < 80000000h, multiply by sign
        cmp     eax,80000000h       ; 80000000h?
        jnb     endIfMaxD           ; skip if not
        imul    DWORD PTR [ebp-4]   ; make signed number
endIfMaxD:

        popfd                       ; restore flags
        pop     esi                 ; restore registers
        pop     edx
        pop     ebx
        mov     esp, ebp            ; delete local variable space
        pop     ebp
        ret                         ; exit
atodproc    ENDP
```

Figure 7.9 ASCII to doubleword integer conversion *(continued)*

This is implemented with a straightforward *while* loop. Note that **BYTE PTR [esi]** uses register indirect addressing to reference a byte of the source string. Following the *while* loop, ESI points at some non-blank character.

The main idea of the procedure is to compute the value of the integer by implementing the following left-to-right scanning algorithm.

```
value := 0;
while pointing at code for a digit loop
    multiply value by 10;
    convert ASCII character code to integer;
    add integer to value;
    point at next byte in memory;
end while;
```

This design works for an unsigned number; a separate multiplier is used to give the correct sign to the final signed result. The second job of the procedure, after skipping blanks, is to determine this multiplier; 1 for a positive number or -1 for a negative number. The multiplier, stored in local variable space on the stack, is given the default value 1 and changed to -1 if the first non-blank character is a minus sign. If the first non-blank character is either a plus or a minus sign, then the address in ESI is incremented to skip over the sign character.

Now the main design is executed and the value is accumulated in the EAX register. There are no checks for errors—if the number is too large to store in a doubleword, for example, then the returned value will simply be wrong. The main loop terminates as soon as ESI points at any character code other than one for a digit. Thus the memory scan is terminated by a space, comma, letter, null, or *any* nondigit.

If the accumulated value in the EAX registers less than 80000000_{16}, it is multiplied by the saved +1 or -1 sign. If the accumulated value is greater than 80000000_{16}, then the returned value will be incorrect. If it is exactly equal to 80000000_{16} and there was a minus sign, then it already has the correct result ($-2,147,483,648_{10}$); but again, no error checking is done.

Exercise 7.3

1. It was noted above that *atodproc* does not check for errors such as the number being too large to store in a doubleword. How could this partic-

ular error be detected? Can other errors in the input string cause incorrect output? If so, how could these errors be detected?

Programming Exercises 7.3

1. Write a procedure *binToInt* that has a single parameter; the address of a string. This procedure will be similar to *atodproc* except that it will convert a string of characters representing an unsigned binary number to a doubleword-length 2's complement integer in EAX. The procedure should skip leading blanks, and then accumulate a value until a character that does not represent a binary digit (0 or 1 only) is encountered. Follow *cdecl* protocols. Test your procedure with a test driver.

2. Write a procedure *hexToInt* that has a single parameter; the address of a string. This procedure will be similar to *atodproc* except that it will convert a string of characters representing an unsigned hexadecimal number to a doubleword-length 2's complement integer in EAX. The procedure should skip leading blanks, and then accumulate a value until a character that does not represent a hex digit is encountered. (Valid characters are 0 through 9, A through F, and a through f.) Follow *cdecl* protocols. Test your procedure with a test driver.

7.4 Chapter Summary

This chapter has explored various 80x86 instructions that allow bits in a byte, word, or doubleword destination to be manipulated. The logical instructions and, or and xor perform Boolean operations using pairs of bits from a source and destination. Applications of these instructions include setting or clearing selected bits in a destination. The not instruction takes the 1's complement of each bit in its destination operand, changing each 0 to a 1 and each 1 to a 0. The test instruction is the same as the and instruction except that it only affects flags; the destination operand is unchanged.

Shift instructions move bits left or right within a destination operand. These instructions come in single-bit and multiple-bit versions. Single-bit shifts use 1 for the second operand; multiple-bit versions use

CL or an immediate value for the second operand and shift the destination the number of positions specified. Vacated positions are filled by 0 bits in all single-shift operations except for the arithmetic right shift of a negative number for which 1 bit is used. Shift instructions can be used for efficient, convenient multiplication or division by 2, 4, 8, or some higher power of 2.

Rotate instructions are similar to shift instructions. However, the bit that falls off one end of the destination fills the void on the other end. Shift or rotate instructions can be used in combination with logical instructions to extract groups of bits from a location or to pack multiple values into a single byte or word.

CHAPTER 8

String Operations

Computers are frequently used to manipulate character strings as well as numeric data. In data processing, application names, addresses, and so forth must be stored and sometimes rearranged. Text editor and word processor programs must be capable of searching for and moving strings of characters. An assembler must be able to separate assembly language statement elements, identifying those that are reserved mnemonics. Even when computation is primarily numerical, it is often necessary to convert a character string to an internal numerical format when a number is entered at the keyboard, or to convert an internal format to a character string for display purposes.

An 80x86 microprocessor has instructions to manipulate character strings. The same instructions can manipulate strings of words, doublewords, or (in 64-bit mode) quadwords. This chapter covers 80x86 instructions that are used to handle strings, with emphasis on character strings. The tasks that can be accomplished with these instructions can also be completed with the simpler instructions previously covered. String instructions are included partly to illustrate that the 80x86 architecture represents the complex instruction set computer (CISC) class of computers. Many additional complex 80x86 instructions are not covered in this book.

8.1 Using String Instructions

There are five 80x86 instructions designed for string manipulation: **movs** (move string), **cmps** (compare string), **scas** (scan string), **stos** (store string), and **lods** (load string). The **movs** instruction is used to copy a string from one memory location to another. The **cmps** instruction is designed to compare the contents of two strings. The **scas** instruction can be used to search a string for one particular value. The **stos** instruction can store a new value in some position of a string. Finally, the **lods** instruction copies a value out of some position of a string.

A string in the 80x86 architecture refers to a contiguous collection of bytes, words, doublewords, or quadwords in memory. Strings are commonly defined in a program's data segment using such directives as

```
response    BYTE    20 DUP (?)
label1      BYTE    'The results are ', 0
wordString  WORD    50 DUP (?)
arrayD      DWORD   60 DUP (0)
qString     QWORD   40 DUP (?)
```

Note that strings and arrays are actually the same except for the way we look at them.

Each string instruction applies to a source string, a destination string, or both. The bytes, words, doublewords, or quadwords of these strings are processed one at a time by the string instruction. Register indirect addressing is used to locate the individual string elements. The 80x86 instructions access elements of the source string using the address in the source index register ESI. Elements in the destination string are accessed using the address in the destination index register EDI. In 64-bit mode, RSI and RDI are used by default; however, the remainder of this chapter refers to just ESI and EDI.

Since the source and destination addresses of string elements are always given by ESI and EDI, respectively, no operands are needed to identify these locations. Without any operand, however, the assembler cannot tell the size of the string element to be used. For example, just **movs** by itself could say to move a byte, word, doubleword, or quadword. To avoid this ambiguity, special versions of the mnemonics define the element size—instructions that operate on bytes use a b suffix, word string instructions use a w suffix, doubleword string instructions use a d suffix, and quadword string instructions use a q suffix. For example, **movsb** is used to move byte strings and **movsd** is used to move doubleword strings. Any of these instructions assemble as a **movs** and none use an operand because the assembler knows the element size from the mnemonic.

The assembler has an alternative way of distinguishing the operand size, which is to actually include source and destination operands. These operands are ignored except for their size attribute, so they can be misleading. We do not use this alternative coding style.

Although a string instruction operates on only one string element at a time, it always gets ready to operate on the next element. It does this by changing the source index register ESI and/or the destination index register EDI to contain the address of the next element of the string(s). When byte-size elements are being used, the index registers are changed by one; for words, ESI and EDI are changed by two; for doublewords, the registers are changed by four; and for quadwords, the registers are changed by eight. The 80x86 can move either forward through a string (from lower to higher addresses) or backward (from higher to lower addresses). The movement direction is determined by the value of the direction flag DF; bit 10 of the flags register. If DF is set to 1, then the addresses in ESI and EDI are decremented by string instructions, causing right-to-left string operations. If DF is clear (0), then the values in ESI and EDI are incremented by string instructions, so that strings are processed left to right.

The 80x86 has two instructions whose sole purpose is to reset or set the direction flag DF. The **cld** instruction clears DF to 0 so that ESI and EDI are incremented by string instructions and strings are processed left to right. The **std** instruction sets DF to 1 so that ESI and EDI are decremented by string instructions and strings are processed backward. Neither instruction affects any flag other than DF. Data about these instructions appear in Figure 8.1.

Instruction	Opcode	Bytes of Object Code
cld	FC	1
std	FD	1

Figure 8.1 cld and std instructions

Mnemonic	Size	Opcode	Bytes of Object Code
movsb	byte	A4	1
movsw	word	A5	1
movsd	doubleword	A5	1
64-bit mode			
movsq	quadword	A5	1

Figure 8.2 movs instructions

Finally, it is time to present all the details about a string instruction. The move string instruction **movs** copies one string element (byte, word, doubleword, or quadword) from a source string to a destination string. The source element at address ESI is copied to address EDI. After the string element is copied, both index registers are changed by the element size (1, 2, 4, or 8), incremented if the direction flag DF is 0, or decremented if DF is 1. The **movs** instruction does not affect any flag. It comes in **movsb**, **movsw**, **movsd**, and **movsq** versions; Figure 8.2 gives information about each form.

Figure 8.3 gives an example of a program that uses the **movs** instruction. The important part of the example is the procedure *strcopy*. This procedure has two parameters that give the destination and source addresses of byte (character) strings. The source string is assumed to be null-terminated. Procedure *strcopy* produces an exact copy of the source string at the destination location, terminating the destination string by a null byte.

The procedure uses only registers ESI and EDI. The values for ESI and EDI are the arguments that were pushed on the stack; the addresses of the first pair of source and destination string bytes. The direction flag is cleared for left-to-right copying. Since the procedure must clear the direction flag and the caller may be depending on it to have the opposite value, the entry code saves the flags register in addition to ESI and EDI.

After initialization the procedure executes this pseudocode design:

---

while next source byte is not null
    copy source byte to destination;
    increment source index;
    increment destination index;
end while;
put null byte at end of destination string;

```
; strcopy procedure and test driver
; author: R. Detmer
; revised: 7/2008
.586
.MODEL FLAT
.STACK  4096
INCLUDE io.h            ; header file for input/output
.DATA                   ; reserve storage for data
prompt       BYTE    "Original string?  ",0
stringIn     BYTE    80 DUP (?)
displayLbl   BYTE    "Your string was...", 0
stringOut    BYTE    80 DUP (?)
.CODE
_MainProc PROC
          input   prompt, stringIn, 80   ; ask for string
          lea     eax, stringIn    ; source
          push    eax              ; second parameter
          lea     eax, stringOut   ; destination address
          push    eax              ; first parameter
          call    strcopy          ; strcopy(dest, source)
          add     esp, 8           ; remove parameters
          output  displayLbl, stringOut  ; display result
          mov     eax, 0           ; exit with return code 0
          ret
_MainProc ENDP

strcopy   PROC NEAR32
; Procedure to copy string until null byte in source is copied.
; Destination location assumed to be long enough to hold copy.
; Parameters:
;   (1)   address of destination
;   (2)   address of source
          push    ebp             ;save base pointer
          mov     ebp,esp         ;copy stack pointer
          push    edi             ;save registers
          push    esi
          pushfd                  ;save flags

          mov     edi,[ebp+8]     ;destination
          mov     esi,[ebp+12]    ;initial source address
          cld                     ;clear direction flag
whileNoNull:
          cmp     BYTE PTR [esi],0 ;null source byte?
          je      endWhileNoNull   ;stop copying if null
```

(continues)

Figure 8.3 String copy program

```
          movsb                       ;copy  one byte
          jmp      whileNoNull        ;go check next byte
endWhileNoNull:
          mov      BYTE PTR [edi],0   ;terminate destination string

          popfd                       ;restore flags
          pop      esi                ;restore registers
          pop      edi
          pop      ebp
          ret                         ;return
strcopy   ENDP
END
```

Figure 8.3 String copy program *(continued)*

To check whether the next source byte is null, the statement

```
cmp     BYTE PTR [esi],0   ; null source byte?
```

is used. Recall that the notation `[esi]` indicates register indirect addressing, so that the element at the address in ESI is used, that is, the current byte of the source string. The operator **BYTE PTR** is necessary since the assembler cannot tell from the operands whether byte, word, doubleword, or quadword comparison is needed. Copying the source byte and incrementing both index registers is accomplished by the **movsb** instruction. Finally,

```
mov     BYTE PTR [edi],0   ; terminate destination string
```

serves to move a null byte to the end of the destination string since EDI was incremented after the last byte of the source was copied to the destination. Again, the operator **BYTE PTR** tells the assembler that the destination is a byte rather than a word or doubleword.

The program to test *strcopy* simply uses a dialog box to input a string from the keyboard, calls *strcopy* to copy it somewhere else, and finally displays the string copy. The most interesting part of the test driver is the collection of instructions used to call the procedure.

The source string for a **movs** instruction usually does not overlap the destination string. However, occasionally this is useful. Suppose that you want to initialize the 80-character-long string at *starSlash* with the pattern */, repeated 40 times. The following code can do this task.

```
starSlash    BYTE    80 DUP (?)
             ...
             mov    starSlash, '*'      ; first *
             mov    starSlash+1, '/'    ; first /
             lea    esi, starSlash      ; source address
             lea    edi, starSlash+2    ; destination
             cld                        ; process left to right
             mov    ecx, 78            ; characters to copy
forCount:    movsb                      ; copy next character
             loop   forCount            ; repeat
```

In this example, the first time **movsb** is executed, a * from the first string position is copied to the third position. In the next iteration, a / is copied from the second to the fourth position. The third time, a * is copied from the third to the fifth position, and so on. The next section introduces an easier way to repeat a **movs** instruction.

Both the *windows32* and *windows64 output* macros call a C function *showOutput* that in turn calls a library function *MessageBox*. Neither the 32-bit nor the 64-bit *MessageBox* function works correctly if the direction flag is set. As a result the *output* macro model statements include a **cld** instruction. This could affect a program that uses the *output* macro in the middle of a loop that is processing a string backwards.

▨▨▨▨ **Exercises 8.1**

*1. What will be the output of the following *windows32* program?

```
.586
.MODEL FLAT
.STACK  4096
INCLUDE io.h

.DATA
outLbl  BYTE   "The modified string is", 0
string  BYTE   "ABCDEFGHIJ", 0

.CODE
_MainProc PROC
; setup code 1
        lea    esi, string      ; beginning of string
        lea    edi, string+5    ; address of 'F'
        cld                      ; forward movement

        movsb                    ; move 4 characters
```

```
                movsb
                movsb
                movsb
                output  outLbl, string  ; display modified string

                mov     eax, 0          ; exit with return code 0
                ret
_MainProc ENDP
                END
```

2. Repeat Exercise 1, replacing the setup code with

```
; setup code 2
                lea     esi, string     ; beginning of string
                lea     edi, string+2   ; address of 'C'
                cld                     ; forward movement
```

3. Repeat Exercise 1, replacing the setup code with

```
; setup code 3
                lea     esi, string+9   ; end of string
                lea     edi, string+4   ; address of 'E'
                std                     ; backward movement
```

4. Repeat Exercise 1, replacing the procedure setup1 with

```
; setup code 4
                lea     esi, string+9   ; end of string
                lea     edi, string+7   ; address of 'H'
                std                     ; backward movement
```

▨ **Programming Exercises 8.1**

1. Write a *windows32* program that reserves a 1024-byte-long area named *byteArea*. Use a dialog box to input strings one at a time into another 80-byte-long area named *stringIn*. Copy the first string to the beginning of *byteArea*, then append carriage return ($0D_{16}$) and linefeed ($0A_{16}$) characters to the end of the copy. Copy the next string from *stringIn* to *byteArea*, starting right after the first string's linefeed. Terminate input when the first character of *stringIn* is $ and append a null byte to the destination right after the last string's linefeed. Finally, use the *output* macro to display all the characters in *byteArea* in a message box. The result should be the strings that were entered, one per line.

8.2   Repeat Prefixes and More String Instructions

Each 80x86 string instruction operates on one string element at a time. However, the 80x86 architecture includes three **repeat prefixes** that change the string instructions into versions that repeat automatically, either for a fixed number of iterations or until some condition is satisfied. The three repeat prefixes actually correspond to two different single-byte codes; these are not themselves instructions, but supplement machine codes for the primitive string instructions, making new instructions.

Figure 8.4 shows two program fragments, each of which copies a fixed number of characters from *sourceStr* to *destStr*. The number of characters is loaded into the ECX register from *count*. The code in part (a) uses a **loop** instruction. Since the count of characters might be zero, the loop is guarded by a **jecxz** instruction. The body of the loop uses **movsb** to copy one character at a time. The **loop** instruction takes care of counting loop iterations. The program fragment in part (b) is functionally equivalent to the one in part (a). After the count is copied into ECX, it uses the repeat prefix **rep** with a **movsb** instruction; the **rep movsb** instruction does the same thing as the last four lines in part (a).

The **rep** prefix is normally used with the **movs** instructions and with the **stos** instruction (discussed on the next page). It causes the following design to be executed.

```
        lea    esi, sourceStr  ; source string
        lea    edi, destStr    ; destination
        cld                    ; forward movement
        mov    ecx, count      ; count of characters to copy
        jecxz endCopy          ; skip loop if count is zero
copy:   movsb                  ; move 1 character
        loop    copy           ; decrement count and continue
endCopy:
```

(a) movsb iterated in a loop

```
        lea    esi, sourceStr  ; source string
        lea    edi, destStr    ; destination
        cld                    ; forward movement
        mov    ecx, count      ; count of characters to copy
        rep movsb              ; move characters
```

(b) Repeat prefix with movsb

Figure 8.4 Copying a fixed number of characters of a string

```
while count in ECX > 0 loop
     perform primitive instruction;
     decrement ECX by 1;
end while;
```

Note that this is a *while* loop. The primitive instruction is not executed at all if ECX contains zero. It is not necessary to guard a repeated string instruction as you often must do with an ordinary *for* loop implemented with the **loop** instruction.

The other two repeat prefixes are **repe** (with equivalent mnemonic **repz**) and **repne** (same as **repnz**). The mnemonic **repe** stands for "repeat while equal" and **repz** stands for "repeat while zero." Similarly, **repne** and **repnz** mean "repeat while not equal" and "repeat while not zero," respectively. Each of these repeat prefixes is appropriate for use with the two string instructions **cmps** and **scas** that affect the zero flag ZF.

The names of these mnemonics partially describe their actions. Each instruction works the same as **rep**, iterating a primitive instruction while ECX is not zero. However, each also examines ZF after the string instruction is executed. The **repe** and **repz** continue iterating while ZF=1, as it would be following a comparison where two operands were equal. The **repne** and **repnz** continue iterating while ZF=0, as it would be following a comparison where two operands were different. Each new instruction that is formed with a repeat prefix and a primitive string instruction affects flags only as the original primitive string instruction would; that is, there is no additional adjustment resulting from the changes to ECX. The three repeat prefixes are summarized in Figure 8.5. Note that **rep** and **repz** (**repe**) generate exactly the same code.

The **repz** and **repnz** prefixes do not produce true *while* loops with the conditions shown in Figure 8.5. The value in ECX is checked prior to the first iteration of the primitive instruction, as it should be with a *while* loop. However, ZF is not checked until

Mnemonic	Loop While	Opcode	Bytes of Object Code
rep	ECX>0	F3	1
repz/repe	ECX>0 and ZF=1	F3	1
repnz/repne	ECX>0 and ZF=0	F2	1

Figure 8.5 Repeat prefixes

Mnemonic	Element Size	Opcode	Bytes of Object Code
cmpsb	byte	A6	1
cmpsw	word	A7	1
cmpsd	doubleword	A7	1
64-bit mode			
cmpsq	quadword	A7	1

Figure 8.6 cmps instructions (use ESI and EDI)

after the primitive instruction is executed. In practice, this is very convenient since the instruction is skipped for a zero count, but the programmer does not have to do anything special to initialize ZF prior to repeated instructions.

The **cmps** instructions, summarized in Figure 8.6, compare elements of source and destination strings. Chapter 5 explained how a **cmp** instruction subtracts two operands and sets flags based on the difference. Similarly, **cmps** subtracts two string elements and sets flags based on the difference; neither operand is changed. If a **cmps** instruction is used in a loop, it is appropriate to follow **cmps** by several of the conditional jump instructions, depending on the design being implemented. Repeat prefixes are often used with **cmps** instructions. In fact, for the task of finding if two strings are identical, the **repe** prefix is a perfect companion for **cmps**.

It is often necessary to search for one string embedded in another. Suppose that the task at hand is to find the position (if any) at which the string at *key* appears in the string at *target*. One simple algorithm to do this is

```
position := 1;
while position ≤ (targetLength − keyLength + 1) loop
    if key matches the substring of target starting at position
    then
        report success;
        exit process;
    end if;
    add 1 to position;
end while;
report failure;
```

This algorithm checks to see if the key string matches the portion of the target string starting at each possible position. Using 80x86 registers, checking for one match can be done as follows:

```
ESI := address of key;
EDI := address of target + position − 1;
ECX := length of key;

forever loop
    if ECX = 0 then exit loop; end if;
    compare [ESI] and [EDI] setting ZF;
    increment ESI;
    increment EDI;
    decrement ECX;
    if ZF = 0 then exit loop; end if;
end loop;

if ZF = 1
then
    match was found;
end if;
```

The *forever* loop is exactly what is done by the repeated string instruction **repe cmpsb**. Since the loop is terminated when either ECX = 0 or when ZF = 0, it is necessary to be sure that the last pair of characters compared were the same; this is the reason for the extra *if* structure at the end of the design. Figure 8.7 shows a complete program that implements this design.

The scan string instruction **scas** is used to scan a string for the presence or absence of a particular string element. The string that is examined is a destination string; that is, the address of the element being examined is in the destination index register EDI. The accumulator contains the element being scanned for, for example, AL with a **scasb** instruction or EAX with a **scasd**. Figure 8.8 summarizes the **scas** instructions.

```
; program to search for one string embedded in another
; author:  R. Detmer
; revised: 7/2008

.586
.MODEL FLAT
.STACK  4096
INCLUDE io.h

.DATA
prompt1     BYTE   "String to search?", 0
prompt2     BYTE   "Key to search for?", 0
target      BYTE   80 DUP (?)
key         BYTE   80 DUP (?)
trgtLength  DWORD  ?
keyLength   DWORD  ?
lastPosn    DWORD  ?
resultLbl   BYTE   "Search Results", 0
failure     BYTE   "The key does not appear in the string", 0
success     BYTE   "The key appears at position"
position    BYTE   11 DUP (?)
            BYTE   "   in the string.", 0

.CODE
_MainProc   PROC
            input   prompt1, target,80  ; input target string
            lea     eax, target       ; address of target
            push    eax               ; parameter
            call    strlen            ; strlen(target)
            add     esp, 4            ; remove parameter
            mov     trgtLength,eax    ; save length of target
            input   prompt2, key,80   ; input key string
            lea     eax, key          ; address of key
            push    eax               ; parameter
            call    strlen            ; strlen(key)
            add     esp, 4            ; remove parameter
            mov     keyLength,eax     ; save length of key

; calculate last position of target to check
            mov     eax,trgtLength
            sub     eax,keyLength
            inc     eax               ; trgtLength - keyLength + 1
            mov     lastPosn, eax
            cld                       ; left to right comparison
```

(continues)

Figure 8.7 String search program

```
            mov     eax,1              ; starting position
whilePosn:  cmp     eax,lastPosn       ; position <= last_posn?
            jnle    endWhilePosn       ; exit if past last position

            lea     esi,target         ; address of target string
            add     esi,eax            ; add position
            dec     esi                ; address of position to check
            lea     edi,key            ; address of key
            mov     ecx,keyLength      ; number of positions to check
            repe cmpsb                 ; check
            jz      found              ; exit on success
            inc     eax                ; increment position
            jmp     whilePosn          ; repeat
endWhilePosn:

            output resultLbl, failure  ; the search failed
            jmp     quit               ; exit

found:      dtoa    position,eax       ; convert position to ASCII
            output resultLbl, success  ; search succeeded
quit:
            mov     eax, 0             ; exit with return code 0
            ret
_MainProc   ENDP

strlen      PROC
; int strlen(char str[])
            push    ebp                ; establish stack frame
            mov     ebp, esp
            push    ebx                ; save EBX
            sub     eax, eax           ; length := 0
            mov     ebx, [ebp+8]       ; address of string
whileChar:  cmp     BYTE PTR [ebx], 0  ; null byte?
            je      endWhileChar       ; exit if so
            inc     eax                ; increment length
            inc     ebx                ; point at next character
            jmp     whileChar          ; repeat
endWhileChar:
            pop     ebx                ; restore registers
            pop     ebp
            ret                        ; return
strlen      ENDP
END
```

Figure 8.7 String search program *(continued)*

Mnemonic	Element Size	Opcode	Bytes of Object Code
scasb	byte	AE	1
scasw	word	AF	1
scasd	doubleword	AF	1
64-bit mode			
scasq	quadword	AF	1

Figure 8.8 scas instructions (use EDI and accumulator)

The program shown in Figure 8.9 inputs a string and a character and uses **repne scasb** to locate the position of the first occurrence of the character in the string. It then displays the part of the string from the character to the end. The length of the string is calculated using the *strlen* procedure that previously appeared in Figure 8.7; this time, we assume that *strlen* is assembled in a separate file. The **lea** instruction is used to load the offset of the string to be searched and **cld** ensures a forward search.

After the search, the destination index EDI will be one greater than desired since a string instruction always increments index registers regardless of whether flags were set. If the search succeeded, EDI will contain the address of the character following the one that matched with AL, or the address of the character after the end of the string if ECX was decremented to zero. The **dec edi** instruction takes care of both cases, backing up to the position of the matching character if there were one, or to the null byte at the end of the string otherwise. The string length was incremented so that the null character would be included in the search. The output macro displays the last portion of the string, whose address is in EDI.

The store string instruction **stos** copies a byte, a word, a doubleword, or a quadword from the accumulator to an element of a destination string. A **stos** instruction affects no flag, so only the **rep** prefix is appropriate for use with it. When repeated with **rep**, it copies the same value into consecutive positions of a string. For example, the following code will store spaces in the first 30 bytes of string. Information about the **stos** instructions is in Figure 8.10.

```
mov    ecx,30            ; 30 bytes
mov    al, ' '           ; character to store
lea    edi, string       ; address of string
cld                      ; forward direction
rep stosb                ; store spaces
```

```
; Program to locate a character within a string
; The string is displayed from the character to the end
; author: R. Detmer
; revised: 7/2008

.586
.MODEL FLAT
.STACK  4096
INCLUDE io.h
EXTRN strlen:PROC

.DATA
prompt1     BYTE    "String?", 0
prompt2     BYTE    "Character?", 0
string      BYTE    80 DUP (?)
char        BYTE    5 DUP (?)
label1      BYTE    "Rest of the string ", 0

.CODE
_MainProc   PROC
            input   prompt1, string,80     ; get string
            lea     eax, string  ; find length of string
            push    eax          ; parameter
            call    strlen       ; strlen(string)
            add     esp, 4       ; remove argument from stack
            inc     eax          ; include null in string length
            mov     ecx, eax     ; save length of string
            input   prompt2, char,5   ; get character
            mov     al, char     ; character to AL
            lea     edi, string  ; offset of string
            cld                  ; forward movement
            repne scasb          ; scan while character not found
            dec     edi          ; back up to null or matching character
            output label1, [edi] ; output string
            mov     eax, 0       ; exit with return code 0
            ret
_MainProc   ENDP
END
```

Figure 8.9 Program to find character in string

Mnemonic	Element Size	Opcode	Bytes of Object Code
stosb	byte	AA	1
stosw	word	AB	1
stosd	doubleword	AB	1
64-bit			
stosq	quadword	AB	1

Figure 8.10 stos instructions (use EDI and accumulator)

Mnemonic	Element Size	Opcode	Bytes of Object Code
lodsb	byte	AC	1
lodsw	word	AD	1
lodsd	doubleword	AD	1
64-bit			
lodsq	quadword	AD	1

Figure 8.11 lods instructions (use ESI and accumulator)

The load string instruction **lods** is the final string instruction. This instruction copies a source string element to the accumulator. A **lods** instruction sets no flag. It is possible to use a **rep** prefix with **lods** but it is not helpful—all values except for the last string element would be replaced as successive values were copied to the accumulator. If string elements require some processing, it is sometimes convenient to set up a loop whose body starts with a **lods** instruction to get the element, then processes the element, and finally uses a **stos** instruction to store the modified element. The **lods** instructions are summarized in Figure 8.11.

Exercises 8.2

For each exercise below, assume that the data segment contains

```
source    BYTE    "brown"
dest      BYTE    "brine"
```

1. Suppose that the following instructions are executed:

```
lea    esi, source
lea    edi, dest
cld
mov    ecx, 5
repne cmpsb
```

Assuming that 00417000 is the address loaded in ESI and 00417005 is loaded in EDI, what will be the values stored in ESI and EDI following the repne cmpsb instruction? What will be stored in ECX?

*2. Suppose that the following instructions are executed:

```
lea    esi, source
lea    edi, dest
cld
mov    ecx, 5
repe cmpsb
```

Assuming that 00417000 is the address loaded in ESI and 00417005 is loaded in EDI, what will be the values stored in ESI and EDI following the repe cmpsb instruction? What will be stored in ECX?

3. Suppose that the following instructions are executed:

```
mov    al, 'w'
lea    edi, dest
cld
mov    ecx, 5
repe scasb
```

Assuming that 00417005 is the address loaded in EDI, what will be the value stored in EDI following the repe scasb instruction? What will be stored in ECX?

4. Suppose that the following instructions are executed:

```
mov    al, 'n'
lea    edi, dest
cld
mov    ecx, 5
repne scasb
```

Assuming that 00417005 is the address loaded in EDI, what will be the value stored in EDI following the repne scasb instruction? What will be stored in ECX?

*5. Suppose that the following instructions are executed:

```
mov    al, '*'
lea    edi, dest
cld
mov    ecx, 5
rep stosb
```

Assuming that 00417005 is the address loaded in EDI, what will be the value stored in EDI following the rep stosb instruction? What will be stored in ECX? What will be stored in the destination string?

6. Suppose that the following instructions are executed:

```
        lea    esi, source
        lea    edi, dest
        cld
        mov    ecx, 5
for6:  lodsb
        inc    al
        stosb
        loop   for6
endFor6:
```

Assuming that 00417000 is the address loaded in ESI and 00417005 is loaded in EDI, what will be the values stored in ESI and EDI following the *for* loop? What will be stored in ECX? What will be stored in the destination string?

7. Suppose that the following instructions are executed:

```
lea    esi, source
lea    edi, dest
cld
mov    ecx, 3
rep    movsb
```

Assuming that 00417000 is the address loaded in ESI and 00417005 is loaded in EDI, what will be the values stored in ESI and EDI following the rep movsb instruction? What will be stored in ECX? What will be stored in the destination string?

8. Suppose that the following instructions are executed:

```
lea    esi, source+4
lea    edi, dest+4
std
```

```
mov    ecx, 3
rep    movsb
```

Assuming that 00417000 is the address loaded in ESI and 00417005 is loaded in EDI, what will be the values stored in ESI and EDI following the rep movsb instruction? What will be stored in ECX? What will be stored in the destination string?

Programming Exercises 8.2

1. Write a procedure *index* to find the position of the first occurrence of a character in a null-terminated string. Specifically, the procedure must have two parameters: (1) a character (passed as the low-order byte of a doubleword), and (2) the address of a string. Return the position of the character within the string; return zero if the character is not found. Follow the *cdecl* or 64-bit protocol, depending on your environment. Write a short test driver to test your procedure.

2. Write a procedure *append* that will append one null-terminated string to the end of another. Specifically, the procedure must have two parameters: (1) the address of *string1* and (2) the address of *string2*. The procedure will copy the characters of *string2* to the end of *string1* with the first character of *string2* replacing the null byte at the end of string1, and so on. Follow the *cdecl* or 64-bit protocol, depending on your environment. Write a short test driver to test your procedure. (*Warning:* There must be enough space reserved in the data section after the null byte of the first string to hold the characters from the second string.)

3. Write a complete program that prompts for and inputs a person's name in the "LastName, FirstName" format and builds a new string with the name in the format "FirstName LastName". A comma and a space separate the names originally and there is no character (except the null) following FirstName; only a space separates the names in the new string. After you generate the new string in memory, display it.

4. Write a complete program that prompts for and inputs a person's name in the "LastName FirstName" format and builds a new string with the name in the format "FirstName LastName". One or more spaces separate the names originally and there may be spaces following FirstName. Only a single space separates the names in the new string. After you generate the new string in memory, display it.

5. Write a complete program that prompts for and inputs a string and a single character. Construct a new string that is identical to the old one

except that it is shortened by removing each occurrence of the character. After you generate the new string in memory, display it.

6. Write a complete program that prompts for and inputs a sentence and a
single word. Construct a new sentence that is identical to the old one
except that it is shortened by removing each occurrence of the word.
After you generate the new sentence in memory, display it.

7. Write a complete program that prompts for and inputs a sentence and
two words. Construct a new sentence that is identical to the old one
except that each occurrence of the first word is replaced by the second
word. After you generate the new sentence in memory, display it.

8.3   Character Translation

Sometimes character data are available in one format but need to be in another format
for processing. One instance of this occurs when characters are transmitted between
two computer systems, one normally using ASCII character codes and the other normally
using EBCDIC character codes. Another time character codes need to be altered is to
transmit them to a device that cannot process all possible codes; it is sometimes easier
to replace the unsuitable codes by acceptable codes than to delete them entirely.

The 80x86 instruction set includes the **xlat** instruction to translate one character to another character. In combination with other string-processing instructions, it can
easily translate characters in a string.

The **xlat** instruction requires only 1 byte of object code, the opcode D7. Prior to
execution, the character to be translated is in the AL register. The instruction works by
using a translation table in the data segment to look up the translation of the byte in AL.
This translation table normally contains 256 bytes of data, one for each possible 8-bit
value in AL. The byte at offset zero in the table (the first byte) is the character to which
00 is translated. The byte at offset one is the character to which 01 is translated. In general, **xlat** uses the character being translated as a zero-based index into the table, and
the byte at that index then replaces the character in AL.

The **xlat** instruction has no operand. The EBX register must contain the
address of the translation table. (RBX is used in 64-bit mode.)

Figure 8.12 lists a short *console32* program that translates each character of
string in place; that is, it replaces each character by its translation using the original
location in memory. This program again makes use of the *strlen* procedure that first
appeared in Figure 8.7. Here it is in a separately assembled file. The heart of the program
is the translation table and the sequence of instructions

```
                mov     ecx, strLength ; string length
                lea     ebx, table     ; address of translation table
                lea     esi, string    ; address of string
                lea     edi, string    ; destination also string
    forIndex:   lodsb                  ; copy next character to AL
                xlat                   ; translate character
                stosb                  ; copy character back into string
                loop    forIndex       ; repeat for all characters
```

```
; Translate upper case letters to lower case; don't change lower
; case letters and digits. Translate other characters to spaces.
; author: R. Detmer
; revised: 7/2008

.586
.MODEL FLAT
.STACK  4096
EXTERN strlen:PROC

.DATA
string      BYTE    "This is a #!$& STRING",0
table       BYTE    48 DUP (' '), "0123456789", 7 DUP (' ')
            BYTE    "abcdefghijklmnopqrstuvwxyz", 6 DUP (' ')
            BYTE    "abcdefghijklmnopqrstuvwxyz", 133 DUP (' ')
.CODE
main        PROC
            lea   eax, string    ; get string length
            push  eax            ; parameter
            call  strlen         ; strlen(string)
            add   esp, 4         ; remove parameter
            mov   ecx, eax       ; string length
            lea   ebx, table     ; address of translation table
            lea   esi, string    ; address of string
            lea   edi, string    ; destination also string
forIndex:   lodsb                ; copy next character to AL
            xlat                 ; translate character
            stosb                ; copy character back into string
            loop  forIndex       ; repeat for all characters

            mov   eax, 0
            ret
main        ENDP
END
```

Figure 8.12 Translation program

These instructions implement a *for* loop with the design

```
for index := 1 to stringLength loop
     load source character into AL;
     translate character in AL;
     copy character in AL to destination;
end for;
```

Each ASCII code is translated to another ASCII code by this program. Upper-case letters are translated to lowercase, lowercase letters and digits are unchanged, and all other characters are translated to spaces. The difficult part of the program is building the translation table. Its construction involves looking at a table of ASCII codes (see Appendix A). For this program the translation table is defined by

```
table       BYTE    48 DUP (' '), "0123456789", 7 DUP (' ')
            BYTE    "abcdefghijklmnopqrstuvwxyz", 6 DUP (' ')
            BYTE    "abcdefghijklmnopqrstuvwxyz", 133 DUP (' ')
```

Careful counting will show that exactly 256 bytes are defined. Recall that a **BYTE** direc-tive stores the ASCII code of each character operand. Each of the first 48 bytes of the table will contain the ASCII code for a space (blank), 20_{16}. Therefore, if the code in the AL register represents any of the first 48 ASCII characters—a control character, or one of the printable characters from 20_{16} (space) to $2F_{16}$ (/)—it will be translated to a space.

Note that it is legal to translate a character to itself. Indeed, this is what will happen for digits; the ASCII codes 30_{16} to 39_{16} for digits 0 through 9 appear at offsets 30_{16} to 39_{16}. The codes for the seven characters : through @ are next in an ASCII chart; each of these will be translated to a space. The next ASCII characters are the uppercase let-ters and the next entries in the table are codes for the lowercase letters. For example, the table contains 61_{16} at offset 41_{16}, so an uppercase A (ASCII code 41_{16}) will be translated to a lowercase a (ASCII code 61_{16}). The next six blanks are at the offsets 91_{16} ([) through 96_{16} ('), so that each of these characters is translated to a blank. The ASCII code for each lowercase letter is assembled at an offset equal to its value, so each lowercase letter is translated to itself. Finally, the translation table contains 133 ASCII codes for blanks;

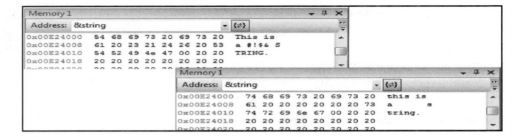

Figure 8.13 Output from translation program

these are the destinations for {, |, }, ~, DEL, and each of the 128-bit patterns starting with a 1, none of them codes for ASCII characters.

Figure 8.13 shows screen dumps from the program running under the debugger, cropped to display just memory starting at the address of string. Notice that "strange" characters are not deleted, they are replaced by blanks.

Exercises 8.3

*1. Here is a partial hexadecimal/EBCDIC conversion table:

81 a	95 n	C1 A	D5 N	40 space
82 b	96 o	C2 B	D6 O	4B .
83 c	97 p	C3 C	D7 P	6B ,
84 d	98 q	C4 D	D8 Q	F0 0
85 e	99 r	C5 E	D9 R	F1 1
86 f	A2 s	C6 F	E2 S	F2 2
87 g	A3 t	C7 G	E3 T	F3 3
88 h	A4 u	C8 H	E4 U	F4 4
89 i	A5 v	C9 I	E5 V	F5 5
91 j	A6 w	D1 J	E6 W	F6 6
92 k	A7 x	D2 K	E7 X	F7 7
93 l	A8 y	D3 L	E8 Y	F8 8
94 m	A9 z	D4 M	E9 Z	F9 9

Give a translation table that would be suitable for xlat translation of EBCDIC codes for letters, digits, space, period, and comma to the corresponding ASCII codes, translating every other EBCDIC code to a null character.

2. Give a translation table that would be suitable for xlat translation of ASCII codes for lowercase letters to the corresponding uppercase letters, leaving all other characters unchanged.

Programming Exercise 8.3

1. In the United States, decimal numbers are written with a decimal point separating the integral part from the fractional part and with commas every three positions to the left of the decimal point. In many European countries, decimal numbers are written with the roles of commas and decimal points reversed. For example, the number 1,234,567.89 would be written 1.234.567,89. Write a *windows32* program that will interchange commas and periods, translating a string of characters representing either format of number to the other format. Use the xlat instruction with a translation table that translates a period to a comma, a comma to a period, each digit to itself, and any other character to a space. Use a dialog box to prompt for and input the number to be translated. Translate the string. Use a message box to display an appropriate label and the reformatted number.

8.4   Converting a 2's Complement Integer to an ASCII String

The *dtoa* macro has been used to convert 2's complement integers to strings of ASCII characters for output. In this section we examine the code for *dtoa* and the *dtoaproc* procedure it calls. The *dtoaproc* uses only one string instruction, but it provides a good example of string manipulation.

The *dtoa* macro expands into the following sequence of instructions.

```
push    ebx             ; save EBX
lea     ebx, dest       ; destination address
push    ebx             ; destination parameter
mov     ebx, [esp+4]    ; in case source was EBX
mov     ebx, source     ; source value
push    ebx             ; source parameter
call    dtoaproc        ; call dtoaproc(source,dest)
add     esp, 8          ; remove parameters
pop     ebx             ; restore EBX
```

These instructions call procedure *dtoaproc* passing source and destination arguments on the stack. The actual source and destination are used in the expanded macro, not the macro parameters *source* and *dest* used in the model statements. So that the user does not need to worry about register contents being altered, EBX is initially saved on the stack and is restored at the end of the sequence. Other registers used by *dtoaproc* are preserved by the procedure itself. There is still a problem if the macro call was **dtoa dest, ebx,** a reasonably likely possibility. To avoid this problem, the original value in EBX is recovered from the stack before the source argument is pushed on the stack. Notice that there is no protection for the less likely possibility of the macro call **dtoa [ebx], source** or some other indirect addressing form using EBX; in this case the macro will not work correctly. The macro could be bypassed, however, using a direct call to *dtoaproc*.

The real work of 2's complement integer to ASCII conversion is done by the procedure *dtoaproc*. The source code, from file *io.asm*, is shown in Figure 8.14. The procedure follows *cdecl* conventions. Entry code preserves the flags register since the direction flag will be cleared by the body, and the caller may be assuming the opposite value.

The basic idea of the procedure is to build a string of characters right to left by repeatedly dividing the number by 10, using the remainder to determine the rightmost character. For instance, dividing the number 2895 ($B4F_{16}$) by 10 gives a remainder of 5 and a quotient of 289 (121_{16}), the last digit of the number, and a new number with which to repeat the process. This scheme works nicely for positive numbers, but a negative number must be changed to its absolute value before starting the division loop. To complicate things further, the bit pattern 80000000_{16} represents the negative number $-2,147,483,648_{10}$, but $+2,147,483,648$ cannot be represented in 2's complement form in a doubleword.

After the entry code, the source value parameter is copied to EAX and the destination address to EDI. The procedure then checks for the special case 80000000_{16}. If this is the source, then the ASCII codes for -2147483648 are moved one at a time to the destination, using the fact that the destination address is in EDI. The location for the minus sign is in the EDI register, so register indirect addressing can be used to put this character in the correct memory byte. The location for the character 2 is one byte beyond the address contained in EDI; this address is referenced by **[edi+1]**. The remaining nine characters are similarly put in place, and the procedure is exited.

The general case of the procedure starts by putting 10 leading blanks in the 11-byte-long destination field. The procedure does this with a **rep stosb** that uses EDI to point to successive bytes in the destination field. Note that EDI is left pointing at the last byte of the destination field.

```
; dtoaproc(source, dest)
; convert double (source) to string of 11 characters at destination address
dtoaproc      PROC   NEAR32
              push   ebp                ; save base pointer
              mov    ebp, esp           ; establish stack frame
              push   eax                ; Save registers
              push   ebx                ;   used by
              push   ecx                ;   procedure
              push   edx
              push   edi
              pushfd                    ; save flags

              mov    eax, [ebp+8]       ; first parameter (source double)
              mov    edi, [ebp+12]      ; second parameter (dest addr)
ifSpecialD:   cmp    eax,80000000h      ; special case -2,147,483,648?
              jne    EndIfSpecialD      ; if not, then normal case
              mov    BYTE PTR [edi],'-' ; manually put in ASCII codes
              mov    BYTE PTR [edi+1],'2' ;   for -2,147,483,648
              mov    BYTE PTR [edi+2],'1'
              mov    BYTE PTR [edi+3],'4'
              mov    BYTE PTR [edi+4],'7'
              mov    BYTE PTR [edi+5],'4'
              mov    BYTE PTR [edi+6],'8'
              mov    BYTE PTR [edi+7],'3'
              mov    BYTE PTR [edi+8],'6'
              mov    BYTE PTR [edi+9],'4'
              mov    BYTE PTR [edi+10],'8'
              jmp    ExitDToA           ; done with special case
EndIfSpecialD:

              push   eax                ; save source number

              mov    al,' '             ; put blanks in
              mov    ecx,10             ;   first ten
              cld                       ;   bytes of
              rep stosb                 ;   destination field

              pop    eax                ; copy source number
              mov    cl,' '             ; default sign (blank for +)
IfNegD:       cmp    eax,0              ; check sign of number
              jge    EndIfNegD          ; skip if not negative
              mov    cl,'-'             ; sign for negative number
              neg    eax                ; number in EAX now >= 0
```

(continues)

Figure 8.14 Doubleword to ASCII conversion procedure

```
EndIfNegD:

            mov     ebx,10                ; divisor

WhileMoreD: mov     edx,0                 ; extend number to doubleword
            div     ebx                   ; divide by 10
            add     dl,30h                ; convert remainder to character
            mov     [edi],dl              ; put character in string
            dec     edi                   ; move forward to next position
            cmp     eax,0                 ; check quotient
            jnz     WhileMoreD            ; continue if quotient not zero

            mov     [edi],cl              ; insert blank or "-" for sign

ExitDToA:   popfd                         ; restore flags and registers
            pop     edi
            pop     edx
            pop     ecx
            pop     ebx
            pop     eax
            pop     ebp
            ret                           ;exit
dtoaproc    ENDP
```

Figure 8.14 Doubleword to ASCII conversion procedure *(continued)*

The procedure then stores the correct "sign" in the CL register. A blank is used for a number greater than or equal to zero, and minus character (−) is used for a negative number. A negative number is also negated, giving its absolute value for subsequent processing.

Finally the main idea is executed. The divisor 10 is placed in the EBX register. The nonnegative number is extended to a doubleword by putting 0 in EDX. Division by the 10 in EBX gives a remainder from 0 to 9 in EDX, the last decimal digit of the number. This is converted to the corresponding ASCII code by adding 30_{16}—recall that the ASCII codes for digits 0 through 9 are 30_{16} through 39_{16}. The ASCII code is then placed in the destination string, and EDI is decremented to point at the next position to the left.

This process is repeated until the quotient is 0. Finally the "sign" stored in CL (blank or −) is copied to the immediate left of the last code for a digit. Other positions to the left, if any, were previously filled with blanks.

Exercises 8.4

*1. Why does *dtoaproc* use a destination string 11 bytes long?

2. Suppose that negative numbers are not changed before the division loop of *dtoaproc* begins, and that an `idiv` instruction is used rather than a `div` instruction in this loop. Recall that when a negative number is divided by a positive number, both quotient and remainder will be negative. For instance, $-1273 = 10*(-127) + (-3)$. How could the rest of the division loop be modified to produce the correct ASCII codes for both positive and negative numbers?

Programming Exercises 8.4

1. Rewrite *dtoaproc*, adding a length parameter. Specifically, the new *dtoaNew* will be a procedure with three parameters:

    (1) The 2's complement number to convert to ASCII characters (a doubleword).

    (2) The address of the ASCII string (a doubleword).

    (3) The desired length of the ASCII string (a doubleword).

    The number will be converted to a string of ASCII characters starting at the offset in the data segment. Do not use a blank in front of a positive number. If the length is less than the actual number of characters needed to display the number, fill the entire field with pound signs (#). If the length is larger than needed, pad with extra spaces to the left of the number.

8.5 Chapter Summary

The word *string* refers to a collection of consecutive bytes, words, double-words, or quadwords in memory. The 80x86 instruction set includes five instructions for operating on strings: `movs` (to move or copy a string from a source to a destination location), `cmps` (to compare two strings), `scas` (to scan a string for a particular element), `stos` (to store a given value in a string), and `lods` (to copy a string element into the accumulator). Each of these has mnemonic forms ending with b, w, d, or q to give the size of the string element.

A string instruction operates on one string element at a time.

When a source string is involved, the source index register ESI contains the address of the string element. When a destination string is involved, the destination index register EDI contains the address of the string element. An index register is incremented or decremented after the string element is accessed, depending on whether the direction flag DF is reset to zero or set to one; the `cld` and `std` instructions are used to give the direction flag a desired value.

Repeat prefixes `rep`, `repe` (`repz`) and `repne` (`repnz`) are used with some string instructions to cause them to automatically repeat. The number of times to execute a primitive instruction is placed in the ECX register. The conditional repeat forms use the count in ECX but will also terminate instruction execution if the zero flag gets a certain value; these are appropriate for use with the `cmps` and `scas` instructions which set or reset ZF.

The `xlat` instruction is used to translate the characters of a string. It requires a 256-byte-long translation table that starts with the destination byte to which the source byte 00 is translated and ends with the destination byte to which the source byte FF is translated. The `xlat` instruction can be used for such applications as changing ASCII codes to EBCDIC codes, or for changing the case of letters within a given character coding system.

The *dtoa* macro expands to code that calls a procedure *dtoaproc*. Basically this procedure works by repeatedly dividing a nonnegative number by 10, and using the remainder to get the rightmost character of the destination string.

The 80x86 microprocessors are classified as complex instruction set computers. The string instructions provide good illustrations of why they are CISC machines.

CHAPTER 9

Floating Point Operations

This book has concentrated on integer representations of numbers since all 80x86 microprocessors have a variety of instructions to manipulate integers. Most 80x86 microprocessors also have instructions to manipulate numbers stored in floating point formats.

The first section of this chapter describes the floating point formats used in the 80x86 architecture. Section 9.2 describes the floating point architecture, which has a completely new set of registers and instructions. Section 9.3 tells how to convert floating point values to and from readable formats. Section 9.4 describes the single-instruction multiple-data registers and instructions that provide an alternative way to do some floating point operations. Finally, Section 9.5 illustrates how to use assembly language procedures with C/C++ programs in the Visual Studio environment.

9.1 Floating Point Formats

Floating point schemes store numbers in forms that correspond closely to scientific notation. Section 1.5 described the IEEE single-precision format, one of the three floating point formats used in 80x86 processors. Recall that it is a 32-bit format consisting of a sign bit, an 8-bit biased exponent (the actual exponent in a normalized binary exponential format plus 127), and a 23-bit fraction (the fraction in the exponential format without the leading 1 bit). Section 1.5 gave the following steps to convert a decimal number to single-precision format:

1. Use a leading 0 bit for a positive number or 1 for a negative number.

2. Write the unsigned decimal number in binary.

3. Write the binary number in binary scientific notation $f_{23}.f_{22} \ldots f_0 \times 2^e$, where $f_{23} = 1$. There are 24 fraction bits, including trailing 0's.

4. Add a bias of 127_{10} to the exponent e. This sum, in binary form, is the next 8 bits of the floating point number, following the sign bit.

5. The fraction bits $f_{22}f_{21} \ldots f_0$ form the last 23 bits of the floating point number. The leading bit f_{23} (which is always 1) is dropped.

In the data section of an assembly language program, the **REAL4** directive generates 4 bytes of storage, optionally initialized to a single floating point value. For example,

```
number1 REAL4    78.375
```

results in

```
00000000 429CC000   number1 REAL4    78.375
```

in the listing file.

The second floating point format the 80x86 uses is the 64-bit IEEE **double-precision** format. It is very similar to the single-precision format except the exponent has a bias of 1023 and is stored in 11 bits, and the fraction is stored in 52 bits. Using -78.375, the negative of the example in Section 1.5,

$$-78.375_{10} = -1.001110011 \times 2^6$$

The sign bit is 1, the exponent is $6 + 1023 = 1029 = 100\ 0000\ 0101$, and the fraction is $00111001100 \ldots 0$ with enough trailing zeros to make 52 bits. Piecing this together into a quadword and regrouping gives 1100 0000 0101 0011 1001 1000 0000 . . . 0000 or C053980000000000 in hex.

In the data section of an assembly language program, the **REAL8** directive generates 8 bytes of storage, optionally initialized to a double-precision floating point value. For example,

        number2 REAL8   -78.375

results in

        00000004   number2 REAL8   -78.375
                   C053980000000000

in the listing file. The statement is displayed on two lines because of its length.

The third 80x86 floating point format is an 80-bit format known as **double extended-precision**. It again starts with the sign bit. It uses a 15-bit exponent with a bias of 16,383. The fraction is 64 bits long and, different from the single- and double-precision formats, *does* include the leading 1 bit. Again using 78.375 as an example

$$78.375_{10} = 1.001110011 \times 2^6$$

The sign bit is 0, the exponent is $6+16383 = 16389 = 100\ 0000\ 0000\ 0101$, and the fraction is 100111001100 . . . 0 with enough trailing zeros to make 64 bits. Piecing this together into 10 bytes and regrouping gives 0100 0000 0000 0101 1001 1100 1100 0000. . .0000 or 40059CC0000000000000 in hex.

In the data section of an assembly language program, the **REAL10** directive generates 10 bytes of storage, optionally initialized to an extended real floating point value. For example,

        number3 REAL10 78.375

results in

        0000000C   number3 REAL10 78.375
                   40059CC0000000000000

in the listing file. Again, the statement is displayed on two lines because of its length.

Using a bias in the exponent's representation is an alternative to storing a signed number in 2's complement form. With single format, the largest biased exponent FF (eight 1 bits) and the smallest biased exponent 00 are reserved to represent special values. In general, an exponent of all 0 bits or all 1 bits is special for each floating point format. This means that the largest actual exponent in single format is 254–127, or 127. The largest fraction is $1.11111111111111111111111_2$, which is almost $10.0_2 = 2_{10}$. This means that the largest single floating point value is approximately 2×2^{127} or about 3.40×10^{38}. Verification of other minima and maxima is left as exercises.

The single format has 24 significant fraction bits, the implied leading 1 bit plus the 23 bits that are stored, for 2^{23} distinct patterns. Since $2^{23} = 8{,}388{,}608$, the single format has about seven decimal digits of precision. Verification of other precision calculations are left as exercises. Figure 9.1 summarizes information about the three floating point formats.

The formats described above are for **normalized** representations, ones where the binary scientific notation mantissa is written starting with 1 and the binary point. These are the commonly used representations. Obviously zero cannot be normalized. A pattern of all 0 bits represents +0. A 1 followed by 0 bits represents −0. The IEEE standards and the 80x86 architecture provide for other non-normalized values. The IEEE standards even define formats for +∞ and −∞, and NaN ("not a number"), a format that is used when a calculation leads to a nonrepresentable value.

Obviously not all real numbers can be represented in any given floating point system—there are infinitely many real numbers and only a finite number of bit patterns in 32, 64, or 80 bits. Many decimal numbers, such as our example 73.375 and all whole numbers unless the magnitude is too large, have exact representations. The numbers that can be exactly represented are not evenly distributed. On the real number line, they are very dense around 0.0 and then become more and more sparse as you move toward larger and larger values. In other words, for a real number without an exact representation, if it is close to 0.0, the floating point approximation will be very close, but if it is

Format	Total Bits	Exponent Bits	Fraction Bits	Approximate Maximum	Approximate Minimum	Approximate Decimal Precision
Single	32	8	23	3.40×10^{38}	1.18×10^{-38}	7 digits
Double	64	11	52	1.79×10^{308}	2.23×10^{-308}	15 digits
Extended Double	80	15	64	1.19×10^{4932}	3.37×10^{-4932}	19 digits

Figure 9.1 Floating point formats

huge, the difference in the number and its best floating point approximation may be large in an absolute sense.

▨▨▨▨ Exercises 9.1

Find the single-precision floating point representation of each of the following numbers:

1. 175.5
2. −1.25
*3. −11.75
4. 45.5

5. 0.09375
6. −0.0078125
7. 3160.0
8. −31.0

Find the double-precision floating point representation of each of the following numbers:

9. 175.5
10. −1.25
11. −11.75
12. 45.5

*13. 0.09375
14. −0.0078125
15. 3160.0
16. −31.0

Find the extended double-precision floating point representation of each of the following numbers:

17. 175.5
18. −1.25
19. −11.75
*20. 45.5

21. 0.09375
22. −0.0078125
23. 3160.0
24. −31.0

Find the decimal number corresponding to each of the following single-precision floating point representations:

25. C26A0000
26. 46FB0800

Find the decimal number corresponding to each of the following double-precision floating point representations:

27. 407A44570A3D70A4
*28. BFA4000000000000

Find the decimal number corresponding to each of the following extended double-precision floating point representations:

29. 4008FA00000000000000
30. BFFEA0000000000000009

31. Show that 1.18×10^{-38} is the approximate minimum value for a normalized single-precision floating point number.

32. Show that 1.79×10^{308} is the approximate maximum value for a normalized double-precision floating point number.

*33. Show that 2.23×10^{-308} is the approximate minimum value for a normalized double-precision floating point number.

34. Show that 1.19×10^{4932} is the approximate maximum value for a normalized extended double-precision floating point number.
35. Show that 3.37×10^{-4932} is the approximate minimum value for a normalized extended double-precision floating point number.
36. Show that the decimal precision for a double-precision floating point number is approximately 15 digits.
*37. Show that the decimal precision for an extended double-precision floating point number is approximately 19 digits.
38. Most decimal fractions do not have exact binary representations. Suppose that x is a decimal number with $0 < x < 1$. One way to get a good n-bit binary approximation is to repeatedly check if 2^{-j} "fits" in x for $j = 1$, $2, \ldots n$. If it does, put a 1 in the representation and subtract 2^{-j} from x; if not, put a 0 in the representation. Expand this idea to a complete pseudocode algorithm.

9.2   80x86 Floating Point Architecture

The **floating point unit** (FPU) of an 80x86 microprocessor is almost independent of the rest of the chip. It has its own internal registers, separate from the registers used by integer operations. It executes instructions to perform floating point arithmetic operations, including commonplace operations such as addition or multiplication, and more complicated operations such as evaluation of some transcendental functions like sine or logarithm. Not only can it transfer floating point operands to or from memory, it can also transfer integer or binary coded decimal (BCD) operands to or from the coprocessor, converting between formats as part of the transfer.

The FPU has eight data registers, each 80 bits long. The extended double-precision floating point format is used for values stored in these registers. The registers are organized as a stack—for example, when the **fld** (floating load) instruction is used to transfer a value from memory to the floating point unit, the value is loaded into the register at the top of the stack, and data stored in the stack top and other registers are pushed down one register. However, some instructions can access registers below the stack top, so that the organization is not a pure stack.

The names of the eight floating point registers are

- ST, the stack top, also called ST(0);
- ST(1), the register just below the stack top;
- ST(2), the register just below ST(1);

- ST(3), ST(4), ST(5), ST(6); and
- ST(7), the register at the bottom of the stack.

In addition to the eight data registers, the floating point unit has several 16-bit control registers, one of which is the **status word**. Some of the status word bits are assigned values by floating point comparison instructions, and these bits must be examined in order for the 80x86 to execute conditional jump instructions based on floating point comparison.

Before considering the floating point instructions, a few notes are in order. Each floating point mnemonic starts with the letter F, a letter that is not used as the first character of any non-floating instruction. Most floating point instructions act on the stack top ST, or on ST and one other operand in another floating point register, or in memory. No floating point instruction can transfer data between an 80x86 general register (such as EAX) and a floating point register—transfers must be made using a memory location for intermediate storage. (There is, however, an instruction to transfer the status word or to AX.)

The floating point instructions are examined in groups, starting with instructions to push operands onto the stack. Figure 9.2 lists these mnemonics. This book does not include opcodes of number of bytes of object code for floating point instructions. Most of the instructions have 1- or 2-byte opcodes, and no additional bytes of object code unless there is a memory operand.

Mnemonic	Operand	Action
`fld`	memory (real)	real value from memory pushed onto stack
`fild`	memory (integer)	integer value from memory converted to floating point and pushed onto stack
`fld`	st(*num*)	contents of floating point register pushed onto stack
`fld1`	(none)	1.0 pushed onto stack
`fldz`	(none)	0.0 pushed onto stack
`fldpi`	(none)	π (pi) pushed onto stack
`fldl2e`	(none)	$\log_2(e)$ pushed onto stack
`fldl2t`	(none)	$\log_2(10)$ pushed onto stack
`fldlg2`	(none)	$\log_{10}(2)$ pushed onto stack
`fldln2`	(none)	$\log_e(2)$ pushed onto stack

Figure 9.2 Floating point load instructions

Some examples illustrate how these instructions work. Suppose that the floating point register stack contains

1.0	ST
2.0	ST(1)
3.0	ST(2)
	ST(3)
	ST(4)
	ST(5)
	ST(6)
	ST(7)

with values shown in decimal rather than in IEEE floating point format. (As you will see shortly, the debugger also shows floating point register contents in decimal.) If the data segment contains

```
fpValue    REAL4   10.0
intValue   DWORD   20
```

then the values assembled will be 41200000 for *fpValue* and 00000014 for *intValue*. If the instruction **fld fpValue** is executed, the register stack will contain

10.0	ST
1.0	ST(1)
2.0	ST(2)
3.0	ST(3)
	ST(4)
	ST(5)
	ST(6)
	ST(7)

The original values have all been pushed down one register position on the stack. Starting with these values, if the instruction **fld st(2)** is now executed, the register stack will contain

2.0	ST
10.0	ST(1)
1.0	ST(2)
2.0	ST(3)
3.0	ST(4)
	ST(5)
	ST(6)
	ST(7)

Notice that the value 2.0 from ST(2) has been pushed onto the top of the stack, but not removed from the stack. Starting with these values, assume that the instruction **fild intValue** is executed. The new contents of the register stack will be

20.0	ST
2.0	ST(1)
10.0	ST(2)
1.0	ST(3)
2.0	ST(4)
3.0	ST(5)
	ST(6)
	ST(7)

What is not obvious here is that the 32-bit value 00000014 is converted to an 80-bit extended double-precision floating point value. An integer operand must be word length, doubleword length, or quadword length—byte-length integer operands are not allowed.

Finally, if the instructions **fldz** and **fldpi** are executed in this order, the FPU register stack will contain

3.14...	ST
0.0	ST(1)
20.0	ST(2)
2.0	ST(3)
10.0	ST(4)
1.0	ST(5)
2.0	ST(6)
3.0	ST(7)

The stack is now full. No further value can be pushed onto the stack unless some value is popped from the stack, or the stack is cleared. The instruction **finit** initializes the floating point unit and clears the contents of all eight registers. Often a program that uses the floating point unit will include the statement

```
finit      ; initialize the FPU
```

near the beginning of the code. It may be desirable to reinitialize the floating point unit at points in the code, but normally this is not required since values will be popped from the floating point stack, not allowed to accumulate on the stack.

The debugger lets you trace floating point operations. Floating point register contents are shown by right-clicking in the Registers windows and selecting Floating Point. Figure 9.3 shows a screen dump following execution of the code shown in the fig9-3.asm window. Notice that floating point register contents are shown as decimal numbers in an E-format, rather than in hex representing the actual bits.

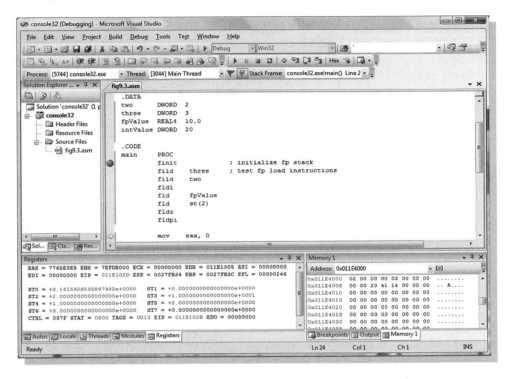

Figure 9.3 Debugger view of floating point execution

Figure 9.4 lists the floating point instructions that are used to copy data from the stack top to memory, or to another floating point register. These instructions are mostly paired—one instruction of each pair simply copies ST to its destination while the other instruction is identical, except that it copies ST to its destination and also pops ST off the register stack.

A few examples illustrate the actions of and the differences between these instructions. Assume that the directive

```
intValue   DWORD ?
```

Mnemonic	Operand	Action
fst	st(*num*)	replaces contents of ST(*num*) by copy of value from ST; only ST(*num*) is affected
fstp	st(*num*)	replaces contents of ST(*num*) by copy of value from ST; ST popped off the stack
fst	memory (real)	copy of ST stored as real value in memory; the stack is not affected
fstp	memory (real)	copy of ST stored as real value in memory; ST popped off the stack
fist	memory (integer)	copy of ST rounded to integer and stored in memory
fistp	memory (integer)	copy of ST rounded to integer and stored in memory; ST popped off the stack
fisttp	memory (integer)	copy of ST truncated to integer and stored in memory; ST popped off the stack

Figure 9.4 Floating point data store instructions

is coded in the data segment. Suppose that the floating point register stack contains

10.0	ST
20.0	ST(1)
30.0	ST(2)
40.0	ST(3)
	ST(4)
	ST(5)
	ST(6)
	ST(7)

The left diagram shows the resulting stack if **fist intValue** is executed and the right diagram shows the resulting stack if **fistp intValue** is executed. In both cases, the contents of *intValue* will be 0000000A, the doubleword 2's complement integer version of the floating point number 10.0.

After `fist`		*After* `fistp`		
10.0	ST	20.0	ST	
20.0	ST(1)	30.0	ST(1)	
30.0	ST(2)	40.0	ST(2)	
40.0	ST(3)		ST(3)	
	ST(4)		ST(4)	
	ST(5)		ST(5)	
	ST(6)		ST(6)	
	ST(7)		ST(7)	

The situation is a bit more confusing when the destination is one of the floating point registers. Suppose that at execution time the floating register stack contains

1.0	ST
2.0	ST(1)
3.0	ST(2)
4.0	ST(3)
	ST(4)
	ST(5)
	ST(6)
	ST(7)

The left diagram shows the resulting stack if `fst st(2)` is executed and the right diagram shows the resulting stack if `fstp st(2)` is executed. In the first case, a copy of ST has been stored in ST(2). In the second case, the copy has been made, and then the stack has been popped.

After `fst`		After `fstp`	
1.0	ST	2.0	ST
2.0	ST(1)	1.0	ST(1)
1.0	ST(2)	4.0	ST(2)
4.0	ST(3)		ST(3)
	ST(4)		ST(4)
	ST(5)		ST(5)
	ST(6)		ST(6)
	ST(7)		ST(7)

In addition to the load and store instructions previously listed, the floating point unit has an **fxch** instruction that will exchange the contents of ST with another floating point register. With no operand,

```
fxch            ; exchange ST and ST(1)
```

will exchange the contents of the stack top and ST(1) just below ST on the stack. With a single operand, for example,

```
fxch   st(3)  ; exchange ST and ST(3)
```

will interchange ST with the specified register. The instruction cannot be used to exchange ST with a value in memory.

Figure 9.5 shows the floating point addition instructions. There are versions for adding the contents of ST to another register, contents of any register to ST, a real number from memory to ST, or an integer number from memory to ST. The **faddp** instruction pops the stack top after adding it to another register, so that both operands are destroyed.

Mnemonic	Operand(s)	Action
fadd	(none)	pops both ST and ST(1); adds these values; pushes sum onto the stack
fadd	st(*num*), st	adds ST(*num*) and ST; replaces ST(*num*) by the sum
fadd	st, st(*num*)	adds ST and ST(*num*); replaces ST by the sum
fadd	memory (real)	adds ST and real number from memory; replaces ST by the sum
fiadd	memory (integer)	adds ST and integer from memory; replaces ST by the sum
faddp	st(*num*), st	adds ST(*num*) and ST; replaces ST(*num*) by the sum; pops ST from stack

Figure 9.5 Floating point addition instructions

A few examples illustrate how the floating point addition instructions work. Suppose that the data segment contains the directives

```
fpValue    REAL4   5.0
intValue   DWORD   1
```

and that the floating point register stack contains

10.0	ST
20.0	ST(1)
30.0	ST(2)
40.0	ST(3)
	ST(4)
	ST(5)
	ST(6)
	ST(7)

After the instruction

```
fadd    st, st(3)
```

is executed, the stack contains

50.0	ST
20.0	ST(1)
30.0	ST(2)
40.0	ST(3)
	ST(4)
	ST(5)
	ST(6)
	ST(7)

Starting with these stack values, after the two instructions

```
fadd    fpValue
fiadd   intValue
```

are executed, the contents of the stack are

56.0	ST
20.0	ST(1)
30.0	ST(2)
40.0	ST(3)
	ST(4)
	ST(5)
	ST(6)
	ST(7)

Finally, if the instruction

```
faddp   st(2),st
```

is executed, the stack will contain

20.0	ST
86.0	ST(1)
40.0	ST(2)
	ST(3)
	ST(4)
	ST(5)
	ST(6)
	ST(7)

Subtraction instructions are displayed in Figure 9.6. The first six instructions are very similar to the corresponding addition instructions. The next six subtraction instructions are the same except that the operands are subtracted in the opposite order. This is convenient because subtraction is not commutative.

An example illustrates the difference between the parallel subtraction instructions. Suppose that the floating point register stack contains

15.0	ST
25.0	ST(1)
35.0	ST(2)
45.0	ST(3)
55.0	ST(4)
	ST(5)
	ST(6)
	ST(7)

Mnemonic	Operand(s)	Action
`fsub`	(none)	pops ST and ST(1); calculates ST(1) − ST; pushes difference onto the stack
`fsub`	st(*num*), st	calculates ST(*num*) − ST; replaces ST(*num*) by the difference
`fsub`	st, st(*num*)	calculates ST − ST(*num*); replaces ST by the difference
`fsub`	memory (real)	calculates ST − real number from memory; replaces ST by the difference
`fisub`	memory (integer)	calculates ST − integer from memory; replaces ST by the difference
`fsubp`	st(*num*), st	calculates ST(*num*) − ST; replaces ST(*num*) by the difference; pops ST from the stack
`fsubr`	(none)	pops ST and ST(1); calculates ST − ST(1); pushes difference onto the stack
`fsubr`	st(*num*), st	calculates ST − ST(*num*); replaces ST(*num*) by the difference
`fsubr`	st, st(*num*)	calculates ST(*num*) − ST; replaces ST by the difference
`fsubr`	memory (real)	calculates real number from memory − ST; replaces ST by the difference
`fisubr`	memory (integer)	calculates integer from memory − ST; replaces ST by the difference
`fsubpr`	st(*num*), st	calculates ST − ST(*num*); replaces ST(*num*) by the difference; pops ST from the stack

Figure 9.6 Floating point subtraction instructions

The following two diagrams show the results after executing the instructions **fsub st,st(3)** and **fsubr st,st(3)**.

	After **fsub st,st(3)**			*After* **fsubr st,st(3)**	
−30.0	ST		30.0	ST	
25.0	ST(1)		25.0	ST(1)	
35.0	ST(2)		35.0	ST(2)	
45.0	ST(3)		45.0	ST(3)	
55.0	ST(4)		55.0	ST(4)	
	ST(5)			ST(5)	
	ST(6)			ST(6)	
	ST(7)			ST(7)	

Multiplication and division instructions are listed in Figures 9.7 and 9.8, respectively. Multiplication instructions have the same forms as the addition instructions in

Mnemonic	Operand(s)	Action
fmul	(none)	pops ST and ST(1); multiplies these values; pushes product onto the stack
fmul	st(*num*), st	multiplies ST(*num*) and ST; replaces ST(*num*) by the product
fmul	st, st(*num*)	multiplies ST and ST(*num*); replaces ST by the product
fmul	memory (real)	multiplies ST and real number from memory; replaces ST by the product
fimul	memory (integer)	multiplies ST and integer from memory; replaces ST by the product
fmulp	st(*num*), st	multiplies ST(*num*) and ST; replaces ST(*num*) by the product; pops ST from stack

Figure 9.7 Floating point multiplication instructions

Mnemonic	Operand(s)	Action
fdiv	(none)	pops ST and ST(1); calculates ST(1) / ST; pushes quotient onto the stack
fdiv	st(*num*), st	calculates ST(*num*) / ST; replaces ST(*num*) by the quotient
fdiv	st,st(*num*)	calculates ST / ST(*num*); replaces ST by the quotient
fdiv	memory (real)	calculates ST / real number from memory; replaces ST by the quotient
fidiv	memory (integer)	calculates ST / integer from memory; replaces ST by the quotient
fdivp	st(*num*),st	calculates ST(*num*) / ST; replaces ST(*num*) by the quotient; pops ST from the stack
fdivr	(none)	pops ST and ST(1); calculates ST / ST(1); pushes quotient onto the stack
fdivr	st(*num*),st	calculates ST / ST(*num*); replaces ST(*num*) by the quotient
fdivr	st,st(*num*)	calculates ST(*num*) / ST; replaces ST by the quotient
fdivr	memory (real)	calculates real number from memory / ST; replaces ST by the quotient
fidivr	memory (integer)	calculates integer from memory / ST; replaces ST by the quotient
fdivpr	st(*num*),st	calculates ST / ST(*num*); replaces ST(*num*) by the quotient; pops ST from the stack

Figure 9.8 Floating point division instructions

Figure 9.5. Division instructions have the same forms as subtraction instructions in Figure 9.6, that is, the *R* versions reverse the operands' dividend and divisor roles.

Figure 9.9 describes four miscellaneous floating point instructions. Additional instructions including trigonometric, exponential, and logarithmic functions are not listed in this book.

The floating point unit provides a collection of instructions to compare the stack top ST to a second operand. These are listed in Figure 9.10. Recall that the floating point unit has a 16-bit control register called the *status word*. The comparison instructions

Mnemonic	Operand(s)	Action
fabs	(none)	ST := | ST | (absolute value)
fchs	(none)	ST := − ST (change sign)
frndint	(none)	rounds ST to an integer value
fsqrt	(none)	replace the contents of ST by its square root

Figure 9.9 Miscellaneous floating point instructions

Mnemonic	Operand(s)	Action
fcom	(none)	compares ST and ST(1)
fcom	st(num)	compares ST and ST(num)
fcom	memory (real)	compares ST and real number in memory
ficom	memory (integer)	compares ST and integer in memory
fcomp	(none)	compares ST and ST(1); then pops stack
fcomp	st(num)	compares ST and ST(num); then pops stack
fcomp	memory (real)	compares ST and real number in memory; then pops stack
ficomp	memory (integer)	compares ST and integer in memory; then pops stack
fcompp	(none)	compares ST and ST(1); then pops stack twice
ftst	(none)	compares ST and 0.0

Figure 9.10 Floating point comparison instructions (set C3, C2, C0)

assign values to bits 14, 10, and 8 in the status word; these "condition code" bits are named C3, C2, and C0, respectively. These flags are set as follows:

Result of Comparison	C3	C2	C0
ST > operand	0	0	0
ST < operand	0	0	1
ST = operand	1	0	0
not comparable	1	1	1

The "not comparable" alternative can occur if one of the operands is the IEEE representation for NaN (not a number), for example.

If a comparison is made in order to determine program flow, simply setting flags in the status word is no help. Conditional jump instructions look at bits in the flag register in the 80x86, not the status word in the floating point unit. Consequently, the status word must be copied to memory or to the AX register before its bits can be examined by an 80x86 instruction, perhaps with a **test** instruction. There is also a **sahf** instruction (below) that copies AH into the flag register so that conditional jump instructions can be used without testing AX. The floating point unit has two instructions to store the status word; these are summarized in Figure 9.11.

Here is an example sequence of instructions for comparing floating point numbers:

```
fcom              ; ST > ST(1)?
fstsw ax          ; copy condition code bits to AX
sahf              ; shift condition code bits to flags
jna    endGT      ; skip if not
```

The new instruction here is **sahf**, which copies AH into the low-order 8 bits of the EFLAGS register. Conveniently, this puts C3 (originally bit 14) in the ZF position (bit 6), C2 (bit 10) in the PF position (bit 2), and C0 (bit 8) in the CF position (bit 0). Now you can use the conditional jump instructions that examine bits in the flags register. Recall the mnemonics listed as appropriate for use after comparison of unsigned operands in Figure 5.6. These examine combinations of ZF and CF and are exactly the ones to use for floating point comparisons. Since C2 now corresponds to PF, you could use **jp** or **jnp** to do a "safety check" for a valid comparison.

The **sahf** instruction is not valid in 64-bit mode. However, there is another option that also works in 64-bit mode and in later 32-bit processors. The **fcomi** and **fcomip** instructions work just like **fcom** and **fcomp** for ST and another stack value,

Mnemonic	Operand(s)	Action
fstsw	memory word	copies status register to memory word
fstsw	AX	copies status register to AX

Figure 9.11 FPU status word access

Mnemonic	Operand(s)	Action
`fcomi`	st, st(*num*)	compares ST and ST(*num*)
`fcomip`	st, st(*num*)	compares ST and ST(*num*), pops stack

Figure 9.12 Floating point comparison instructions (set ZF, PF, CF)

except that they directly set ZF, PF, and CF, avoiding the need for the `fstsw` and `sahf` steps illustrated earlier. These instructions are shown in Figure 9.12.

This section concludes by utilizing some of the floating point instructions in a complete example. Recall that for the quadratic equation

$$ax^2 + bx + c = 0$$

the quadratic formula gives two roots

$$x = \frac{-b \pm \sqrt{b^2 - 4ac}}{2a}$$

The following algorithm incorporates the quadratic formula to compute the roots, if they exist.

```
discr := b*b − 4*a*c;
if discr ≥ 0
then
    x1 := (−b + sqrt(discr))/2*a;
    x2 := (−b − sqrt(discr))/2*a;
end if;
```

Figure 9.13 lists a *console32* program that implements this algorithm. Each of the variables a, b, c, *discr*, $x1$, and $x2$ has storage reserved in memory. (The coefficients a, b, and c have been coded as **aa**, **bb**, and **cc** partly because they are more visible, but mostly because the 32-bit assembler treats **c** as a reserved word.) The screenshot in Figure 9.14 shows this program's state just before the second root is stored and popped

```
; compute roots of quadratic equation
; author: R. Detmer
; date: 7/2008

.586
.MODEL FLAT
.STACK 4096

.DATA
aa      REAL4    2.0
bb      REAL4    -1.0
cc      REAL4    -15.0
discr   REAL4    ?
x1      REAL4    ?
x2      REAL4    ?
four    DWORD    4
two     DWORD    2

.CODE
main    PROC
        finit              ; initialize FPU
        fld     bb         ; b in ST
        fmul    bb         ; b*b
        fild    four       ; 4.0 in ST
        fmul    aa         ; 4*a
        fmul    cc         ; 4*a*c
        fsub               ; b*b-4*a*c
        fldz               ; 0.0 in ST
        fxch               ; b*b-4*a*c in ST; 0.0 in ST(1)
        fcom    st(1)      ; b*b-4*a*c >= 0 ?
        fstsw   ax         ; copy condition code bits to AX
        sahf               ; shift condition code bits to flags
        jnae    endGE      ; skip if not
        fsqrt              ; sqrt(b*b-4*a*c) in ST
        fst     st(1)      ; copy to ST(1)
        fsub    bb         ; -b + sqrt(b*b-4*a*c)
        fdiv    aa         ; (-b + sqrt(b*b-4*a*c))/a
        fidiv   two        ; (-b + sqrt(b*b-4*a*c))/(2*a)
        fstp    x1         ; save and pop stack
        fchs               ; -sqrt(b*b-4*a*c)
        fsub    bb         ; -b -sqrt(b*b-4*a*c)
        fdiv    aa         ; (-b + sqrt(b*b-4*a*c))/a
        fidiv   two        ; (-b + sqrt(b*b-4*a*c))/(2*a)
        fstp    x2         ; save and pop stack
endGE:
        mov     eax, 0     ; exit
        ret
main    ENDP
END
```

Figure 9.13 Find roots of quadratic equation

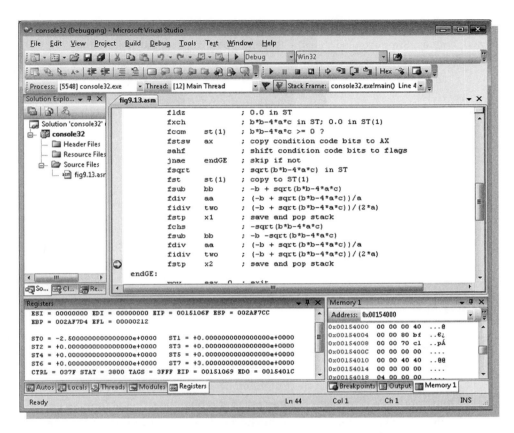

Figure 9.14 Find roots of quadratic equation

from the stack—you can see its value (-2.5) in ST (ST0). Input and output will be added
to this program in the next section.

▬▬▬ Exercises 9.2

1. Suppose that a program's data segment contains

```
fpValue     REAL4     0.5
intValue    DWORD     6
```

and that code executed so far by the program has not changed these values. Suppose also that the floating point register stack contains

9.0	ST
12.0	ST(1)
23.0	ST(2)
24.0	ST(3)
35.0	ST(4)
	ST(5)
	ST(6)
	ST(7)

Assume that these values are correct before each of the following instructions is executed; do *not* use the "after" state of one problem as the "before" state of the next problem. Draw a picture to show the contents of the floating point register stack and give the value of *fpValue* (as a decimal number) and of *intValue* (as an integer) after execution of the instruction.

(a)	fld	st(2)	(n)	fsub	fpValue
*(b)	fld	fpValue	(o)	fisub	intValue
(c)	fild	intValue	(p)	fisubr	intValue
(d)	fldpi		*(q)	fsubp	st(3), st
(e)	fst	st(4)	(r)	fmul	st, st(4)
*(f)	fstp	st(4)	(s)	fmul	
(g)	fst	fpValue	(t)	fmul	fpValue
(h)	fistp	intValue	(u)	fdiv	
(i)	fxch	st(3)	(v)	fdivr	
*(j)	fadd		*(w)	fidiv	intValue
(k)	fadd	st(3), st	(x)	fdivp	st(2), st
(l)	fadd	st, st(3)	(y)	fchs	
(m)	faddp	st(3),st	(z)	fsqrt	

2. Suppose that a program's data segment contains

```
fpValue     REAL4    1.5
intValue    DWORD    9
```

and that code executed so far by the program has not changed these values. Suppose also that the floating point register stack contains

9.0	ST
12.0	ST(1)
23.0	ST(2)
24.0	ST(3)
35.0	ST(4)
	ST(5)
	ST(6)
	ST(7)

Assume that these values are correct before each of the following instructions is executed. Give the contents of the status word flags C3, C2, and C0 after execution of the instruction.

*(a) fcom   (c) fcom   fpValue

 (b) fcom   st(3)   (d) ficom intValue

For the next two parts, also give the contents of the stack following execution of the instructions.

*(e) fcomp   (f) fcompp

Programming Exercises 9.2

1. Modify the coefficients in the program in Figure 9.13 so that there will be exactly one real root. Trace execution of the program.

2. Modify the coefficients in the program in Figure 9.13 so that there will be no real root. Trace execution of the program.

3. The following algorithm approximates the cube root of a real number *x*.

```
root := 1.0;
repeat
    oldRoot := root;
    root := (2.0*root + x/(root*root)) / 3.0;
until (|root − oldRoot| < smallValue);
```

Implement this design in a *console32* program, embedding the value for *x* in the data section, using 0.001 for *smallValue*, and leaving *root* in ST where you can easily examine it with the debugger. Test your program with different values for *x*.

9.3   Converting Floating Point to and from ASCII

This section describes a procedure to facilitate conversion of decimal numbers to floating point format from a readable (ASCII) format, and a procedure that converts from floating point to ASCII. With these procedures and the *input* and *output* macros from *io.h*, we then modify the quadratic equation solver in Figure 9.13 to input coefficients and output roots. Section 9.5 covers an alternative way of providing I/O—by making the equation solver a procedure that is called from C and C++ main programs that do the I/O.

The ASCII to floating point conversion algorithm is given in Figure 9.15. It is similar to the algorithm used for the procedure *atodproc* described in Section 7.3. It scans memory at the address given by its parameter, interpreting the characters as a floating point number. It looks for a leading minus sign and a decimal point. The scan is terminated by a nondigit.

This algorithm is implemented in a procedure *atofproc* with one parameter, the address of the string. It returns the floating point value in ST. The procedure code appears in Figure 9.16, along with a simple *console32* test driver.

This implementation of the ASCII to floating point algorithm (Figure 9.16) uses ST for *value* and ST(1) for *divisor* except for one short segment where they are reversed in order to modify *divisor*. After the procedure entry code, the instructions

```
fld1            ; divisor := 1.0
fldz            ; value := 0.0
```

```
value := 0.0;
divisor := 1.0;
point := false;
minus := false;

point at first character of source string;
if source character = '−'
then
    minus := true;
    point at next character of source string;
end if;

while (source character is a digit or a decimal point) loop
    if source character = '.'
    then
        point := true;
    else
        convert ASCII digit to 2's complement digit;
        value := 10*value + float(digit);
        if point
        then
            multiply divisor by 10;
        end if;
    end if;
    point at next character of source string;
end while;

value := value/divisor;

if minus
then
    value := − value;
end if;
```

Figure 9.15 ASCII to floating point algorithm

```
; ASCII to floating point code
; author:  R. Detmer
; revised:  7/2008
.586
.MODEL FLAT
.STACK  4096

.DATA
source      BYTE    "-78.375", 0
result      REAL4   ?

.CODE
main        PROC
            lea  eax, source      ; address parameter
            push eax               ; push parameter
            call atofproc          ; atof(source)
            add  esp, 4            ; remove parameter
            fstp result            ; get result from FPU
            mov  eax, 0            ; exit
            ret
main        ENDP

atofproc  PROC
; convert ASCII string to floating point number
; Parameter passed on the stack: address of ASCII source string
; After an optional leading minus sign, only digits 0-9 and a decimal
; point are accepted — the scan terminates with any other character.
; The floating point value is returned in ST.
; Local variables are stored on the stack:
;    ten    [EBP-4]  — always 10 after initial code
;    point  [EBP-8]  — Boolean, -1 for true, 0 for false
;    minus  [EBP-12] — Boolean, -1 for true, 0 for false
;    digit  [EBP-16] — next digit as an integer

            push ebp                     ; establish stack frame
            mov  ebp, esp
            sub  esp, 16                 ; stack space for local variables
            push eax                     ; save registers
            push esi

            mov  DWORD PTR [ebp-4], 10   ; ten := 10
            fld1                         ; divisor := 1.0
            fldz                         ; value := 0.0
            mov  DWORD PTR [ebp-8], 0    ; point := false
            mov  DWORD PTR [ebp-12], 0   ; minus := false
```

(continues)

Figure 9.16 ASCII to floating point code

```
            mov   esi, [ebp+8]                ; address of first source character
            cmp   BYTE PTR [esi], '-'         ; leading minus sign?
            jne   endifMinus                  ; skip if not
            mov   DWORD PTR [ebp-12], -1      ; minus := true
            inc   esi                         ; point at next source character
endifMinus:

whileOK:    mov   al, [esi]                   ; get next character
            cmp   al, '.'                     ; decimal point?
            jne   endifPoint                  ; skip if not
            mov   DWORD PTR [ebp-8], -1       ; point := true
            jmp   nextChar
endifPoint:
            cmp   al, '0'                     ; character >= '0'
            jnge  endwhileOK                  ; exit if not
            cmp   al, '9'                     ; character <= '9'
            jnle  endwhileOK                  ; exit if not
            and   eax, 0000000fh             ; convert ASCII to integer value
            mov   DWORD PTR [ebp-16], eax    ; put integer in memory
            fimul DWORD PTR [ebp-4]          ; value := value * 10
            fiadd DWORD PTR [ebp-16]         ; value := value + digit
            cmp   DWORD PTR [ebp-8], -1      ; already found a decimal point?
            jne   endifDec                    ; skip if not
            fxch                              ; divisor in ST and value in ST(1)
            fimul DWORD PTR [ebp-4]          ; divisor := divisor * 10
            fxch                              ; value to ST; divisor back to ST(1)
endifDec:
nextChar:   inc   esi                         ; point at next source character
            jmp   whileOK
endwhileOK:

            fdivr                             ; value := value / divisor
            cmp   DWORD PTR [ebp-12], -1     ; was there a minus sign?
            jne   endifNeg
            fchs                              ; value := -value
endifNeg:
            pop   esi                         ; restore registers
            pop   eax
            mov   esp, ebp
            pop   ebp
            ret                               ; return
atofproc    ENDP
            END
```

Figure 9.16 ASCII to floating point code *(continued)*

initialize these two variables. Note that the value 1.0 for divisor ends up in ST(1) because it is pushed down by the **fldz** instruction.

Other local variables are stored on the stack at the locations shown in the program comments. Notice that they are coded using not only [ebp−x] but also with the size and type of the operand.

The design element

value := 10*value + float(digit);

is implemented by the code

```
fimul DWORD PTR [ebp-4]      ; value := value * 10
fiadd DWORD PTR [ebp-16]     ; value := value + digit
```

Note that the floating point unit converts the integer 10 to floating point for the multiplication and the integer version of *digit* to floating point for the addition.

To implement "multiply *divisor* by 10," the number to be multiplied must be in ST. The instructions

```
fxch                     ; divisor in ST and value in ST(1)
fimul DWORD PTR [ebp-4] ; divisor := divisor * 10
fxch                     ; value to ST; divisor back to ST(1)
```

take care of swapping *divisor* and *value*, carrying out the multiplication in ST, and then swapping back.

When it is time to execute "*value* := *value* / *divisor*" the instruction

```
fdivr           ; value := value / divisor
```

pops *value* from ST and divisor from ST(1), computes the quotient, and pushes it back to ST. Notice that the **fdiv** version of this instruction would incorrectly compute "*divisor/value*." The instruction **fchs** changes the sign of value if a leading minus sign was noted in the ASCII string.

The code in Figure 9.16 includes a simple test driver for *atofproc*. Figure 9.17 shows the execution state in the debugger after *atofproc* is called and just before the result is popped from the floating point stack. It is instructive to trace the entire program and watch the value accumulate in ST.

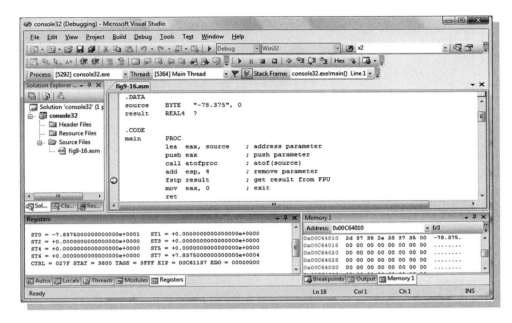

Figure 9.17 ASCII to floating point execution

Next we look at a procedure to convert a single floating point parameter to "E notation." The procedure generates a 12-byte-long ASCII string consisting of

- A leading minus sign or a blank
- A digit
- A decimal point
- Five digits
- The letter *E*
- A plus sign or a minus sign
- Two digits

This string represents the number in base 10 scientific notation. For example, for the decimal value 145.8798, the procedure would generate the string *b*1.45880E+02 (where *b* represents a blank.) Notice that the ASCII string contains a rounded value.

Figure 9.18 presents the design for the floating to ASCII procedure. After the leading space or minus sign is generated, most of the work necessary to get the remaining characters is done before they are actually produced. The value is repeatedly multiplied or divided by 10 until it is at least 1.0 but less than 10.0. Multiplication is used if the

```
point at first destination byte;

if value ≥ 0
then
    put blank in destination string;
else
    put minus in destination string;
    value := −value;
end if;
point at next destination byte;

exponent := 0;
if value ≠ 0
then
    if value ≥ 10
    then
        repeat
            divide value by 10;
            add 1 to exponent;
        until value < 10 loop
    else
        while value < 1 loop
            multiply value by 10;
            subtract 1 from exponent;
        end while;
    end if;
end if;

add 0.000005 to value;    { for rounding }
if value ≥ 10
then
    divide value by 10;
    add 1 to exponent;
end if;
```

(continues)

Figure 9.18 Floating point to ASCII conversion algorithm

```
digit := int(value);        { truncate to integer }
convert digit to ASCII and store in destination string;
point at next destination byte;
store "." in destination string;
point at next destination byte;

for i := 1 to 5 loop
    value := 10 * (value − float(digit));
    digit := int(value);
    convert digit to ASCII and store in destination string;
    point at next destination byte;
end for;
store E in destination string;
point at next destination byte;
if exponent ≥ 0
then
    put + in destination string;
else
    put − in destination string;
    exponent := −exponent;
end if;
point at next destination byte;

convert exponent to two decimal digits;
convert two decimal digits of exponent to ASCII;
store characters of exponent in destination string;
```

Figure 9.18 Floating point to ASCII conversion algorithm *(continued)*

value is initially less than 1; the number of multiplications gives the negative power of 10 required for scientific notation. Division is used if the value is initially 10.0 or more; the number of divisions gives the positive power of 10 required for scientific notation.

Only five digits will be displayed after the decimal point. The value between 1.0 and 10.0 is rounded by adding 0.000005; if the sixth digit after the decimal point is 5 or greater, this will be reflected in the digits that are actually displayed. It is possible that this addition gives a sum of 10.0 or more; if this happens, the value is divided by 10 again and the exponent is incremented.

With a value at least 1.0 but under 10.0, truncating to an integer gives the digit that goes before the decimal point. This digit and the decimal point are placed in the destination string. Then the remaining five digits can be generated by repeatedly subtracting the whole part from the value, multiplying the remaining fraction by 10, and truncating the new value to an integer.

After the "fraction" of the ASCII string is generated, the letter E, a plus or minus sign for the exponent, and the exponent digits are generated. The exponent will contain at most two digits—the single IEEE notation provides for numbers as large as 2^{128}, which is less than 10^{39}.

Figure 9.19 shows this design implemented in a procedure named *ftoaproc*, along with a short *console32* test driver. The procedure has two parameters: (1) the floating point value to be converted and (2) the address of the destination string.

After customary procedure entry code, the destination address is copied to EDI and the value to be converted to ASCII is copied to ST. Most of the code is a straightforward implementation of the design. Once the value is adjusted to be at least 1.0 but less than 10.0, truncating the value gives the digit that goes before the decimal point. This is done with the **fisttp** instruction, but it is necessary to copy the value first since the truncating integer store doesn't come in a "non-pop" version. This single digit is easily converted to the corresponding ASCII code. After subtracting the integer value from the whole value and multiplying by 10.0, the process can be repeated to get the next digit. Notice that if the number being converted is 0.0, this process simply results in a string of 0 characters.

Changing the exponent to two ASCII characters uses a "trick." The exponent in AX is nonnegative and less than 40 when the following code is executed.

```
div   byteTen          ; convert exponent to 2 digits
or    ax, 3030h         ; convert both digits to ASCII
mov   BYTE PTR [edi], al  ; store characters in destination
mov   BYTE PTR [edi+1], ah
```

Dividing by 10 puts the quotient (the high-order base-10 digit) in AL and the remainder (the low-order digit) in AH. These are simultaneously converted to ASCII by the **or** instruction, and are then stored in the destination string. This technique will work whenever the number being converted is in AX and is 99 or less.

Figure 9.20 shows the debugger's display of this program right before it exits. The *memory 1* window shows memory starting at the address of *source*. You can see the result string starting in the fifth byte.

```
; floating point to ASCII code
; author: R. Detmer
; revised: 7/2008
.586
.MODEL FLAT
.STACK   4096

.DATA
source        REAL4    145.8798
result        BYTE     12 DUP (?)

.CODE
main          PROC
              lea    eax, result    ; address of result
              push   eax            ; parameter 2
              push   source         ; parameter 1, floating point value
              call   ftoaproc       ; ftoa(source, result)
              add    esp, 8         ; remove parameters
              mov    eax, 0         ; exit
              ret
main          ENDP

; procedure ftoaproc(source, result)
; convert floating point number to ASCII string
; Parameters passed on the stack:
;    (1) 32-bit floating point value
;    (2) address of ASCII destination string
; ASCII string with format [blank/-]d.dddddE[+/-]dd is generated.
; (The string is always 12 characters long.)

.DATA
ten      REAL4  10.0
one      REAL4  1.0
round    REAL4  0.000005
digit    DWORD  ?
exponent DWORD  ?
byteTen  BYTE   10

.CODE
ftoaproc  PROC
          push ebp                  ; establish stack frame
          mov  ebp, esp
          push eax                  ; save registers
          push ebx
```

(continues)

Figure 9.19 Floating to ASCII procedure and test driver

```
            push ecx
            push edi

            finit                   ; initialize FPU
            mov  edi, [ebp+12]      ; destination string address
            fld  REAL4 PTR [ebp+8]  ; value to ST
            ftst                    ; value >= 0?
            fstsw   ax              ; status word to AX
            sahf                    ; condition code bits to flags
            jnae elseNeg            ; skip if negative
            mov  BYTE PTR [edi], ' '  ; blank for positive
            jmp  endifNeg           ; exit if
elseNeg:    mov  BYTE PTR [edi], '-'  ; minus for negative
            fchs                    ; make number positive
endifNeg:
            inc  edi                ; point at next destination byte

            mov  exponent, 0        ; exponent := 0
            ftst                    ; value = 0?
            fstsw ax                ; status word to AX
            sahf                    ; condition code bits to flags
            jz   endifZero          ; skip if zero
            fcom ten                ; value > 10?
            fstsw ax                ; status word to AX
            sahf                    ; condition code bits to flags
            jnae elseLess           ; skip if value not >= 10
untilLess:
            fdiv ten                ; value := value/10
            inc  exponent           ; add 1 to exponent
            fcom ten                ; value < 10?
            fstsw ax                ; status word to AX
            sahf                    ; condition code bits to flags
            jnb  untilLess          ; continue until value < 10
            jmp  endifBigger        ; exit if
elseLess:
whileLess:
            fcom one                ; value < 1?
            fstsw ax                ; status word to AX
            sahf                    ; condition code bits to flags
            jnb  endwhileLess       ; exit if not less
            fmul ten                ; value := 10*value
```

(continues)

Figure 9.19 Floating to ASCII procedure and test driver *(continued)*

```
              dec   exponent           ; subtract 1 from exponent
              jmp   whileLess          ; continue while value < 1
endwhileLess:
endifBigger:
endifZero:

              fadd round               ; add rounding value
              fcom ten                 ; value > 10?
              fstsw ax                 ; status word to AX
              sahf                     ; condition code bits to flags
              jnae endifOver           ; skip if not
              fdiv ten                 ; value := value/10
              inc   exponent           ; add 1 to exponent
endifOver:

; at this point 1.0 <= value < 10.0 (or value = 0.0)
              fld   st                 ; copy value
              fisttp digit             ; store integer part
              mov   ebx, digit         ; copy integer to EBX
              or    ebx, 30h           ; convert digit to character
              mov   BYTE PTR [edi], bl  ; store character in destination
              inc   edi                ; point at next destination byte
              mov   BYTE PTR [edi], '.'     ; decimal point
              inc   edi                ; point at next destination byte

              mov   ecx, 5             ; count of remaining digits
forDigit: fisub digit                  ; subtract integer part
              fmul ten                 ; multiply by 10
              fld   st                 ; copy value
              fisttp digit             ; store integer part
              mov   ebx, digit         ; copy integer to EBX
              or    ebx, 30h           ; convert digit to character
              mov   BYTE PTR [edi], bl  ; store character in destination
              inc   edi                ; point at next destination byte
              loop forDigit            ; repeat 5 times

              mov   BYTE PTR [edi], 'E'  ; exponent indicator
              inc   edi                ; point at next destination byte
              mov   eax, exponent      ; get exponent
              cmp   eax, 0             ; exponent >= 0 ?
              jnge NegExp
              mov   BYTE PTR [edi], '+'  ; non-negative exponent
              jmp   endifNegExp
```

(continues)

Figure 9.19 Floating to ASCII procedure and test driver *(continued)*

```
NegExp:   mov   BYTE PTR [edi], '-'   ; negative exponent
          neg   eax                   ; change exponent to positive
endifNegExp:
          inc   edi                   ; point at next destination byte

          div   byteTen               ; convert exponent to 2 digits
          or    eax, 3030h            ; convert both digits to ASCII
          mov   BYTE PTR [edi], al    ; store characters in destination
          mov   BYTE PTR [edi+1], ah

          pop   edi                   ; restore registers
          pop   ecx
          pop   ebx
          pop   eax
          pop   ebp
          ret                         ; return
ftoaproc ENDP
         END
```

Figure 9.19 Floating to ASCII procedure and test driver *(continued)*

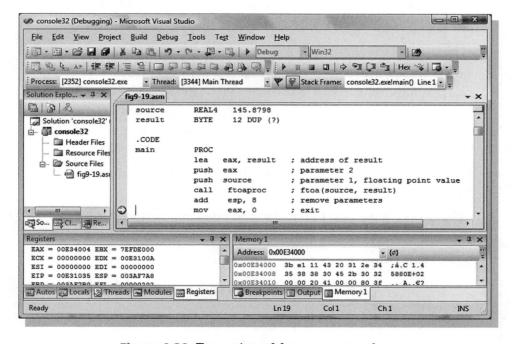

Figure 9.20 Execution of *ftoaproc* procedure

Now we combine code already written into a complete *windows32* program that prompts for the coefficients of a quadratic equation, solves the equation, and displays the roots. Getting each coefficient is a two-part process, first using the *input* macro to get the coefficient as a string of ASCII characters, then using *atofproc* to interpret this string as a floating point number. Display of the roots is similar—*ftoaproc* gives the ASCII string corresponding to a root and the *output* macro displays the string.

Figure 9.21 lists the program. The *ftoaproc* and *atofproc* procedures have been put in separate files. The heart of the main program is the same as the quadratic equation solver in Figure 9.13, with input code before and output code after. The inset shows the output window from a sample run solving the equation $2x^2 - x - 15 = 0$.

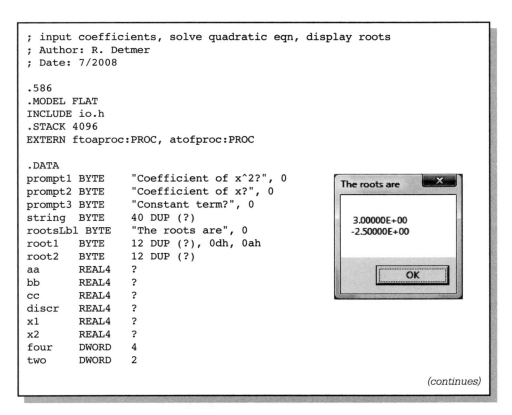

```
; input coefficients, solve quadratic eqn, display roots
; Author: R. Detmer
; Date: 7/2008

.586
.MODEL FLAT
INCLUDE io.h
.STACK 4096
EXTERN ftoaproc:PROC, atofproc:PROC

.DATA
prompt1 BYTE     "Coefficient of x^2?", 0
prompt2 BYTE     "Coefficient of x?", 0
prompt3 BYTE     "Constant term?", 0
string  BYTE     40 DUP (?)
rootsLbl BYTE    "The roots are", 0
root1   BYTE     12 DUP (?), 0dh, 0ah
root2   BYTE     12 DUP (?)
aa      REAL4    ?
bb      REAL4    ?
cc      REAL4    ?
discr   REAL4    ?
x1      REAL4    ?
x2      REAL4    ?
four    DWORD    4
two     DWORD    2
```

(continues)

Figure 9.21 Quadratic equation solver with I/O

```
.CODE
_MainProc PROC
        input   prompt1, string, 40 ; first coefficient
        lea     ebx, string     ; parameter for ftoaproc
        push    ebx
        call    atofproc  ; ftoaproc(string)
        add     esp, 4  ; remove parameter
        fstp    aa      ; store x*x coefficient

        input   prompt2, string, 40 ; second coefficient
        push    ebx     ; source address parameter
        call    atofproc  ; ftoaproc(string)
        add     esp, 4  ; remove parameter
        fstp    bb      ; store x coefficient

        input   prompt3, string, 40  ; third coefficient
        push    ebx     ; source address parameter
        call    atofproc  ; ftoaproc(string)
        add     esp, 4  ; remove parameter
        fstp    cc      ; store constant

        finit           ; initialize FPU
        fld     bb      ; b in ST
        fmul    bb      ; b*b
        fild    four    ; 4.0 in ST
        fmul    aa      ; 4*a
        fmul    cc      ; 4*a*c
        fsub            ; b*b-4*a*c
        fldz            ; 0.0 in ST
        fxch            ; b*b-4*a*c in ST; 0.0 in ST(1)
        fcom    st(1)   ; b*b-4*a*c >= 0 ?
        fstsw   ax      ; copy condition code bits to AX
        sahf            ; shift condition code bits to flags
        jnae    endGE   ; skip if not
        fsqrt           ; sqrt(b*b-4*a*c) in ST
        fst     st(1)   ; copy to ST(1)
        fsub    bb      ; -b + sqrt(b*b-4*a*c)
        fdiv    aa      ; (-b + sqrt(b*b-4*a*c))/a
        fidiv   two     ; (-b + sqrt(b*b-4*a*c))/(2*a)
        fstp    x1      ; save and pop stack
        fchs            ; -sqrt(b*b-4*a*c)
        fsub    bb      ; -b -sqrt(b*b-4*a*c)
        fdiv    aa      ; (-b + sqrt(b*b-4*a*c))/a
```

(continues)

Figure 9.21 Quadratic equation solver with I/O *(continued)*

```
        fidiv   two     ; (-b + sqrt(b*b-4*a*c))/(2*a)
        fstp    x2      ; save and pop stack
endGE:
        lea     ebx, root1   ; address for first root
        push    ebx     ; 2nd parameter
        push    x1      ; 1st parameter, fp source
        call    ftoaproc    ; ftoaproc(x1, root1)
        add     esp, 8  ; remove parameters
        lea     ebx, root2   ; address for second root
        push    ebx     ; 2nd parameter
        push    x2      ; 1st parameter, fp source
        call    ftoaproc    ; ftoaproc(x1, root1)
        add     esp, 8  ; remove parameters
        output  rootsLbl, root1

        mov     eax, 0  ; exit
        ret
_MainProc ENDP
END
```

Figure 9.21 Quadratic equation solver with I/O *(continued)*

Exercises 9.3

1. What will procedure *atofproc* return for a null-terminated character string containing "1234" and no other character? In other words, what will it do if there is no decimal point?

*2. What will procedure *atofproc* return for a null-terminated character string containing "12..34" and no other character? In other words, what will it do if there are two decimal points?

3. What will procedure *atofproc* return for a null-terminated character string containing "--12.34" and no other character? In other words, what will it do if there are two leading plus signs?

4. Why was procedure *ftoaproc* designed to produce six significant decimal digits and a two-digit exponent?

Programming Exercises 9.3

1. Write a complete *windows32* program that will prompt for and input a decimal value for the radius of a circle, and will calculate and display the circumference and the area of the circle. Use the *input* macro and

atofproc procedure for input and the *ftoaproc* procedure and *output* macro for output.

2. The following algorithm approximates the cube root of a real number *x*.

```
root := 1.0;
until (|root − oldRoot| < smallValue) loop
oldRoot := root;
root := (2.0*root + x/(root*root)) / 3.0;
end until;
```

Write a complete *windows32* program to input a value for *x* and display *root*, using 0.001 for *smallValue*. Use the *input* macro and *atofproc* procedure for input and the *ftoaproc* procedure and *output* macro for output.

3. Improve the quadratic equation solver program (Figure 9.21), so that it displays "no solution" if $b^2 - 4ac < 0$.

4. Design and implement a procedure *dbltoaproc* that is similar to *ftoaproc* except that it works for a double floating point value. What is the appropriate format for the destination string? (*Hint:* See Figure 9.1.) Parameters will be (1) the *address* of a double floating point value and (2) the address of the ASCII destination string. Write a short test driver for your procedure, and view the results with the debugger.

5. Write a procedure *ftoaproc1* that will convert a single floating point number to an ASCII string in fixed point format. Specifically, the procedure will have four parameters:

    1) A single floating point value
    2) The address of the destination string
    3) A doubleword containing the total number *n* of characters in the string to be generated
    4) A doubleword containing the number of digits *d* to be generated after the decimal point

The output string will consist of a leading blank or minus sign, the integer part of the value in $n-d-2$ positions (with leading blanks as needed), a decimal point, and the fractional part of the value rounded to *d* positions.

Write a short *console32* or *windows32* test driver for your procedure, and view the results with the debugger.

9.4. Single-Instruction Multiple-Data Instructions

Single-instruction multiple-data (SIMD) instructions operate on several operands at once with a single instruction. The 80x86 family has had some form of SIMD instructions since the Pentium II, starting with MMX technology and continuing through several generations of **streaming SIMD extensions** (SSE). All current 80x86 CPUs include these features.

MMX technology added eight 64-bit register designations; MM0 through MM8. These were *not* independent registers—they were physically the same as the registers in the floating point stack, basically ignoring the high-order 16 bits of each floating point register. The contents of a single MMX register can be viewed as eight byte-size integers, four word-size integers, two doubleword-size integers, or one quadword-size integer. The MMX instruction set includes instructions to pack multiple values into an MMX register (`pinsrw`, for example), or to unpack the parts. Other instructions can simultaneously operate on all the components in two operands. For example, after four words are loaded into each of MM0 and MM1, then the single instruction `paddw mm0, mm1` simultaneously adds the four pairs of integers, putting the sums in MM0. MMX technology is not further covered in this book.

SSE first appeared in the Pentium III processor. Its features include eight new 128-bit registers; XMM0 through XMM7. These are not aliased to any floating point or other registers—they are actually new storage. The 64-bit architecture added eight more XMM registers; XMM8 through XMM15. In the original SSE architecture, a single 128-bit register could hold four 32-bit floating point numbers, and a typical SSE instruction would simultaneously operate on four pairs of floating point numbers. Later SSE extensions added several other ways of viewing a single XMM register as multiple components, but these are not covered in this book.

Figure 9.22 lists selected SSE instructions. Most of these come in "scalar" (ss) and "packed" (ps) versions. The packed versions operate simultaneously on four pairs of floating point operands. The scalar versions operate only on the low-order operand, ignoring the other three. The scalar instructions are often used in 64-bit programming for floating point operations instead of using the floating point unit, which is the reason for including SSE in this book.

Programming floating point operations with SSE is similar to programming integer operations with general registers in the 32-bit or 64-bit mode. Figure 9.23 shows a *console64* program to compute $\sqrt{b^2 - 4ac}$, given single-precision floating point values for a, b, and c in memory. The result is stored in memory at *discr*.

Figure 9.24 is a screenshot showing the program halted just before exiting. The XMM registers are displayed by right-clicking in the Registers display window and then

Mnemonic	Operand 1 (destination)	Operand 2 (source)	Action
movss	xmmreg or mem32	xmmreg or mem32	destination := source (at least one operand must be a register)
addss	xmmreg	xmmreg or mem32	destination := destination + source
subss	xmmreg	xmmreg or mem32	destination := destination − source
mulss	xmmreg	xmmreg or mem32	destination := destination * source
divss	xmmreg	xmmreg or mem32	destination := destination / source
sqrtss	xmmreg	xmmreg or mem32	destination := sqrt(source)
rcpss	xmmreg	xmmreg or mem32	destination := 1/source
comiss	xmmreg	xmmreg or mem32	compare operand1 and operand2; set flags
movups	xmmreg or mem128	xmmreg or mem128	destination := source (at least one operand must be a register)
addps	xmmreg	xmmreg or mem128	destination := destination + source (four additions)
subps	xmmreg	xmmreg or mem128	destination := destination − source (four subtractions)
mulps	xmmreg	xmmreg or mem128	destination := destination * source (four multiplications)
divps	xmmreg	xmmreg or mem128	destination := destination / source (four divisions)

Figure 9.22 Selected SSE instructions

```
; compute discriminant using SSE instructions
; author: R. Detmer
; date: 7/2008

.DATA
a          REAL4    2.0
b          REAL4    -1.0
c          REAL4    -15.0
discr      REAL4    ?
four       REAL4    4.0

.CODE
main       PROC
           movss    xmm0, b       ; copy b
           mulss    xmm0, xmm0    ; b*b
           movss    xmm1, four    ; 4.0
           mulss    xmm1, a       ; 4*a
           mulss    xmm1, c       ; 4*a*c
           subss    xmm0, xmm1    ; b*b-4*a*c
           sqrtss   xmm0, xmm0    ; sqrt(b*b-4*a*c)
           movss    discr, xmm0   ; store result

           mov      rax, 0        ; exit
           ret
main       ENDP
END
```

Figure 9.23 Compute $\sqrt{b^2 - 4ac}$ using SSE

selecting SSE. Note that each XMM register is displayed as 32 hex digits (128 bits) and as four decimal values. For instance, XMM0 shows 11.0, the value that has been computed for *discr*.

The **comiss** comparison instruction sets flags exactly as **fcomi** does for the floating point unit. This means that the "unsigned" conditional jump instructions are appropriate following these instructions.

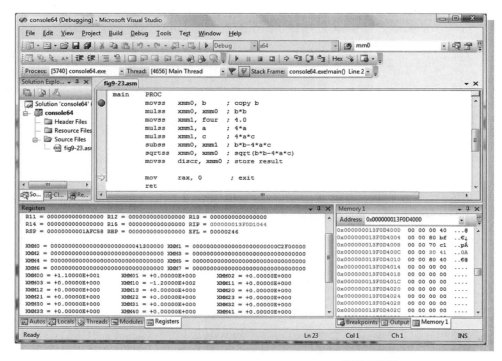

Figure 9.24 Execution of program to compute $\sqrt{b^2 - 4ac}$ using SSE

Exercises 9.4

For each of these exercises, assume the following contents of XMM0 and XMM1 before the instruction is executed.

XMM0			
XMM00	XMM01	XMM02	XMM03
5.0	–10.5	3.7	4.6

XMM1			
XMM10	XMM11	XMM12	XMM13
4.0	4.5	–7.3	8.3

What will be in XMM0 following execution of each instruction given?

*1. `movss xmm0, xmm1`   2. `addss xmm0, xmm1`

 3. `subss xmm0, xmm1`   *4. `mulss xmm0, xmm1`

 5. `divss xmm0, xmm1`   6. `sqrtss xmm0, xmm1`

 7. `rcpss xmm0, xmm1`   8. `addps xmm0, xmm1`

*9. `subps xmm0, xmm1`   10. `mulps xmm0, xmm1`

11. `divps xmm0, xmm1`

1. The *geometric mean* of two numbers x and y is defined by $\sqrt{xy}$. Write a *console64* program that starts with single-precision floating point values for x and y in memory and uses SSE instructions to compute the geometric mean and store it at *mean*.

2. The *harmonic mean* of two numbers x and y is defined by

$$\frac{1}{\dfrac{1}{x}+\dfrac{1}{y}}$$

Write a *console64* program that starts with single-precision floating point values for x and y in memory and uses SSE instructions to compute the harmonic mean and store it at *mean*.

9.5. Floating Point Assembly Language Procedures with C/C++

Sometimes the power of assembly language makes it possible or easier or more efficient to code parts of a program in assembly language than in a high-level language. These parts may need critical optimization, or may implement low-level algorithms that would be difficult or impossible to code in the high-level language. However, the bulk of programming is better done in a high-level language. Section 6.3 showed some examples of calling an assembly language procedure from a C function, and a C function from an assembly language procedure. This section extends the information in Section 6.3 to floating point examples.

First, we take the quadratic equation-solving program and make it into a procedure *roots*. The listing of this procedure is in Figure 9.25. The C-style function header describes its five parameters, the first three being the single-precision floating point coefficients a, b, and c of the quadratic equation $ax^2 + bx + c = 0$, and the fourth and fifth being the addresses to put the floating point roots. The procedure name is decorated with a leading underscore since it will be called from a 32-bit C program. The code that finds the roots is exactly what we have seen before in this chapter.

```
; compute roots of quadratic equation
; author: R. Detmer
; date: 7/2008
.586
.MODEL FLAT
.DATA
four    DWORD    4
two     DWORD    2
.CODE
; void roots(float a, float b, float c, float* x1, float* x2)
_roots  PROC
        push    ebp      ; save base register
        mov     ebp, esp ; establish stack frame
        push    eax      ; save EAX

        finit            ; initialize FPU
        fld     REAL4 PTR [ebp+12]     ; b in ST
        fmul    REAL4 PTR [ebp+12]     ; b*b
        fild    four            ; 4.0 in ST
        fmul    REAL4 PTR [ebp+8]      ; 4*a
        fmul    REAL4 PTR [ebp+16]     ; 4*a*c
        fsub              ; b*b-4*a*c
        fldz              ; 0.0 in ST
        fxch              ; b*b-4*a*c in ST; 0.0 in ST(1)
        fcom    st(1)    ; b*b-4*a*c >= 0 ?
        fstsw   ax       ; copy condition code bits to AX
        sahf             ; shift condition code bits to AL
        jnae    endGE    ; skip if not
        fsqrt            ; sqrt(b*b-4*a*c) in ST
        fst     st(1)    ; copy to ST(1)
        fsub    REAL4 PTR [ebp+12]      ; -b + sqrt(b*b-4*a*c)
        fdiv    REAL4 PTR [ebp+8]       ; (-b + sqrt(b*b-4*a*c))/a
        fidiv   two      ; (-b + sqrt(b*b-4*a*c))/(2*a)
        mov     eax, [ebp+20]    ; address of x1
        fstp    REAL4 PTR [eax]        ; save and pop stack
        fchs              ; -sqrt(b*b-4*a*c)
        fsub    REAL4 PTR [ebp+12]       ; -b -sqrt(b*b-4*a*c)
        fdiv    REAL4 PTR [ebp+8]        ; (-b + sqrt(b*b-4*a*c))/a
        fidiv   two      ; (-b + sqrt(b*b-4*a*c))/(2*a)
        mov     eax, [ebp+24]    ; address of x2
        fstp    REAL4 PTR [eax]        ; save and pop stack
endGE:

        pop     eax      ; restore registers
        pop     ebp
        ret
_roots  ENDP
END
```

Figure 9.25 Quadratic equation-solving procedure

```
/* C program to provide I/O for quadratic equation solver */
/* author: R. Detmer */
/* date: 7/2008 */

#include <stdio.h>

void roots(float a, float b, float c, float* x1, float* x2);
/* find roots of quadratic equation */

int main()
{
    float a, b, c;
    float root1, root2;

    printf("please enter coefficients: ");
    scanf("%f %f %f", &a, &b, &c);
    roots(a, b, c, &root1, &root2);
    printf("\nroot 1 %f\nroot 2 %f\n", root1, root2);
    return 0;
}
```

Figure 9.26 C test driver for *roots* procedure

Figure 9.26 shows a simple C program to input coefficient values and display results. This program and *roots* are part of the same *console32* project. Figure 9.27 shows a sample run of the program.

If you prefer C++ to C, you can use the C++ test driver shown in Figure 9.28, combined in a *console32* project with the assembly language *roots* procedure in Figure 9.22. The only notable feature of this C++ code is the "C" specification in the **extern** directive. This tells the C++ compiler to call *roots* using C linkage conventions. Figure 9.29 shows a sample run.

In the 32-bit environment a procedure that returns a single floating point value does so in ST. This is analogous to returning a single integer value in the accumulator. We have seen several examples of how floating point arguments are passed in a 32-bit environment—basically on the stack exactly as integer arguments are passed.

We now take a brief look at how floating point arguments are passed in a 64-bit environment. In 64-bit mode, a single floating point value is returned in XMM0. The first four floating point parameters are passed in XMM0, XMM1, XMM2, and XMM3. If floating point and integer parameters are mixed, then RCX, RDX, R8, and R9 are used for the integer parameters, and the XMM registers are used for the floating point parameters.

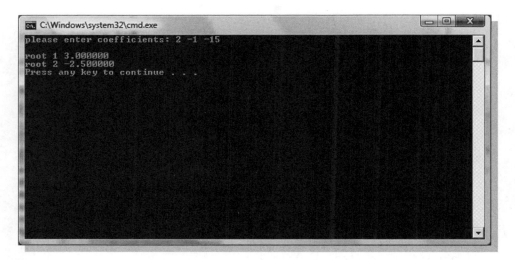

Figure 9.27 Sample run of C/assembly program

```cpp
// C++ program to provide I/O for quadratic equation solver
// author: R. Detmer
// date: 7/2008

#include <iostream>
using namespace std;

extern "C" void roots(float a, float b, float c, float& x1,
float& x2);
// find roots of quadratic equation

int main()
{
    float a, b, c;
    float root1, root2;

    cout << "please enter coefficients: ";
    cin >> a >> b >> c;
    roots(a, b, c, root1, root2);
    cout << "\nroot 1 " << root1 << "\nroot 2 " << root2 << endl;
    return 0;
}
```

Figure 9.28 C++ test driver for *roots* procedure

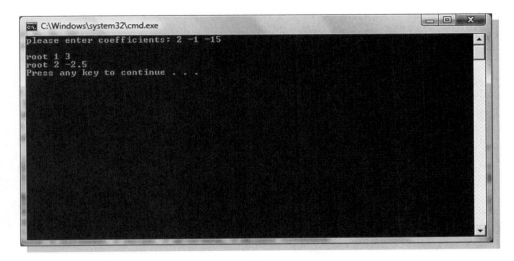

Figure 9.29 Sample run of C++/assembly program

For example, if there are three parameters, an integer and two floats, in this order, then the integer would be passed in RCX, the first float in XMM1, and the second float in XMM2. If, on the other hand, the three parameters were a float, an integer, and a float, in this order, then the first float would be passed in XMM0, the integer in RDX, and the second float in XMM2. Parameters beyond four are passed on the stack.

Figure 9.30 shows *roots* implemented as a value-returning procedure in a *console64* program. Note how the parameters are passed: floating point coefficients *a* in XMM0, *b* in XMM1, and *c* in XMM2, but the address of *x1* in R9 since an address is an integer. The fifth parameter, the address of *x2*, is passed on the stack. This procedure works with either the C driver shown in Figure 9.26 or the C++ driver shown in Figure 9.28—neither requires any change in the source code, although obviously the 32-bit and 64-bit C and C++ compilers generate very different code.

Some high-level language compilers have the ability to translate a program that includes in-line assembly code. This permits most of a program to be written in the high-level language, with a few parts written in assembly language. With Visual Studio 2008, the 32-bit C++ compiler allows in-line assembly, but the 64-bit C++ compiler does not. With the 32-bit compiler, the embedded assembly language code format looks like

```
    __asm
    {
        ; assembly language statements
        ; that can use variables in the C++ program
    }
```

```
; compute roots of quadratic equation
; author: R. Detmer
; date: 7/2008

.DATA
four    REAL4    4.0
two     REAL4    2.0
zero    REAL4    0.0

.CODE
; void roots(float a, float b, float c, float* x1, float* x2)
roots   PROC
        movss    xmm3, xmm1  ; copy b
        mulss    xmm3, xmm3  ; b*b
        movss    xmm4, four  ; 4.0
        mulss    xmm4, xmm0  ; 4*a
        mulss    xmm4, xmm2  ; 4*a*c
        subss    xmm3, xmm4  ; b*b-4*a*c
        comiss   xmm3, zero  ; b*b-4*a*c >= 0?
        jnae     endGE       ; skip if not
        sqrtss   xmm3, xmm3  ; sqrt(b*b-4*a*c)
        movss    xmm4, zero  ; 0
        subss    xmm4, xmm1  ; -b
        addss    xmm4, xmm3  ; -b + sqrt(b*b-4*a*c)
        divss    xmm4, xmm0  ; (-b + sqrt(b*b-4*a*c))/a
        divss    xmm4, two   ; (-b + sqrt(b*b-4*a*c))/(2*a)
        movss    REAL4 PTR [r9], xmm4    ; store root1
        movss    xmm4, zero  ; 0
        subss    xmm4, xmm1  ; -b
        subss    xmm4, xmm3  ; -b - sqrt(b*b-4*a*c)
        divss    xmm4, xmm0  ; (-b - sqrt(b*b-4*a*c))/a
        divss    xmm4, two   ; (-b - sqrt(b*b-4*a*c))/(2*a)
        mov      r9, [rsp+40] ; addr of root2
        movss    REAL4 PTR [r9], xmm4    ; store root2
endGE:
        ret
roots   ENDP
END
```

Figure 9.30 Quadratic equation-solving procedure (64-bit version)

The in-line assembly language code is preceded by the __asm keyword (beginning with two underscores), and braces surround the assembly language statements. The assembly language statements can reference C++ variables declared outside the braces. Almost any statements can appear in in-line assembly language, including integer instructions, floating point instructions, and statements with labels.

Programming Exercises 9.5

Any of these exercises can be done in a 32-bit or a 64-bit environment.

1. Write a complete program that will prompt for and input a decimal value for the radius of a circle, and will calculate and display (appropriately labeled) the circumference and the area of the circle. Do the input and output with C or C++. Write two assembly language procedures, *circumference* and *area*, each with one floating point parameter giving the radius, and each returning the appropriate value. Call these procedures from your C/C++ program to do the floating point calculations.

2. The volume of a pyramid with a square base b units on a side and a height h is given by $\frac{1}{3}b^2h$. Write an assembly language procedure *pVolume* with two floating point parameters, the base and the height, and returning the volume of the pyramid. Call this procedure from a C or C++ driver that inputs values for the base and height and outputs the volume.

3. The *roots* procedure will fail if $b^2 - 4ac < 0$. Modify the procedure to add a sixth Boolean parameter *success* that will be set to *false* if the procedure fails and to *true* if it succeeds. A modified C header would look like

   ```
   void roots(float a, float b, float c, float* x1, float* x2,
   int* success)
   ```

   and would return -1 for *true* and 0 for *false*. A modified C++ header would look like

   ```
   void roots(float a, float b, float c, float& x1, float& x2,
   bool& success)
   ```

   and the assembly language procedure will treat success as the address of a byte-size integer and store 1 for *true* or 0 for *false*.

4. The following algorithm approximates the cube root of a real number *x*.

```
root := 1.0;
until (Iroot − oldRootI < smallValue) loop
    oldRoot := root;
    root := (2.0*root + x/(root*root)) / 3.0;
end until;
```

Implement this algorithm as a value-returning assembly language procedure *cuberoot* with two float parameters: (1) *x* and (2) *smallValue*. Write a C or C++ program to input values for *x* and *smallValue*, call *cuberoot*, and display the computed value.

9.6 Chapter Summary

The 80x86 uses three formats for floating point numbers, single (32 bits), double (64 bits), and extended double (80 bits). Each format consists of a sign, a biased exponent, and a fraction.

The 80x86 floating point unit (FPU) contains eight 80-bit data registers, organized as a stack. Each register stores an extended real floating point value. The FPU executes a variety of instructions from load and store, to simple arithmetic, to complex transcendental functions.

Conversion between floating point and ASCII representations is similar to that previously described for integers. The easiest ASCII format to scan is a simple decimal format. The simplest ASCII format to produce is E-notation.

Several generations of 80x86 processors have included single-instruction multiple-data instructions. The streaming SIMD extensions (SSE) add XMM registers and floating point instructions that are often used in the 64-bit environment.

Assembly language procedures can be called from C or C++ programs using standard linkage conventions. A single float is returned on the top of the floating point stack in 32-bit mode, or in the XMM0 register in 64-bit mode. In 32-bit mode, parameter passing is the same for integers and floats. However, in 64-bit mode, float parameters are passed in XMM registers.

Hexadecimal/ASCII Conversion

00	NUL	(null)	20	space	40	@	60	`	
01	SOH		21	!	41	A	61	a	
02	STX		22	"	42	B	62	b	
03	ETX		23	#	43	C	63	c	
04	EOT		24	$	44	D	64	d	
05	ENQ		25	%	45	E	65	e	
06	ACK		26	&	46	F	66	f	
07	BEL	(bell)	27	' (apostrophe)	47	G	67	g	
08	BS	(backspace)	28	(	48	H	68	h	
09	HT	(tab)	29	)	49	I	69	i	
0A	LF	(linefeed)	2A	*	4A	J	6A	j	
0B	VT		2B	+	4B	K	6B	k	
0C	FF	(form feed)	2C	, (comma)	4C	L	6C	l	
0D	CR	(return)	2D	–	4D	M	6D	m	
0E	SO		2E	.	4E	N	6E	n	
0F	SI		2F	/	4F	O	6F	o	
10	DLE		30	0	50	P	70	p	
11	DC1		31	1	51	Q	71	q	
12	DC2		32	2	52	R	72	r	
13	DC3		33	3	53	S	73	s	
14	DC4		34	4	54	T	74	t	
15	NAK		35	5	55	U	75	u	
16	SYN		36	6	56	V	76	v	
17	ETB		37	7	57	W	77	w	
18	CAN		38	8	58	X	78	x	
19	EM		39	9	59	Y	79	y	
1A	SUB		3A	:	5A	Z	7A	z	
1B	ESC	("escape")	3B	;	5B	[	7B	{	
1C	FS		3C	<	5C	\	7C			
1D	GS		3D	=	5D	]	7D	}	
1E	RS		3E	>	5E	^	7E	~	
1F	US		3F	?	5F	_	7F	DEL	

Assembler Reserved Words

Words that are reserved only for the 32-bit assembler are in *italics*. Words that are reserved only for the 64-bit assembler are in **bold**. All other words are reserved with both assemblers.

$	.CODE	.ERRNDEF	**.PUSHFRAME**
%OUT	.CONST	.ERRNZ	**.PUSHREG**
.	*.CONTINUE*	*.EXIT*	.RADIX
.186	.CREF	.FARDATA	*.REPEAT*
.286	.DATA	.FARDATA?	.SAFESEH
.286C	.DATA?	*.FPO*	.SALL
.286P	*.DOSSEG*	*.IF*	**.SAVEREG**
.287	*.ELSE*	*.K3D*	**.SAVEXMM128**
.386	*.ELSEIF*	.LALL	*.SEQ*
.386C	*.ENDIF*	.LFCOND	**.SETFRAME**
.386P	**.ENDPROLOG**	.LIST	.SFCOND
.387	*.ENDW*	.LISTALL	*.STACK*
.486	.ERR	.LISTIF	*.STARTUP*
.486P	.ERR1	.LISTMACRO	.TFCOND
.586	.ERR2	.LISTMACROALL	.TYPE
.586P	.ERRB	*.MMX*	*.UNTIL*
.686	.ERRDEF	*.MODEL*	*.UNTILCXZ*
.686P	.ERRDIF	*.MSFLOAT*	*.WHILE*
.8086	.ERRDIFI	*.NO87*	.XALL
.8087	.ERRE	.NOCREF	.XCREF
.ALPHA	.ERRIDN	.NOLIST	.XLIST
.ALLOCSTACK	.ERRIDNI	.NOLISTIF	*.XMM*
.BREAK	.ERRNB	.NOLISTMACRO	?

@B	BLENDPD	CMOVE	CMPLTSS
@F	BLENDPS	CMOVG	CMPNEQPD
AAA	BLENDVPD	CMOVGE	CMPNEQPS
AAD	BLENDVPS	CMOVL	CMPNEQSD
AAM	*BOUND*	CMOVLE	CMPNEQSS
AAS	BP	CMOVNA	CMPNLEPD
ADC	**BPL**	CMOVNAE	CMPNLEPS
ADD	BSF	CMOVNB	CMPNLESD
ADDPD	BSR	CMOVNBE	CMPNLESS
ADDPS	BSWAP	CMOVNC	CMPNLTPD
ADDR	BT	CMOVNE	CMPNLTPS
ADDSD	BTC	CMOVNG	CMPNLTSD
ADDSS	BTR	CMOVNGE	CMPNLTSS
ADDSUBPD	BTS	CMOVNL	CMPORDPD
ADDSUBPS	BX	CMOVNLE	CMPORDPS
AESDEC	BYTE	CMOVNO	CMPORDSD
AESDECLAST	*C*	CMOVNP	CMPORDSS
AESENC	CALL	CMOVNS	CMPPD
AESENCLAST	*CARRY?*	CMOVNZ	CMPPS
AESIMC	CATSTR	CMOVO	CMPS
AESKEYGENASSIST	CBW	CMOVP	CMPSB
AH	CDQ	CMOVPE	CMPSD
AL	**CDQE**	CMOVPO	**CMPSQ**
ALIAS	CH	CMOVS	CMPSS
ALIGN	CL	CMOVZ	CMPSW
ALTENTRY	CLC	CMP	CMPUNORDPD
AND	CLD	CMPEQPD	CMPUNORDPS
ANDNPD	CLFLUSH	CMPEQPS	CMPUNORDSD
ANDNPS	CLGI	CMPEQSD	CMPUNORDSS
ANDPD	CLI	CMPEQSS	CMPXCHG
ANDPS	CLTS	CMPLEPD	*CMPXCHG8B*
ARPL	CMC	CMPLEPS	**CMPXCHG16B**
ASSUME	CMOVA	CMPLESD	**CMPXCHG8B**
AX	CMOVAE	CMPLESS	**CODE**
BASIC	CMOVB	CMPLTPD	COMISD
BH	CMOVBE	CMPLTPS	COMISS
BL	CMOVC	CMPLTSD	COMM

COMMENT	CVTTSD2SI	**DR9**	*ESC*
CPUID	CVTTSS2SI	DS	ESI
CQO	CWD	DT	ESP
CR0	CWDE	DUP	EVEN
CR2	CX	DW	EXITM
CR3	*DAA*	DWORD	EXTERN
CR4	*DAS*	DX	EXTERNDEF
CR10	DB	EAX	EXTRACTPS
CR11	DD	EBP	EXTRN
CR12	DEC	EBX	EXTRQ
CR13	DF	ECHO	F2XM1
CR14	DH	ECX	FABS
CR15	DI	EDI	FADD
CR8	**DIL**	EDX	FADDP
CR9	DIV	ELSE	FAR
CRC32	DIVPD	ELSEIF	*FAR16*
CS	DIVPS	ELSEIF1	*FAR32*
CVTDQ2PD	DIVSD	ELSEIF2	FBLD
CVTDQ2PS	DIVSS	ELSEIFB	FBSTP
CVTPD2DQ	DL	ELSEIFDEF	FCHS
CVTPD2PI	*DOSSEG*	ELSEIFDIF	FCLEX
CVTPD2PS	DPPD	ELSEIFDIFI	FCMOVB
CVTPI2PD	DPPS	ELSEIFE	FCMOVBE
CVTPI2PS	DQ	ELSEIFIDN	FCMOVE
CVTPS2DQ	DR0	ELSEIFIDNI	FCMOVNB
CVTPS2PD	DR1	ELSEIFNB	FCMOVNBE
CVTPS2PI	DR2	ELSEIFNDEF	FCMOVNE
CVTSD2SI	DR3	EMMS	FCMOVNU
CVTSD2SS	DR6	END	FCMOVU
CVTSI2SD	DR7	ENDIF	FCOM
CVTSI2SS	**DR10**	ENDM	FCOMI
CVTSS2SD	**DR11**	ENDP	FCOMIP
CVTSS2SI	**DR12**	ENDS	FCOMP
CVTTPD2DQ	**DR13**	ENTER	FCOMPP
CVTTPD2PI	**DR14**	EQ	FCOS
CVTTPS2DQ	**DR15**	EQU	FDECSTP
CVTTPS2PI	**DR8**	ES	FDISI

FDIV	FNCLEX	*FSTENVD*	IDIV
FDIVP	FNDISI	FSTENVW	IF
FDIVR	FNENI	FSTP	IF1
FDIVRP	FNINIT	FSTSW	IF2
FEMMS	FNOP	FSUB	IFB
FENI	FNSAVE	FSUBP	IFDEF
FFREE	*FNSAVED*	FSUBR	IFDIF
FFREEP	FNSAVEW	FSUBRP	IFDIFI
FIADD	FNSTCW	FTST	IFE
FICOM	FNSTENV	FUCOM	IFIDN
FICOMP	*FNSTENVD*	FUCOMI	IFIDNI
FIDIV	FNSTENVW	FUCOMIP	IFNB
FIDIVR	FNSTSW	FUCOMP	IFNDEF
FILD	FOR	FUCOMPP	IMAGEREL
FIMUL	FORC	FWAIT	IMUL
FINCSTP	*FORTRAN*	FWORD	IN
FINIT	FPATAN	FXAM	INC
FIST	FPREM	FXCH	INCLUDE
FISTP	FPREM1	FXRSTOR	INCLUDELIB
FISTTP	FPTAN	FXSAVE	INS
FISUB	**FRAME**	FXTRACT	INSB
FISUBR	FRNDINT	FYL2X	INSD
FLAT	FRSTOR	FYL2XP1	INSERTPS
FLD	*FRSTORD*	GE	INSERTQ
FLD1	FRSTORW	GETSEC	INSTR
FLDCW	FS	GOTO	INSW
FLDENV	FSAVE	*GROUP*	INT
FLDENVD	*FSAVED*	GS	*INTO*
FLDENVW	FSAVEW	GT	INVD
FLDL2E	FSCALE	HADDPD	INVEPT
FLDL2T	FSETPM	HADDPS	INVLPG
FLDLG2	FSIN	HIGH	INVLPGA
FLDLN2	FSINCOS	HIGH32	*INVOKE*
FLDPI	FSQRT	HIGHWORD	INVVPID
FLDZ	FST	HLT	IRET
FMUL	FSTCW	HSUBPD	IRETD
FMULP	FSTENV	HSUBPS	IRETDF

IRP	LAHF	LOOPZ	MOVAPD
IRPC	LAR	LOOPZD	MOVAPS
JA	LDDQU	*LOOPZW*	MOVD
JAE	LDMXCSR	LOW	MOVDDUP
JB	*LDS*	LOW32	MOVDQ2Q
JBE	LE	LOWWORD	MOVDQA
JC	LEA	*LROFFSET*	MOVDQU
JCXZ	LEAVE	LSL	MOVHLPS
JE	LENGTH	LSS	MOVHPD
JECXZ	LENGTHOF	LT	MOVHPS
JG	*LES*	LTR	MOVLHPS
JGE	LFENCE	LZCNT	MOVLPD
JL	LFS	MACRO	MOVLPS
JLE	LGDT	MASK	MOVMSKPD
JMP	LGS	MASKMOVDQU	MOVMSKPS
JNA	LIDT	MASKMOVQ	MOVNTDQ
JNAE	LLDT	MAXPD	MOVNTDQA
JNB	LMSW	MAXPS	MOVNTI
JNBE	LOCAL	MAXSD	MOVNTPD
JNC	LOCK	MAXSS	MOVNTPS
JNE	LODS	MFENCE	MOVNTQ
JNG	LODSB	MINPD	MOVNTSD
JNGE	LODSD	MINPS	MOVNTSS
JNL	**LODSQ**	MINSD	MOVQ
JNLE	LODSW	MINSS	MOVQ2DQ
JNO	LOOP	MM0	MOVS
JNP	LOOPD	MM1	MOVSB
JNS	LOOPE	MM2	MOVSD
JNZ	LOOPED	MM3	MOVSHDUP
JO	*LOOPEW*	MM4	MOVSLDUP
JP	LOOPNE	MM5	**MOVSQ**
JPE	LOOPNED	MM6	MOVSS
JPO	*LOOPNEW*	MM7	MOVSW
JRCXZ	LOOPNZ	MMWORD	MOVSX
JS	LOOPNZD	MOD	**MOVSXD**
JZ	*LOOPNZW*	MONITOR	MOVUPD
LABEL	*LOOPW*	MOV	MOVUPS

MOVZX	PADDB	PEXTRB	PMADDWD
MPSADBW	PADDD	PEXTRD	PMAXSB
MUL	PADDQ	**PEXTRQ**	PMAXSD
MULPD	PADDSB	PEXTRW	PMAXSW
MULPS	PADDSW	PF2ID	PMAXUB
MULSD	PADDUSB	PF2IW	PMAXUD
MULSS	PADDUSW	PFACC	PMAXUW
MWAIT	PADDW	PFADD	PMINSB
NAME	PAGE	PFCMPEQ	PMINSD
NE	PALIGNR	PFCMPGE	PMINSW
NEAR	PAND	PFCMPGT	PMINUB
NEAR16	PANDN	PFMAX	PMINUD
NEAR32	*PARITY?*	PFMIN	PMINUW
NEG	*PASCAL*	PFMUL	PMOVMSKB
NOP	PAUSE	PFNACC	PMOVSXBD
NOT	PAVGB	PFPNACC	PMOVSXBQ
OFFSET	PAVGUSB	PFRCP	PMOVSXBW
OPATTR	PAVGW	PFRCPIT1	PMOVSXDQ
OPTION	PBLENDVB	PFRCPIT2	PMOVSXWD
OR	PBLENDW	PFRSQIT1	PMOVSXWQ
ORG	PCLMULHQHDQ	PFRSQRT	PMOVZXBD
ORPD	PCLMULHQLQDQ	PFSUB	PMOVZXBQ
ORPS	PCLMULLQHDQ	PFSUBR	PMOVZXBW
OUT	PCLMULLQLQDQ	PHADDD	PMOVZXDQ
OUTS	PCLMULQDQ	PHADDSW	PMOVZXWD
OUTSB	PCMPEQB	PHADDW	PMOVZXWQ
OUTSD	PCMPEQD	PHMINPOSUW	PMULDQ
OUTSW	PCMPEQQ	PHSUBD	PMULHRSW
OVERFLOW?	PCMPEQW	PHSUBSW	PMULHRW
OWORD	PCMPESTRI	PHSUBW	PMULHUW
PABSB	PCMPESTRM	PI2FD	PMULHW
PABSD	PCMPGTB	PI2FW	PMULLD
PABSW	PCMPGTD	PINSRB	PMULLW
PACKSSDW	PCMPGTQ	PINSRD	PMULUDQ
PACKSSWB	PCMPGTW	**PINSRQ**	POP
PACKUSDW	PCMPISTRI	PINSRW	*POPA*
PACKUSWB	PCMPISTRM	PMADDUBSW	*POPAD*

POPAW	PSUBSW	**R12B**	REAL10
POPCNT	PSUBUSB	**R12D**	REAL4
POPCONTEXT	PSUBUSW	**R12W**	REAL8
POPF	PSUBW	**R13**	RECORD
POPFD	PSWAPD	**R13B**	REP
POR	PTEST	**R13D**	REPE
PREFETCH	PTR	**R13W**	REPEAT
PREFETCHNTA	PUBLIC	**R14**	REPNE
PREFETCHT0	PUNPCKHBW	**R14B**	REPNZ
PREFETCHT1	PUNPCKHDQ	**R14D**	REPT
PREFETCHT2	PUNPCKHQDQ	**R14W**	REPZ
PREFETCHW	PUNPCKHWD	**R15**	RET
PROC	PUNPCKLBW	**R15B**	*RETD*
PROTO	PUNPCKLDQ	**R15D**	RETF
PSADBW	PUNPCKLQDQ	**R15W**	*RETN*
PSHUFB	PUNPCKLWD	**R8**	*RETW*
PSHUFD	PURGE	**R8B**	ROL
PSHUFHW	PUSH	**R8D**	ROR
PSHUFLW	*PUSHA*	**R8W**	ROUNDPD
PSHUFW	*PUSHAD*	**R9**	ROUNDPS
PSIGNB	*PUSHAW*	**R9B**	ROUNDSD
PSIGND	PUSHCONTEXT	**R9D**	ROUNDSS
PSIGNW	*PUSHD*	**R9W**	**RSI**
PSLLD	PUSHF	**RAX**	RSM
PSLLDQ	PUSHFD	**RBP**	**RSP**
PSLLQ	PUSHW	**RBX**	RSQRTPS
PSLLW	PXOR	RCL	RSQRTSS
PSRAD	QWORD	RCPPS	SAHF
PSRAW	**R10**	RCPSS	SAL
PSRLD	**R10B**	RCR	SAR
PSRLDQ	**R10D**	**RCX**	SBB
PSRLQ	**R10W**	**RDI**	SBYTE
PSRLW	R11	RDMSR	SCAS
PSUBB	**R11B**	RDPMC	SCASB
PSUBD	**R11D**	RDTSC	SCASD
PSUBQ	**R11W**	RDTSCP	**SCASQ**
PSUBSB	**R12**	**RDX**	SCASW

SDWORD	SHLD	STRUC	VARARG
SECTIONREL	SHORT	STRUCT	VERR
SEG	SHR	SUB	VERW
SEGMENT	SHRD	SUBPD	VMCALL
SETA	SHUFPD	SUBPS	VMCLEAR
SETAE	SHUFPS	SUBSD	*VMCLI*
SETB	SI	SUBSS	*VMCPUID*
SETBE	SIDT	SUBSTR	*VMDXDSBL*
SETC	*SIGN?*	SUBTITLE	*VMDXENBL*
SETE	**SIL**	SUBTTL	*VMGETINFO*
SETG	SIZE	**SWAPGS**	*VMHLT*
SETGE	SIZEOF	SWORD	*VMIRETD*
SETL	SIZESTR	SYSCALL	VMLAUNCH
SETLE	SKINIT	*SYSENTER*	VMLOAD
SETNA	SLDT	*SYSEXIT*	VMMCALL
SETNAE	SMSW	SYSRET	VMPOPFD
SETNB	SP	**SYSRETQ**	*VMPTRLD*
SETNBE	**SPL**	TBYTE	VMPTRST
SETNC	SQRTPD	TEST	*VMPUSHFD*
SETNE	SQRTPS	TEXTEQU	VMREAD
SETNG	SQRTSD	THIS	VMRESUME
SETNGE	SQRTSS	TITLE	VMRUN
SETNL	SQWORD	*TR3*	VMSAVE
SETNLE	SS	*TR4*	*VMSDTE*
SETNO	ST	*TR5*	*VMSETINFO*
SETNP	STC	*TR6*	*VMSGDT*
SETNS	STD	*TR7*	*VMSIDT*
SETNZ	STDCALL	TYPE	*VMSLDT*
SETO	STGI	TYPEDEF	*VMSPLAF*
SETP	STI	UCOMISD	*VMSTI*
SETPE	STMXCSR	UCOMISS	*VMSTR*
SETPO	STOS	UD2	VMWRITE
SETS	STOSB	UNION	VMXOFF
SETZ	STOSD	UNPCKHPD	VMXON
SFENCE	**STOSQ**	UNPCKHPS	WAIT
SGDT	STOSW	UNPCKLPD	WBINVD
SHL	STR	UNPCKLPS	WHILE

WIDTH	XMM2	**XMM14**	XMMWORD
WORD	XMM3	**XMM15**	XOR
WRMSR	XMM4	**XMM2**	XORPD
XADD	XMM5	**XMM3**	XORPS
XCHG	XMM6	**XMM4**	XRSTOR
XGETBV	XMM7	**XMM5**	XSAVE
XLAT	**XMM10**	**XMM6**	XSAVEOPT
XLATB	**XMM11**	**XMM7**	XSETBV
XMM0	**XMM12**	**XMM8**	*ZERO?*
XMM1	**XMM13**	**XMM9**	

C

Answers to Selected Exercises

Exercises 1.1 (page 7)

2. 1010 1101   <u>AD</u>   <u>173</u>
8. <u>1010 0101 0010 1110</u>   A52E   <u>42286</u>
14. <u>10 1110 1010 1011</u>   <u>2EAB</u>   11947
18. 03:46:32

Exercises 1.2 (page 11)

1. (b) 29522 or sR
2. (b) 47 65 6f 72 67 65 20 73 61 69 64 2c 20 22 4f 75 63 68 21 22
3. (c) June 11, 1947CRLF

Exercises 1.3 (page 16)

1. (a) 00000F22
2. (d) FFF6
3. (b) 6F
4. (b) −509 signed; 4,294,966,787 unsigned
5. (c) 28,448 signed or unsigned
6. (a) −31 signed; 225 unsigned
8. (a) −32,768 to +32,767; (b) 0 to 65,535

Exercises 1.4 (page 23)

1. 003F + 02A4

    sum: 02E3, no overflow, no carry

    signed and unsigned check: 63 + 676 = 739

    unsigned check: 32766 + 2 = 32768

5. FF07 + 06BD

    sum: 05C4, no overflow, carry

    signed check: $-249 + 1725 = 1476$

    unsigned check: $65287 + 1725 = 67012 \neq 1476$

9. FFF1 + 8005

    sum: 7FF6, overflow, carry

    signed check: $-15 + (-32763) = -32778 \neq 32758$

    unsigned check: $65521 + 32773 = 98294 \neq 32758$

13. EBBC $-$ 791C = EBBC + 86E4

    difference: 72A0, overflow, no borrow

    signed check: $-5188 - 31004 = -36192 \neq 29344$

    unsigned check: $60348 - 31004 = 29344$

Exercises 1.5 (page 27)

1. 00AF
2. FF50
5. 00 00 02 30
11. C13C0000

Exercises 2.1 (page 32)

2. $2 \times 3^{20} = 2^{31} = 80000000_{16}$, so the last address is 000000007FFFFFFF
4. (a) 2B8C0 + 8D21 = 345E1

Exercises 2.2 (page 38)

3.

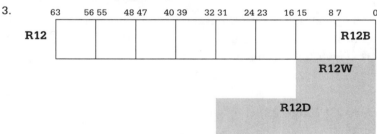

4. (b) EAX: FFFFFF72   CF 0   OF 0   SF 1   ZF 0
    (e) EAX: 00000000   CF 1   OF 0   SF 0   ZF 1

Exercises 2.3 (page 40)

2. 65,535

Exercises 3.1 (page 50)

2. (c) more: OK   (e) 2much: not allowed (starts with numeral)

Exercises 3.3 (page 62)

1. B7
3. B7
7. 44
10. 3E 3C 3E 3C 3E 3C 3E 3C 3E 3C (shown as 00000005 [3E3C])
17. FFF0BDC0
21. 00000000 00000001 00000002 00000003
30. 0001 0001 0001 0001 0001 0001 0001 0001 (shown as 00000008 [0001])
33. FFFFFFFFFFFFFFF6

Exercises 3.4 (page 67)

1. direct, immediate
4. register, register indirect
7. direct, immediate

Exercises 3.6 (page 79)

2. (a) 2D 35 37 38   (b) FFFFFDBE

Exercises 4.1 (page 102)

1.
   (a) EBX: 00 00 01 A2, ECX: 00 00 01 A2
   (d) AX: 00 4B
   (h) RAX: FF FF FF FF FF FF FF FF
2.
   (a) opcode 8B, 2 bytes
   (d) opcode B4, 2 bytes
   (h) opcode C7, 7 bytes

3.

- (a) *mod-reg-r/m* byte D9 = 1101 1001 = 11 011 001, *mod* 11 for register to register, *reg* 011 for EBX and *r/m* 001 for ECX
- (d) no *mod-reg-r/m* byte

4.

- (a) EBX: 00 00 01 A2, ECX: 00 00 FF 75
- (d) AX: D9 4B, BX: 5C 01

5.

- (a) opcode 87, 2 bytes
- (d) opcode 86, 2 bytes

Exercises 4.2 (page 116)

1.

- (a) opcode 03, 7 bytes
- (g) opcode 2A, 2 bytes
- (l) opcode FE, 2 bytes
- (o) opcode F7, 6 bytes

2.

- (d) opcode 81, 11 bytes
- (e) opcode FE, 3 bytes

3.

- (a) EBX: 00 00 01 17, ECX: 00 00 01 A2, SF=0, ZF=0, CF=1, OF=0
- (e) EAX: 00 00 00 00, SF=0, ZF=1, CF=0, OF=0
- (i) EAX: 00 00 00 00, SF=0, ZF=1
- (q) R11: 00 00 00 00 00 00 00 04, SF=0, ZF=0

Exercises 4.3 (page 128)

1.

- (b) EAX: 00 00 15 A8, EDX: FF FF FF 1E, CF=OF=1
- (f) EAX: 00 00 0F FE, DX: 00 00 00 00, CF=OF=0
- (j) AX: 04 74, CF=OF=1

2.

- (b) opcode F7, 6 bytes
- (f) opcode F7, 6 bytes
- (j) opcode F6, 2 bytes

3.

    (a) BX: 00 00 0F FE, CF=OF=0

    (c) EAX: 00 00 EB 6E, CF=OF=0

    (h) EBX: FFFF FF74, CF=OF=0

4.

    (a) opcode 0F AF, 3 bytes

    (c) opcode 6B, 3 bytes

    (h) opcode 6B, 3 bytes

Exercises 4.4 (page 139)

1.

    (a) EDX: 00 00 00 04, EAX: 00 00 00 0A

    (d) division error

    (h) EDX: 00 00 00 05, EAX: 00 00 00 2B

2.

    (a) opcode F7, 2 bytes

    (d) opcode F7, 3 bytes

    (h) opcode F7, 2 bytes

Exercises 5.1 (page 148)

2. jmp doAgain (after 3 instructions), relative short

    jmp doAgain (after 200 instructions), relative near

    jmp addrStore, memory indirect

    jmp eax, register indirect

    jmp DWORD PTR [edi], memory indirect

Exercises 5.2 (page 159)

1. (a) no jump   (e) no jump

2.

    (a)

```
            cmp ecx, 0        ; count = 0 ?
            jne endifa        ; skip if not
            mov ecx, value    ; count := value
        endifa:
```

(d)

```
                cmp edx, -1000  ; value <= -1000 ?
                jle thend       ; do it if so
                cmp edx, 1000   ; value >= 1000 ?
                jnge endifd     ; skip if not
        thend:  mov edx, 0      ; value := 0
        endifd:
```

Exercises 5.3 (page 168)

1. (b)

```
                mov  sum, 0       ; sum := 0
                mov  ecx, 1       ; count := 1
        whileB: cmp  sum, 1000    ; sum < 1000 ?
                jnl  endwhileB    ; exit if not
                cmp  ecx, 50      ; count <= 50 ?
                jnle endwhileB    ; exit if not
                add  sum, ecx     ; add count to sum
                inc  ecx          ; add 1 to count
                jmp  whileB       ; repeat
        endwhileB:
```

2. (c)

```
                mov  sum, 0       ; sum := 0
                mov  ecx, 1       ; count := 1
        untilC: add  sum, ecx     ; add count to sum
                inc  ecx          ; add 1 to count
                cmp  sum, 5000    ; sum >= 5000 ?
                jnge untilC       ; repeat if not
                cmp  ecx, 40      ; count > 40 ?
                jng  untilC       ; repeat if not
        enduntilC:
```

3. (b)

```
                mov  sum, 0       ; sum := 0
                mov  ecx, -10     ; count := -10
        forB:   cmp  ecx, 50      ; count <= 50 ?
                jnle endforB      ; exit if not
                add  sum, ecx     ; add count to sum
                inc  ecx          ; add 1 to count
                jmp  forB         ; repeat
        endforB:
```

Exercises 5.4 (page 175)

1.

(b) 1

(d) 4,294,967,295

2. (b)
```
            mov   sum, 0      ; sum := 0
            mov   ecx, 50     ; loop index
     forB:  mov   eax, 51     ; count = 51 - index
            sub   eax, ecx
            add   sum, eax    ; add count to sum
            loop  forB        ; repeat
```

Exercises 5.5 (page 184)

3. (a) ModR/M = 94 = 10 010 100, mod 10 and R/M=100 to require SIB, reg 010 for EDX source. SIB = B3 = 10 110 011, scale 10 for 4, index 110 for ESI, base 011 for EBX

Exercises 6.1 (page 197)

1. (c) opcode 55, 1 byte

2.

    (a)

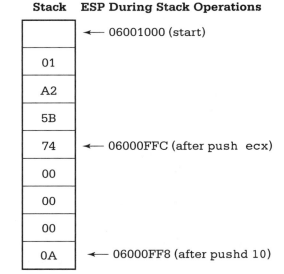

Exercises 6.2 (page 206)

1. return address on stack: 00402005
   ESP: 00405FFC

Exercises 6.3 (page 220)

1. ```
   push  ebp        ; establish stack frame
   mov   ebp, esp
   sub   esp, 8     ; 8 bytes local variable space
   ...
   mov   esp, ebp   ; remove local variables
   pop   ebp        ; restore EBP
   ret              ; return
   ```

   local double variables are accessed by [ebp-4] and [ebp-8]

Exercises 6.4 (page 228)

1. (b) in R8   (d) at [RSP+56]
2. (b) in R8   (d) at [RSP+72]
3. (b) in R8   (d) at [RSP+120]

Exercises 6.5 (page 236)

1. (a) ```
   mov   eax, 25
   add   eax, ebx
   ```

2. (a) ```
   push eax
   mov   eax, value1
   xchg eax, value2
   mov   value1, eax
   pop   eax
   ```

3. (a) ```
   mov   eax, value1
   cmp   eax, value2
   jle   ??000A
   mov   eax, value2
   ??000A:
   ```

Exercises 7.1 (page 248)

1. (a) BX: 3000, SF 0, ZF 0   (b) BX: FB77, SF 1, ZF 0
   (c) BX: CB77, SF 1, ZF 0   (d) BX: 058A

3. ```
   mov   ebx, eax    ; copy value
   and   ebx, 111b   ; value mod 8
   ```

4. (b) ```
   and   flags, 0FFF6FFDFh
         ;1111 1111 1111 0110 1111 1111 1101 1111
   ```

5. (b) ```
   and   bl, 1011111b   ; 5fh
   ```

### Exercise 7.2 (page 261)

1. (a) AX: 516A, CF 1, OF 1        (c) AX: D45A, CF 1, OF 0
   (d) AX: 516B, CF 1              (k) AX: 516B, CF 1
   ```

2. (a) 5 + 5 + 2 = 12 bytes

3. (b) 3 bytes

4. (b) one of many solutions

```
mov   value3, al    ; copy value3
and   value3, 01111111b ; mask 8th bit
ror   ax, 7          ; move value2 to right
mov   value2, al    ; copy value2
and   value2, 00001111b ; mask all but 4 bits
ror   ax, 4          ; move value3 to right
mov   value1, al    ; copy value1
and   value1, 00011111b ; mask all but 5 bits
ror   ax, 5          ; restore AX to original value
```

5.
```
; multiply by 9
mov  ebx, eax       ; value
shl  eax, 3         ; 8*value
add  add, ebx       ; 9*value
```

Exercises 8.1 (page 275)

1. Message box with title "the modified string is" displaying
   "ABCDEABCDJ"

Exercises 8.2 (page 285)

2. ESI = 00417003, EDI = 00417008, ECX = 00000002

5. EDI = 0041700A, ECX = 00000000, memory at dest 2a 2a 2a 2a 2a

Exercises 8.3 (page 292)

1.
```
toASCII BYTE 64 DUP (0), ' ', 10 DUP (0), '.', 31 DUP (0), ','
        BYTE 21 DUP (0), "abcdefghi", 7 DUP (0), "jklmnopqr"
        BYTE 8 DUP (0), "stuvwxyz", 23 DUP (0), "ABCDEFGHI"
        BYTE 7 DUP (0), "JKLMNOPQR", 8 DUP (0), "STUVWXYZ"
        BYTE 6 DUP (0), "0123456789", 6 DUP (0)
```

Exercises 8.4 (page 297)

1. Because −2147483648 and some other large negative numbers have 11
   characters.

Exercises 9.1 (page 303)

3. C13C0000

13. 3FB8000000000000

20. 4004B600000000000000

28. −0.0390625

33. A biased exponent of 00000000001 corresponds to an actual exponent of −1022. To be normalized, the fraction must start with a 1 bit, so that the smallest actual fraction is 1.0_2 or 1_{10}. This gives a minimum value of 1×2^{-1022}, which is approximately 2.23×10^{-308}.

37. 64 fraction bits corresponds to 2^{64} possible values, between 10^{19} and 10^{20} values.

Exercises 9.2 (page 323)

1. (b)

0.5	ST	*fpValue:* 0.5
9.0	ST(1)	*intValue:* 6
12.0	ST(2)	
23.0	ST(3)	
24.0	ST(4)	
35.0	ST(5)	
	ST(6)	
	ST(7)	

(f)

12.0	ST	*fpValue:* 0.5
23.0	ST(1)	*intValue:* 6
24.0	ST(2)	
9.0	ST(3)	
	ST(4)	
	ST(5)	
	ST(6)	
	ST(7)	

(j)

21.0	ST	*fpValue:* 0.5
23.0	ST(1)	*intValue:* 6
24.0	ST(2)	
35.0	ST(3)	
	ST(4)	
	ST(5)	
	ST(6)	
	ST(7)	

(q)

12.0	ST	*fpValue:* 0.5
23.0	ST(1)	*intValue:* 6
15.0	ST(2)	
35.0	ST(3)	
	ST(4)	
	ST(5)	
	ST(6)	
	ST(7)	

(w)

1.5	ST	*fpValue:* 0.5
12.0	ST(1)	*intValue:* 6
23.0	ST(2)	
24.0	ST(3)	
35.0	ST(4)	
	ST(5)	
	ST(6)	
	ST(7)	

2. (a) ST < ST(1) so C3 = 0, C2 = 0, C0 = 1

(e) ST < ST(1) so C3 = 0, C2 = 0, C0 = 1

12.0	ST
23.0	ST(1)
24.0	ST(2)
35.0	ST(3)
	ST(4)
	ST(5)
	ST(6)
	ST(7)

Exercises 9.3 (page 341)

2. 414570a4 or 12.34

Exercises 9.4 (page 346)

1.

XMM00	XMM01	XMM02	XMM03
4.0	−10.5	3.7	4.6

4.

XMM00	XMM01	XMM02	XMM03
20.0	−10.5	3.7	4.6

9.

XMM00	XMM01	XMM02	XMM03
1.0	−1.5	11.0	−3.7

Index